The American Law of Slavery, 1810–1860

★★★

The American Law of Slavery
1810-1860

★★★

CONSIDERATIONS OF HUMANITY AND INTEREST

★★★

MARK V. TUSHNET

PRINCETON UNIVERSITY PRESS
PRINCETON, NEW JERSEY

To my mother and to the memory of my father

Contents

viii ★ Contents

Acknowledgments

THIS WORK has been gestating for an inordinately long time. It began as a seminar paper for Eugene Genovese and was expanded into another for C. Vann Woodward. Other obligations led me to put it aside, but I returned to the work and published a first extended effort in the *Law & Society Review* 10 (Fall, 1975): 119-84.[1] Along the way, Professors Genovese and Woodward made helpful comments, as did David Trubek, Willard Hurst, and the editor of the *Review*, Robert Gordon. The present work incorporates some of the material that I included in that article, but the analytical framework has, I think, been substantially clarified, and some of the arguments have been changed in important ways. Parts of Chapters I and II were presented at the Annual Meetings of the Organization of American Historians, New York, April 12-15, 1978, and have appeared in *Civil War History* 25 (Dec., 1979): 329-38.[2] In addition, some of the ideas in Chapter I were sketched in the *University of Chicago Law Review* 45 (Summer 1978): 906-18.[3]

Professor Genovese encouraged me to expand my earlier work into this book. The immediate impulse was provided by similar encouragement from Stanley Katz and Robert Cover. Colleen Higgins provided important research assistance, and Kay Heinrichs typed the manuscript with admirable care. I am indebted, too, to the intellectual currents that flow through the Conference of Critical Legal Studies. My greatest debt, as always, is to Elizabeth Alexander, both for her historical and legal insight and for her immense capacity for emotional support. The book's dedication carries out a promise I made to myself a long time ago; the book could equally honestly have been dedicated to Elizabeth, Rebecca, and Laura.

The American Law of Slavery, 1810–1860

INTRODUCTION

IN JANUARY 1852, James Gorman, a Georgia slaveowner, hired out his slave London to Charles Campbell for $15 a month.[1] The slave had worked as a steamboat hand for several months when, on May 19, he was drowned. Although custom barred slaves from working in the water to remove obstructions, London had been attempting to cut a log in order to open up a new passage so that the steamboat, which had been tied up for several days, could proceed. After London had been working on the log for about thirty minutes, the captain, who had been watching London's work, noticed that the log was about to be carried downstream. The captain called to London several times, and London jumped to another log, which, however, was itself carried downstream. One witness thought that London fell off while reaching for his hat, but in any event London drowned in water about four feet deep. Because London's tongue was badly bitten when his body was recovered, some witnesses thought that he might have had an epileptic fit.

Gorman sued Campbell for the value, approximately $500, of the dead slave. The trial judge charged the jury that, had the captain been in charge of "a bale or box of goods or other inanimate object," he would have been obliged to put it on the bank in a safe place, but that the rule was different in cases of slaves. They were "sentient being[s], capable of volition and locomotion." Thus, the judge told the jury, Campbell was liable if the captain commanded or permitted London to work in the water, but was not liable if London had done so "of his own free will" after being forbidden to work in the water. After all, the alternative would have been to keep London in chains "if they were to be made responsible for any act of his . . . which might end disastrously." The jury returned a verdict finding no liability.

On Gorman's appeal, Justice Joseph Lumpkin, who had sat on the Georgia Supreme Court since its creation in 1845 and who was the court's most influential figure,[2] wrote the opinion reversing the judgment on the ground that the jury had not been correctly instructed. He noted acerbically that the witnesses carefully refrained from testifying that the captain was aware of London's activity in the water, and said that the captain's presence made the jury instructions incomplete. According to Justice Lumpkin, permission to work should have been implied, "[f]or to neglect to exercise authority to forbid a thing, is to permit it." Justice Lumpkin then addressed the special problems posed by the fact that the slave had volition. Whether working in the water was customary or not,

> it is still the duty of the hirer to exercise proper care in the supervision of the slave. And he not only *may* use coercion even to chains, if necessary, for the protection of the property from peril, but it is his duty to do so. . . . And humanity to the slave, as well as a proper regard for the interest of the owner, alike demand that the rules of law, regulating this contract, should not be relaxed. We must enforce the obligation which this contract imposes, by making it the interest of all who employ slaves, to watch over their lives and safety. Their improvidence demands it. They are incapable of self-preservation, either in danger or in disease.— This office devolves upon those who are entrusted, for the time being, with their custody and control. And if they fail faithfully to perform it, it becomes a high and solemn duty of all courts to enforce the trust by the only means in their power—a direct appeal to the pocket of the delinquent party.

The court concluded that if London had been killed while doing the service he was hired out for, Campbell would be liable only if the captain had been grossly culpable, but because London was engaged in more dangerous activity than that which had been stipulated in the contract, the hirer was liable. "And it is no protection that the loss arose from the voluntary act of the slave."

Gorman v. *Campbell* is not an especially noteworthy case; it set no great precedents, nor gave special shape to slave law. Yet, perhaps just because it is an ordinary case, it reveals a great deal about what Southern slave law had to deal with: the relation between the contract for and the use of the slave, difficulties in managing slaves, and the need for rules that conformed to party expectations. I will examine *Gorman* in detail in Chapter II. For now, it will serve to introduce the central issue in slave law. Justice Lumpkin, an ardent secessionist in 1860, wrote of the demands of humanity in dealing with slaves; the law, he argued, had to provide inducements for hirers to take care of those in their charge, by appeal to their pockets if necessary. Those inducements had two effects. In the name of humanity, they would lead the hirer to put the slave in chains, and they also, as it happened, protected the interest of the master. But the appeal to humanity cannot be dismissed as high irony or reduced to the protection of interest. If the owner's economic interest were all that had to be considered, the opinion would have focused, not on the captain's misbehavior, but on the expectations of Gorman in entering into the contract of hire. It might have argued, as other cases that we will examine did, that Gorman was not entitled to recover because the contract price included or should have included a risk premium that took account of the fact that the slave might exercise his volition in dangerous ways. Or it might have justified the result the court reached by pointing to the expectation that London would be used only as a boathand, and that the hirer's liability flowed directly, albeit with some judicial assistance in order to reduce the complexity of contracts, from the deviation from the expected use.

Justice Lumpkin's opinion, then, if not the court's result, can be understood only if we take the dual invocation of humanity and interest seriously. Southern slave law as a whole can be viewed as reproducing this interplay between humanity and interest. In some settings, where legal problems arose from transactions within a single household or plantation, considerations of humanity came to the fore; this emphasis is most apparent in manumission cases, but it is found in some others as well. In other settings, masters engaged in ordinary market transactions, and considerations of interest were emphasized in developing the law, as in cases involving hired slaves injured by coworkers. I will examine cases across a range of settings and will show that in all of them, slave law responded to the competing pressures of humanity and interest.

Developing a stable body of law proved extremely difficult. A sketch of the social and material basis of law in bourgeois and slave society will indicate why that was so. The short explanation is that concern with humanity arose from one set of social relations whereas concern for interest arose from another set, and although those social relations coexisted in the slave South, they could not be integrated into a unified social formation, one that lacked internal contradiction. The law thus reproduced the contradictions of Southern slave society.

Social relations in slave society rest upon the interaction of owner with slave; the owner, having total dominion over the slave, relates to the entire personality of the slave. In contrast, bourgeois social relations rest upon the paradigmatic instance of market relations, the purchase by a capitalist of a worker's labor power; that transaction implicates only a part of the worker's personality. Slave social relations are total, engaging the master and the slave in exchanges where each must take account of the entire range of belief, feeling, and interest embodied in the other; bourgeois social relations are partial, requiring only that participants in a market evaluate their general productive characteristics without regard to aspects of personality unrelated to production. Ways of interpreting slave conduct are developed from slave social relations and are ultimately embodied in the law, although of course altered by the fact that legal doctrine is part of a specialized and professional enterprise.[3]

It was the dilemma of Southern slave law that slave relations generated a totalistic concern for both humanity and interest at the same time that Southern society was inserted into a bourgeois world economy whose well-developed bourgeois world-view pervaded the consciousness of all who took part in trade in the world markets. Even worse from the Southern point of view, the slave South was locked into a political union with a dynamic bourgeois economy. Southern slave law thus had to respond to the double reality that the South was a slave society and that it was inextricably bound up, politically and economically, with bourgeois society. The War of 1861-65 embodied one attempted solution: the tensions would be resolved by breaking the connecting links.[4] In the sphere of ideology, similar attempts were made, but Eugene Genovese's analysis of the thought of George Fitzhugh has shown how very difficult it would have been to develop a comprehensive alternative to bourgeois ideology.[5] Fitzhugh and other ideologues had a certain type of freedom and irresponsibility; they could build their schemes constrained only by their need to make the schemes persuasive to those still partly bound by bourgeois thought. Further, we look to ideologues as exemplary and often isolated individuals whose genius has led them to see better than most what had to be done. And even then we find men like Fitzhugh faced with a massive weight of bourgeois thought from which they cannot entirely free themselves.

The problem in the sphere of law was worse. The solution, represented in one form by the Civil War and in another by Fitzhugh, of a total break with bourgeois law was simply impossible in the time available to Southern judges. First, most judges were, in the nature of things, merely ordinary thinkers; the law they generated, when taken as a whole, could not be founded upon a deep, systematic, and extraordinarily difficult reconstruction of the premises of a slave, rather than a bourgeois, society. Second, the professional norms of the law required a certain kind of continuity, through adherence to precedent, or its rejection on a relatively small number of grounds, that inhibited the development of sharp alterations in doctrine. Talented judges could and did manipulate rules developed and supported by bourgeois practices into forms that were consistent with the experience of slave society, but again, there could not be enough judges with such abilities to shape Southern slave law when viewed as a whole. Finally, many, perhaps most, of the cases that gave courts the opportunity to develop the law arose in settings, like that of *Gorman* v. *Campbell*, where market and slave relations were both present; the ethos of slavery, after all, conduced to, although it did not compel, the solution of problems lacking market connections on the plantations where they arose.

Although Southern slave law did not develop an alternative view of the world to displace bourgeois law and its worldview, it moved haltingly, and at different rates in different geographic and legal areas, toward a resolution of the tensions between law generated by totalistic views of master-slave relations and law generated by partial views that treated masters and slaves as special classes of employers and employees. The resolution amounted to bracketing slave law off from other areas of the law: for example, a judge deciding a case involving injury to a hired slave would look only to cases involving slaves and not to the law of accidental injuries generally. By isolating slave cases from the general body of law, Southern judges could confine the influence of market notions that were giving shape to the law of contracts and of accidents. The development of a distinct category of slave law was supported, in addition, by the pervasive need of mediocre judges to have simple tools at hand; the new category made the judges' search for relevant analogies a shorter one. In the end, however, using the special category of slave law probably would not have solved the conceptual problems that Southern judges faced, because those problems arose from the contradiction between slave relations and the world and national political economy into which they were inserted: even masters, that is, took part in transactions in a market that had to be thought of in bourgeois terms, bourgeois market relations regarding slaves were internally inconsistent, and Southern slave law could not escape that inconsistency, though it continually sought ways to avoid confronting it.

This book examines Southern slave law. Its aims and limitations should be identified at the outset. I regard this study as one in Southern history, in legal history, and in the historical sociology of law. It is guided by an explicit reliance on Marxist theoretical constructs whose utility, I believe, is demonstrated throughout. The initial chapter develops the perspective on the legal system that guides this book, through a critical examination of the perspectives that have guided earlier students of slave law. Those students, I must emphasize, have greatly enhanced our understanding of slavery, and my critical comments are designed, not to deprecate their work, but to indicate what they have given us to build upon. My concern for explicit theory leads, perhaps unfortunately, to some blurring of lines that historians would like to draw. Thus, I am primarily concerned with the "general" law of slavery, a sort of "Restatement of the Law of Slavery," and am less concerned with its local variances except as they illuminate general propositions. Similarly, I give little attention to the political and social backgrounds of individual judges, which seem homogeneous enough to ignore in view of my purposes; other scholars, such as A. E. Keir Nash, have other goals for which detailed attention to judicial biography is needed.

After developing the conceptual framework that I use by means of this historiographical excursion, I turn to an examination of the structure of Southern slave law. I have selected four cases to illustrate that structure. They are illustrative and not typical, however, although the subsequent analysis shows how pervasive the structure really was. The cases were decided in three different states, from civil-law Louisiana to sophisticated common-law North Carolina, and at widely separated times, from 1818 to 1858. In all of them, we can see an effort, successful in varying degrees, to develop a rigid separation between law and sentiment, which parallels a separation between market and slave relations.

The final part of the book expands the scope of inquiry in order to show that the law/sentiment and market/slave structure was pervasive in Southern law. I have examined every reported appellate opinion[6] listed in Helen Catterall's compilation[7] for the period 1810 to 1860[8] that was decided in the secession South exclusive of South Carolina and Tennessee.[9] The study relies on cases across the range of legal areas, including contracts and torts as well as criminal law and manumission law, thus providing a broader base than was used by scholars such as Keir Nash and Michael Hindus.[10] The length of the period studied induces an unfortunate homogenization in the analysis, for it suggests that not much changed during the period. In one sense, that suggestion is correct. After the institution of slavery was given a firm legal basis, a process that was completed by roughly 1800, the courts worked out a substantive law of slavery that was largely uniform, although with some local variants, and that changed little over time. Even in the 1850s, Southern courts neither abandoned old rules nor developed new ones in the face of abolitionist criticism of existing slave law as inhumane. However, the image of stability is inaccurate when we turn from substance to process, for there we can see the increasing use of a sharply defined category of slave law. My primary conclusion, indeed, is that the historical development of slave law is best described by identifying the development of a categorical approach to that law, and that the categorical approach was the general solution arrived at by Southern courts to the problem of reconciling the demands of humanity and interest.

I.   SLAVE LAW AND ITS USES

IN 1827, George Stroud, a Philadelphia abolitionist, published
A Sketch of the Laws Relating to Slavery. In the preface, Stroud
emphasized that he had carefully considered authentic legal
materials, and continued: "Of the *actual* condition of slaves
this sketch does not profess to treat. In representative repub-
lics, however, . . . the *laws* may be safely regarded as con-
stituting a faithful exposition of the sentiments of the people,
and as furnishing, therefore, strong evidence of the practical
enjoyments and privations of those whom they are designed
to govern." Stroud acknowledged, though, that the treatment
of individual slaves would "no doubt, in great degree, take
its complexion from the peculiar disposition of their respective
masters,—a consideration which operates as much *against* as
in *favour* of the slave. . . ."

Stroud stated the two themes that have recurred throughout
the study of the American law of slavery. Laws have been
treated as providing evidence of popular sentiment and of
practical experience. Stroud's qualification regarding actual
treatment is, however, one whose importance cannot be
overstated. This chapter, through an examination of various
uses of slave law in works of legal and historical analysis,
presents the argument that difficulties in interpreting available
legal materials impair their use as evidence of "the actual
condition of slaves," but that judicial opinions in particular
are a useful source of insight into the ideological structures
from which slavery drew support. Subsequent chapters show
that we cannot move directly from opinion to ideology, but
must instead take into account the transformation of thought
that occurs when ideological questions are inserted into legal
institutions.

A. THE LAW AS EVIDENCE OF EXPERIENCE

Broadly speaking, legal materials can be divided into those that openly reveal the facts of day-to-day social relations in the slave system and those that reveal the special set of facts that are the articulated methods by which slave law dealt with the society's problems. The first category includes the statements of facts given by appellate courts in the course of decision and statistics concerning the rate of so-called criminal activity by slaves and the master class's response to that activity. The second category includes the statements of reasons given by appellate courts in deciding cases. This section deals with the use of the first category of materials, for those materials have been the source of some very interesting work. Unfortunately, as they are put to increasingly sophisticated use, they become rather less helpful as evidence of day-to-day social relations.

Helen Catterall's compilation of "cases concerning American slavery" is, because of the simplicity of its criterion for selection, the best place to begin. Catterall included all cases where a slave is mentioned in the statement of facts. One can garner a great deal of information from Catterall's pages; even the routine inventories of estates contain information on slave prices and slave families. Yet a case "concerning" slavery need not implicate the law of slavery. For example, a random choice of two pages in the volume containing Mississippi cases produces ten items.[1] Only four, three criminal and one civil, deal with questions of substantive slave law. The remaining six cases do not involve the law of slavery at all. Rather, they illustrate such things as the informal market in which purchases of slaves were made, the existence of slave-stealing, and the occasional inability of a seller to comply with promises to deliver slaves because the slaves ran away.

Despite my concern with the law of slavery, I have followed Catterall's implicit principles in one respect. In presenting the cases whose substance is my primary concern, I have stated in as much detail as the reports allow the factual settings from which the cases arose. The detail is useful, in part because it sheds light on the context in which the courts faced the substantive questions, but perhaps even more because the vignettes are interesting in themselves as illustrations of what happened in the ordinary course of slave society.

Of course, using the facts of reported cases to illustrate social relationships can be dangerous. There is no a priori reason to think that those facts are representative. Still, when coupled with other sources of evidence, legal materials can reveal what Kenneth Stampp calls the "human drama" of slavery.[2] For example, throughout *The Peculiar Institution* Professor Stampp intersperses examples of master-slave relations taken from Catterall, ordinarily bracketed by references to personal diaries, newspaper accounts, and the like. The fact that reported cases provided the evidence has no special significance. In Stampp's work, representativeness is assured by the integrity of the conscientious historian, who presents selected pieces of evidence backed by guarantees that the historian has examined a broad range of materials and that the selections are indeed representative.

Although this use of legal materials is wholly unexceptionable, it does not exploit them to their fullest. In particular, it does not build on the fact that, for something to appear in the case reports in the first place, someone had to care enough about what was at stake to assume the expense and bother of litigation. When this consideration is taken into account, some of the material used by Professor Stampp solely for illustrative purposes may take on a broader significance. Most of the legal material in *The Peculiar Institution* is scattered, one citation to illustrate the existence of runaway camps, another to show the slave's need for diversions from routine, and so on. At only one point, apart from the explicit discussion of substantive slave law, is the legal material both concentrated and nearly the exclusive source of evidence. This occurs in the treatment of miscegenation.[3]

The very fact that legal materials are systematically better than other sources for illustrating the occurrence of interracial sexual relations, and are apparently not systematically better on any other point, is quite suggestive.[4] Because Professor Stampp regularly discounts travelers' reports when adverse to the slave system, he is left with diaries, Southern newspapers, and legal materials. The former sources appear to have suppressed slaveowners' perceptions of miscegenation, but the topic could not be kept out of legal materials because it directly posed serious questions of property rights about which it was worth going to court: nearly all of Professor Stampp's examples are taken from disputes among heirs over who should inherit what, or from divorce proceedings involving questions of property division.[5] These disputes were subject to few of the constraints that can lead to nonjudicial resolution of disputes, particularly when questions of bastardy and miscegenation could be raised; the stakes were large, and there were few continuing relations between the parties that would be strained by libelous charges.

Thus, simply by noting the distribution of legal materials in *The Peculiar Institution* and without attending to the content of slave law, we can see an interesting interaction between race relations and property relations. It would appear that, ordinarily, the master class thought itself set apart from the slave class by rigid racial lines, but in fact those lines were permeable. Constraints on revealing information demonstrating that permeability were relaxed where important questions of property rights were at issue. As I argue in Chapter III, a related structural tension between the use of race as a classifying legal criterion and the social relations of slave society pervaded slave law. It is important to note here only that this argument has moved from what Stroud called "actual conditions" to what he called "sentiment." That move will recur throughout this chapter.

Antislavery polemicists made a more complex and problematic use of legal materials as evidence of actual conditions. William Goodell, in *The American Slave Code in Theory and Practice*, relied on them for an "account of the usages and practices current among slaveholders."[6] Yet, although Goodell was an extremely perceptive analyst and an acute dissector of arguments, he did not, because he could not, consistently adhere to an account of practice based on legal materials. For example, he excoriated the slave code for its refusal to acknowledge the right of a slave to marry.[7] We know, however, that at least some slaves maintained nuclear families over long periods of time,[8] which indicates that the slave code did not, as Goodell argued, state the best behavior that could be expected of slaveholders.[9] Further, although the codes did not provide mechanisms for ceremonial marriages among slaves, they did sometimes recognize the incidents of marriage. A North Carolina case suggests, for example, that a slave who found his wife in the act of adultery would have the same defenses that a white man would have if he killed the adulterer.[10] A late case from Georgia, relying on a statute that made the rules of evidence the same in the trials of slaves and whites, held, contrary to the rule elsewhere,[11] that the testimony of a slave's wife should not be admitted against him.[12]

Goodell's implicit response to these problems pointed to the difference between a code that recognized a right to marry and one that allowed an individual master to extend permission to marry. Marriage, to Goodell, entailed mutual promises of protection and respect; which slaves, subject to the whims of their owners, could not make.[13] Once again, we see a significant shift in the use of legal materials. With this response, the law does not measure what actually occurred, but instead demonstrates the emotions and meanings that slaves and masters could attach to what happened—in a word, the "sentiments" and not the "actual conditions" of slave society.

Abolitionists like Goodell inaugurated a tradition of moral evaluation of slavery based upon evidence about day-to-day treatment of slaves drawn from legal materials. They had politically sound reasons for searching for evidence of harsh treatment, which they of course found. But they had difficulty with the expressions running through the materials of concern for the well-being of slaves. Exploring the abolitionist analysis of these expressions illustrates once more the transition from conditions to sentiment and brings out some defects in analysis that have persisted in historians' use of legal materials.

Stroud and Goodell could not honestly deny the existence of laws on the books that, on their face, seemed designed to protect slaves from their masters. Producing an early form of legal realism, they responded that the laws on the books had no relation to what actually happened.[14] But this response was at least incomplete. The abolitionists argued, for example, that slaves themselves were usually the only witnesses who could establish that some protective law had been violated, that slaves could not testify against whites, and that the protective laws were therefore unenforceable.[15] Stroud, however, cited a case in which a master was penalized for failing to provide his slave with adequate food or clothing.[16] An overseer provided the evidence supporting the charge. Enforcement thus could occur on the basis of testimony of whites who saw mistreatment or its results. Further, the cases reveal a persistent undercurrent of tension between masters and overseers, with slaves not infrequently appealing about the latter to the former.[17] Stroud argued that it would be rare for one of these white witnesses to bear the costs of litigation, since most whites were bound up with the slave system and could not be expected to challenge a master's right to treat his slaves as he wished.[18] But legal materials cannot reveal, without much more probing than the abolitionists gave them, the strength of a social conscience that might lead slaveowners to become indignant at mistreatment of slaves generally.[19]

More important, the "realist" response to apparently benevolent expressions in legal materials introduced a fatal ambiguity into the analysis. The ambiguity resulted from the need to decide whether the benevolent or the stern laws failed to describe actual conditions. For political reasons, the abolitionists described the benevolent ones as hypocritical, whereas defenders of slavery noted that extreme cases need not describe common treatment.[20] That same ambiguity has infected recent studies that rely, not on reported appellate opinions, but on statistics dealing with the enforcement of the criminal law at the trial level.

Michael Hindus' study of prosecutions of blacks in South Carolina illustrates the problem.[21] His statistics show that, as seen by the master class and compared with white criminality, theft by slaves was widespread but personal violence among slaves was rare. We do not know, however, why there were relatively few prosecutions of slaves for acts of personal violence, and several of the obvious hypotheses lead to quite different conclusions about the nature of slave society. One hypothesis is that prosecutions were rare because personal violence itself was rare, suggesting that the repressive socialization of slaves was quite effective—the Elkins thesis—or that slave anger was displaced into activities such as messianic Christianity—the Genovese thesis. Another hypothesis is that slave violence occurred but was handled outside the judicial system. Suppose that the violence was directed against someone, slave or free, other than the slave's owner. If punishment occurred without the invocation of formal state procedures, this suggests a sense of class solidarity among slaveowners coupled with a view that state intervention, even in apparent support of slave discipline, could disrupt the relations of personal dependence upon which slavery in the South was thought to rest.[22]

Just as the statistics become interesting, that is, we find them silent. There are other examples. Hindus says that the seventeen appellate decisions involving defendants convicted of killing slaves "indicate that only the most atrocious murders by men of the lowest standing resulted in conviction," and he concludes that blacks were not protected by the appellate courts. Even if one concedes that a rate of affirmance that exceeded 90 percent demonstrates a lack of protection because the cases involved atrocities, one would have to know whether persons of higher social standing went unprosecuted or unconvicted for more run-of-the-mill murders. Another statistical study, Arthur Howington's examination of criminal prosecutions in Tennessee, found roughly equal conviction rates for whites and slaves.[23] Howington concluded that slaves received "fair and impartial" trials, but conviction rates alone will not support that conclusion. We do not know, and have no a priori reason to assume, that the underlying evidence was the same in cases involving blacks and in those involving whites. If blacks were prosecuted on generally flimsy evidence and whites only on substantial evidence, equal rates of conviction would show "unfairness."[24]

There are, then, two major difficulties in using statistics on convictions, and other legal materials, as evidence of day-to-day social relations. First, historians, following the abolitionists' lead, have considered the "fairness" or "justice" of the legal system, embedded though it was in a slave society, to be a relevant dimension of inquiry. To measure fairness, though, we must agree on what would count as fair treatment. Using ordinary moral criteria, we will decide that a system of slave justice is by definition unfair. Using criteria that are sensitive to the conditions of slave society, we will be hard pressed to resist the Whiggish conclusion that slave law in the American South was just about as fair as we can expect it to have been.[25] Neither conclusion is especially interesting and, I argue in the next section, both are variants of the same politically pernicious approach.

The second difficulty with legal materials as evidence of actual conditions is, I think, insurmountable. They are necessarily incomplete. One can use them, as Professor Stampp does, to provide interesting anecdotes, but then one is not concerned with the law of slavery. The incompleteness of legal materials, in this sense, leads inexorably from "actual conditions" to "sentiment," for, as I have argued, every effort to complete the picture of the law drives analysis to the ideology of the slaveholders.

B. The Law as Evidence of Sentiment

Winthrop Jordan has written that "while statutes usually speak falsely as to actual behavior, they afford probably the best single means of ascertaining what a society thinks behavior ought to be," and Eugene Genovese describes the slave cases as having "positive value . . . not in the probability of scrupulous enforcement but in the standards of decency they laid down in a world inhabited, like most worlds, by men who strove to be considered decent."[26] Judicial opinions described the limits of morally tolerable behavior when holding a master liable or not. In addition to defining norms and limits, opinions describe, with varying explicitness, the structures of sentiment and reason used to rationalize—to order and to explain—slave society.

As descriptions of structures of thought, judicial opinions are not incomplete in the way they are as descriptions of practice. Further, because they are public documents designed to convince, judicial opinions set out premises accepted quite widely and attempt to gain assent to a particular result by showing how that result can be derived from those premises. A historian relying on opinions for evidence of sentiment must of course be sensitive to the various audiences for judicial opinions. An extended inquiry into who the judges seem to have thought were their audiences will introduce the method of this book and some of its major themes.

By the 1850s, Southern judges could expect that their published opinions would be scrutinized by abolitionists eager to find evidence of slavery's inhumanity, and a number of opinions seem aware of that audience. For example, when Anthony, a slave, was convicted of manslaughter for killing a free black, Judge Eugenius Nisbet for the Georgia Supreme Court rejected his claim that he was improperly tried by a trial court of general jurisdiction rather than by a special court for blacks, as the state constitution, according to Anthony's attorney, required.[27] The special courts had been eliminated in capital cases by statute in 1850, which, Judge Nisbet said, "reflect[ed] distinguished honor upon the State. . . . Thus it is, that by this Act, as well as by numerous other provisions of the law, whilst they are, in law and in fact, property, they are recognized as human creatures. For the justice and humanity of the slave-holding State of Georgia, an appeal well lies from the slanderous imputations of the ignorant, the fanatical, or the willfully base, to the law which I now re-

view." Not surprisingly, the court found, as the state constitution reasonably read fairly compelled, that Anthony's
argument was insubstantial.

A few years later, the same court again mentioned ignorant
attacks on slave law, in denying that a slave could justify
killing an overseer by showing that the overseer had attacked
the slave with a deadly weapon.[28] Judge Ebenezer Starnes
introduced the discussion of this issue:

> The legal principles which we shall deem it necessary to
> assert, and some of the sentiments which we may think it
> expedient to utter, in this connection, may shock those who
> are prejudiced against the institution of slavery—who are
> unmindful of the causes and the means which influenced,
> and the men who established that institution in our coun-
> try—who are blind to the difficulties in dealing with the
> subject, on the part of those whose interests are involved
> in it, and *their right* to deal with it themselves, according
> to their social responsibilities under which they rest to their
> Maker. But we will not shrink from our duty, nevertheless,
> sincerely convinced, as we are, that it is more important
> to the best interests of the master and slave, where this
> relation exists, that justice should be administered on the
> principles we lay down, than that a diseased sensibility
> should be propitiated.

The slave's obedience to the master was "a primary necessity"
in a slave system and included a duty to submit to moderate
correction. The master, and not the slave, had to judge what
was moderate; the slave had to "trust to the law for his vin-
dication" and could turn against the master only in self-defense when escape was impossible. Contrary to the rule in
North Carolina, examined in Chapter III, Georgia law did
not even reduce the offense from murder to manslaughter.
The reduction was an allowance for human passion, but it
was not morally required. It therefore was available where
it was "wise and expedient," and it would be neither wise nor
expedient to "place [a slave] continually in a state of insub-

ordination" where the slave could judge the reasonableness
of "patriarchal discipline" and have his crime mitigated on
the basis of actions he took after making such a judgment.

Two cases upholding manumissions develop similar themes.
Ann Barclay had been a slave in Louisiana but was sent to
Ohio and freed there in 1839.[29] She immediately returned to
Louisiana, where, by 1857, the legislature had prohibited the
reentry of slaves freed elsewhere as a result, the Louisiana
Supreme Court said, of "injudicious and impertinent assaults
from without upon an institution thoroughly interwoven
with our interior lives." But there had been no limitations on
foreign emancipation in 1839, and Barclay's free status was
confirmed.

Vance v. Crawford, a Georgia case, is more interesting.[30] A
wealthy slaveowner, Marshal Keith, made a will in 1839 in
which, after making several bequests, he directed that his
executors should free his servant Ishmael and Ishmael's sisters,
and, if possible, settle them in Georgia. Ishmael was to receive
enough pr property and goods to establish a farm; he would also
receive the "use" of seven other slaves. Three slaves were left
to the Colonization Society for settlement in Liberia; two of
them would go to Ishmael if they refused to go to Liberia.
Within a year or two, all of the slaves involved had, not
surprisingly, settled in Ohio. The residuary legatees, who had
already received about $40,000, challenged the manumission
provisions as against Georgia policy, in a suit brought five
years after Keith's death. The court, in an opinion by Judge
Joseph Lumpkin, who was later to lead it to much more
extreme positions,[31] held that foreign manumission by will
was legal and, indeed, "in accordance with our declared policy
. . . to prevent the increase of [the black] population." Judge
Lumpkin criticized the will for suggesting that Ishmael might
reside in Georgia:

> Neither humanity, nor religion, nor common justice, re-
> quires of us to sanction or favor domestic emancipation;
> to give our slaves their liberty at the risk of losing our own.
> They are incapable of taking part with ourselves, in the

exercise of self-government. To set up a model empire for the world, God in His wisdom planted on this virgin soil, the best blood of the human family. To allow it to be contaminated, is to be recreant to the weighty and solemn trust committed to our hands. Republican institutions cannot exist in Mexico, or the *commingled* races of South America. And while we concede that the condition of our slaves is humble, still it is infinitely better than it would have been, but for this very system of bondage, better than the lower orders in Europe, and better far than it would be, if they were emancipated here, "destroying others, by themselves destroyed."

By the late 1850s, Judge Lumpkin might have construed the will to create a "quasi-freedom" for Ishmael and have refused to enforce the bequest,[32] but in 1848 it was upheld.

Lumpkin's invocation of the comparison between slave and free labor, a staple in proslavery arguments,[33] occurred elsewhere. The Virginia Court of Appeals, for example, rejected a claim by slaves who had successfully sued for freedom, for the wages they had earned during the time they were wrongfully held, that is, after their former owner had died and his successors knew that they were to be freed pursuant to his will.

A rule giving *mesne* profits to slaves, after a recovery of freedom, would operate harshly and often ruinously in regard to the master. The arrangements, management and expenditures of slave-owners are, in a great measure, essentially different from those of persons who employ free labour in their occupations and service. The latter are, for the most part, in the habit of engaging individuals, from time to time, as the occasion may seem to require, and of dismissing them when found unsuitable or unnecessary; and are in no wise bound to provide gratuitously for their wants and comforts, or the maintenance of their families. The owner of slaves, on the contrary, is usually condemned to a constant, permanent and anxious burthen of care and

expenditure. It seldom happens that more than a small pro-
portion of them are capable of productive labour; while
provision must be made for the food, clothing and shelter
of all; for the helplessness of infancy, the decrepitude of
age, the infirmities of disease; to say nothing of the heed-
lessness, slothfulness and waste natural to persons in their
condition. Hence it is that the scantiness of net profit from
slave labour has become proverbial, and that nothing is
more common than an actual loss, or a benefit merely in
the slow increase of capital from propagation.[34]

If many opinions were characterized by appeals northward,
serious distortions would be introduced into an ideological
analysis of the opinions. Few judges would be so unsophis-
ticated as to arm their opponents with open defenses of all
the rigors of an extremely harsh system of slave justice. Also,
to the extent that the persuasive force of an argument rests
upon the invocation of shared premises, opinions directed to
Northern audiences might well struggle to state premises
shared in both regions and not, therefore, linked to the conditions of slave society. Fortunately, however, such distortions are likely to be infrequent. Even the opinions that seem
to notice the existence of a Northern audience are not really
aimed at that audience. Instead, the internal audience of Southerners was almost certainly more important to the judges.
Slavery was a system in serious tension with prevailing Western notions of justice, and those who by profession had to
manipulate the institutions of slave society found themselves
in an awkward moral position. Their difficulties could be
alleviated by various rhetorical maneuvers, but one maneuver
that would not work was to glory in assertions that they were
moral monsters. The next chapter documents the widespread
struggle to elaborate an alternative morality but shows also
how that struggle did not reach its objective. Failing that,
Southern judges attempted to place slavery in the moral
framework of Western law.

The fact that judicial opinions are arguments of a special
sort helps explain what is perhaps the best-documented con-

clusion in recent studies of the law of slavery, that appellate courts rather consistently enforced the same procedural technicalities in trials of slaves and whites.[35] Of course, technical rules that benefited slaves at least superficially benefited individual masters, who might sell the troublesome slave, perhaps at distress prices, instead of forfeiting the slave's value. But, more important, procedural fairness was a major element in the moral framework of Western law. To abandon for slave cases technicalities developed in cases involving whites would have required the judges to distinguish slaves from free persons. In Chapter III, the tortured course to distinctive treatment of slave law is described; it strongly suggests that the costs of trying to develop moral bases for that distinction were probably not worth bearing in light of the relatively small burdens that procedural rigor placed on the slave system.

With these considerations in mind, it is useful to turn from appellate opinions back to Professor Hindus' work. He found what can be fairly characterized as a pattern of harshness in the administration of slave justice at the local level, as compared with the pattern revealed by appellate opinions. What distinguishes Hindus' evidence is that appellate judges had to explain what they were doing, whereas local magistrates and slave patrols had only to do it. This difference is especially significant in light of the appellate court's reluctance to distinguish slave, and free persons' law. An appellate court ran the risk of diminishing protections given free whites accused of crime if it relaxed procedural rules in slave cases, because it did not have the conceptual tools for distinguishing the situations readily at hand. But local magistrates, under no obligation to articulate the grounds for their decisions, could do what they wished in slave cases without concern for the implications for cases involving whites.

Further, practice in slave cases on the local level differs from articulated judicial opinions in that each opinion had to rationalize individual results with the general body of law, whereas no single prosecution of a slave established any general pattern. Thus, a distinctive body of slave law-in-action developed only through the accumulation of instances, and no one instance would force the distinctiveness of the law-in-action to the consciousness of the local authorities. Practice in slave cases might then never seem all that different from practice in free cases; differences that could not exist unnoticed if appellate judges created them could survive unquestioned at the local level.

The preceding analysis probably exhausts what can usefully be said about the "harshness" of the law of slavery. The difficulty in going forward is that speaking of harshness, fairness, or justice assumes an antecedent agreement on what is harsh, fair, or just. But the judges who decided the cases were, in their own terms, fair and just. It is unclear what advantage we gain by noting that some of them, even while they accepted the conditions of slave society, adopted positions that, on our terms, seem more fair and just than those adopted by other judges.[36] Perhaps more important, the moral evaluative approach to the law of slavery conceals two questionable assumptions. One is that the criteria of justice and fairness can sensibly be invoked to describe the structure of slave law. Part of my strategy in this book is to present such extensive quotations from the opinions that it will be impossible to conclude that the structure of slave law can be described in any simple terms. As the material already presented shows, the law of slavery was both harsh and fair, paternalist and market oriented, and so on. My fundamental enterprise is to pry apart the cases to disclose the ordering implicit in slave law. Criteria of justice and fairness are far too simple as ordering principles.

The other questionable assumption is part of the Whiggishness noted earlier: that contemporary standards of fairness and justice provide adequate moral-evaluative criteria. One legal scholar characterizes the law of slavery as a "literature of nightmare," and suggests:

A legal system . . . has at its heart certain fundamental principles, ideals, and values which are utterly inconsistent with the premises of slavery. . . . [A]s a slave system is more fully expressed in the law, either it becomes less and less a slave system or the more obvious it is that the "legal" system bears little resemblance to any we know, that it is not system of law at all. . . . If slavery is to exist, it must be as the sole concern of the society, subordinating every other value and interest. This institutional truth explains why the South became at last hysterical. . . . It was a totalitarian system founded upon a principle that destroyed every other, including the fundamental principles of legality.[37]

One is tempted to a simple Johnsonian response to such nonsense: Southern courts were open and functioning, deciding cases with all the apparent rationality of any court up to the end. To deny that slave law was law at all is, unless the denial is carefully qualified, to make a pernicious political claim. The claim is that law means bourgeois law, and that any legal system that does not satisfy standards of bourgeois legality is not entitled to the moral respect that a system of law should receive. The study of the law of slavery has attracted such political claims recently,[38] for obvious reasons. Bourgeois law in the recent past has received a severe battering for its unfairness, especially with regard to race. Contrasting bourgeois law with slave law cannot help but make the former appear in a better light, and, since we agree that slavery was awful, we are induced to conclude that bourgeois law is basically all right.

If the identification of bourgeois law with law is put aside, it is possible to find something interesting in the assertion that slave law "destroyed . . . the fundamental principles of [bourgeois] legality." It is of course unsurprising to discover that a nonbourgeois society did not have a bourgeois law, but, as the next chapter shows, spelling out the ways in which slave law differed from bourgeois law yields some very interesting material. To do so, however, we need an adequate account of the linkages between the social and the legal orders. The resurgence of intellectual vitality in the study of the slave South was fed by attempts to provide such synthetic accounts, and the historiographical survey can conclude with them.

C. Law and the Conditions of Society: The Theoretical Turn

The moral critics of slave law, the abolitionists and those who employ terms like "liberalism" or "proslavery" in describing judicial opinions, had a simple model of the relation between law and the social order: the former was a reflex of the latter. That model justified the assumption that the law was evidence of actual conditions and the inverse assumption that because slavery was an unmitigated evil, slave law was equally unmitigated in its evil.

The reflex model can of course be caricatured, but that it is attractive cannot be denied. Even so sophisticated a historian as Stanley Elkins relied on the reflex model, treating the lawmaking process as one form of pluralist politics, with the strongest social group or coalition prevailing.[39] His discussion of the American South began with a section on "The Dynamics of Unopposed Capitalism," describing the inability of religious institutions and the central government to control capitalist tendencies there, and followed with a discussion of "the four major legal categories which defined the status of the American slave." That this structure was intended to imply a causal relationship is shown by Elkins' explicit reliance on the reflex model in describing Latin American slavery: "What it came to was that three formidable interests—the crown, the planter, and the church—were deeply concerned with the system, that these concerns were in certain ways competing, and that the product of this balance of power left its profound impress on the actual legal and customary sanctions governing the status and treatment of slaves."[40] In the United States, the absence of countervailing institutions made the law a reflection of capitalism alone.

Elkins' description of the South as a purely capitalist society has not survived scrutiny,[41] but my concern here is with the model he employed and not with the accuracy of his use of the model. One difficulty might be characterized as a specification problem. Elkins' contrast between Latin America and the South might mean that the reflex model is applicable only where capitalism is unopposed. But the grounds for such a restriction are unclear, and, in any event, the general model is not "capitalism—law" but rather "balance of power—law." This, however, is either so general as to be uninformative or too simple. Elkins treated opposing institutions as mediating the impact of capitalism—or, more generally, the relations of production—on the law. Once we recognize that institutions can modify and transform the impact of the relations of production on various spheres of social activity, though, the reflex model is unsatisfactory. For, if the church in Latin America could oppose capitalism, why cannot the institution of law itself, the traditions of specialized training and selective recruitment, be an opposing force as well?

The reflex model, as Elkins presented it, treats the church and the crown as institutions independent, at least to some extent, of the relations of production. The law can be similarly described as relatively autonomous. The model, no longer presenting law as pure outcome, must then specify what the sources and forms of autonomy are. One source may be the self-interest of bureaucrats seeking to increase their own power by extending the scope of bureaucratic regulation, or lawyers similarly motivated to claim greater jurisdiction for the courts, and so on.[42] The law would be a countervailing force if the income, in money and prestige, of judges were affected by expansionist desires. But their money income has traditionally been insensitive to demand for service, and to assume that a judge would think that prestige increases with the scope of judicial authority is to assume precisely what must be shown, that self-interest leads to countervailing and not supportive power. Indeed, one can interpret the argument in the next chapter as establishing that the logic of slavery would accord the greatest prestige to judges who denied their authority to regulate master-slave relations.

Other sources of autonomy derive from the precedent system and its requirement, already discussed, that judges explain their decisions. The generally shared principles to which opinions appeal may themselves be rooted in the relations of production, but where, as in the slave South, those relations are internally contradictory—joining a slave system to a bourgeois market system—the attempts to reconcile competing roles will lead to the development of general conceptual structures that do not directly reflect any of the underlying relations of production. Further, in a society divided into classes and fractions of classes, the persuasive power of opinions rests on their invocation of principles that transcend the parochial interests of any class or fraction.

Precedent, too, contributes to the autonomy of law, in a way that materialist discussions have not appreciated. Even in the clearest situations, precedents are significantly malleable, and in the typical case, competing lines of precedent are available to support contradictory results. As the detailed analyses of the cases in the remainder of the book show, one of the most fruitful sources of insight into the structure of slave law is indeed the pattern of silences, or arguments unmade and lines of precedent ignored, that the cases establish. Initially, the manipulability of precedent might seem to support the reflex model, for one might wonder on what basis other than interest a judge could decide how to characterize and use the precedents. However, the fact that precedents can be manipulated to any result does not mean that they usually are so manipulated. For not all judges have the capacity to transform precedents into the shape they wish them to have. Only the best can maneuver through the competing lines to reach their own goals. Others, the mediocre who necessarily form the largest group of judges, act as if they were constrained by precedent and, indeed, construct approaches to the law that apparently reduce the confusion created by competing precedents to manageable proportions. Though that effort is doomed by the nature of legal rules, we can see throughout the cases attempts to evade that fate by developing appropriate rules and approaches.

Finally, as Professor Genovese argues, "the law tends to reflect the will of the most politically coherent and determined fraction" of the ruling class.[43] Without exaggerating that coherence, we can still expect the law to embrace positions that are required by the interests of the ruling class as a whole, even as they are inconsistent with the interests of individual members of that class. The law remains linked to the relations of production directly through the political perception of advanced segments of the ruling class and indirectly through the political principles that are ultimately rooted in those relations, but it is a connection better described by the phrase "relative autonomy," as I have tried to elaborate it, than by the image of a mirror that gives the reflex model its force.[44]

The description of the sources of relative autonomy suggests the forms that that autonomy takes. Each source leads to efforts to develop more or less coherently organized complexes of thought and argument. I have called these complexes "structures" in order to convey the sense of internal organization that they have. But they are not logically ordered principles, although logical inconsistency may lead to internal tensions that can be accommodated by adjustment within the structure or resolved by discarding one of the inconsistent elements. Rather, the structures are groupings of ideas connected by repeated association. My arguments will typically indicate how one element in a structure is logically related to, or sociologically explained by, another, and how the second is related to or explained by a third, but they will not establish relations, other than location within a single structure, between the first and the third.

D. A MARXIST INTERPRETATION OF THE STRUCTURE OF SOUTHERN SLAVE LAW

I have argued that judicial opinions provide useful evidence of the structures of thought that animated slave law because they were documents designed to convince by linking specific results to general assumptions. I have also suggested that we should distinguish between structures that are consistent with bourgeois assumptions and those that are consistent with the assumptions of a slave society, and that the important turn toward theory inaugurated by Elkins must be continued by rejecting the theory that would treat the structures as simple reflections of economic interest. Legal institutions mediate the impact of interest on law by creating a profession with its own interests and by making precedent important.

This section and the next elaborate the theoretical perspective that guides the remainder of the book. I must emphasize that separating the theoretical exercise from the examination of the cases falsifies to some extent the process by which my argument was constructed. My initial approaches to the cases were of course not theoretically innocent, but they were informed by a much cruder theory than the one I present here. Accounting for the cases forced reformulations and increasing complexity in the theory to which I was led. I have therefore resorted to some references to material in later chapters as a way of showing that the Marxist analysis given here is rooted in the case material.

Gorman v. *Campbell* and the cases already presented suggest that Southern slave law distinguished between law and sentiment as modes of regulating the institution of slavery. Marxist theory links these alternatives to the market and slave modes of production that were found in the slave South. The theory begins with a psychology of ideology which, though an essential part of a comprehensive understanding of society, has been neglected by prominent Marxist scholars until recently. Important work by Peter Gabel, drawing on Jean-Paul Sartre's late existential-phenomenological Marxism, provides the basis on which the following analysis rests.[45] The fundamental idea is that people must intepret the material conditions of their existence in ways that make their experience coherent. This idea, of course, is widely shared among certain schools of sociology which draw on the work of Alfred Schutz;[46] the contribution of Marxism is to emphasize that the primary, though not exclusive, material conditions that shape interpretations of the world are the material social relations of production. Marx himself developed the argument in the context of capitalist production, in his discussion of the fetishism of commodities.[47] The exchange of labor power for a wage is the basic transaction of bourgeois society, in the sense that it defines that society. In order for a market in labor power to operate, each worker's contribution to the market must be homogenized; a common unit of measurement is used to reduce the varying forms and quality of individual labor to an undifferentiated mass of fungible labor power. Thus, in the defining relations of capitalist production, each worker's individuality is eliminated in favor of an incomplete version of his or her ability. The first characteristic of bourgeois social relations that people must interpret is thus the role of partial relationships among people. This can be seen in more concrete forms as well. For example, the employer is unconcerned with the employee's family life except to the extent that the family situation affects worker productivity and so the value of the worker's labor power. Similarly, relations among workers are restricted to concern for each other's place in the production system.[48] These partial relationships are supported by other characteristics of capitalist production, and in particular are reinforced by the fractionation of the production process, as workers are involved solely in the segment of production that comes before them, rather than in the entire sequence of steps that produces commodities.

In specific historical settings, of course, partial relationships and fragmentation do not fully describe the world that people must interpret. They become more descriptive as capitalism matures, but even then people confront situations where, for example, solidarity, based on totalistic relations in the family or at the workplace, is a part of the experience that must be interpreted. Indeed, to some extent that description is necessarily incomplete, for the social relations of bourgeois society are internally contradictory, as is shown most dramatically by the simultaneous division of labor and unification of the working force in the factory. It is important to emphasize, however, that the description is not an ideal type but rather an abstraction that captures the fundamental relations in bourgeois society.

The interpretation of a world premised on partial relationships has historically taken the form of an ideology of individualism,[49] which, if not the world-view compelled by such relationships, is at least consistent with them. That ideology forms the basis of the bourgeois theory of the rule of law, which allocates to the government a strictly defined and limited set of ends. By so limiting government power, the rule of law defines a sphere of individual autonomy into which intrusions, whether by the state or by other people, are prohibited. For the purposes of this study, it is unnecessary to spell out the details of bourgeois individualism, law, or ideology;[50] they form a complex whose contrast with the fundamental social relations of slave society concerns us here.

When a slaveowner purchases a slave, he or she acquires, not the use of the slave's labor power—not, that is, only part of the slave's activities—but the slave's labor—all the activities in which the slave engages. The fundamental social relation of slave society is thus total, engaging the full personalities of the slaveowner and the slave. As with the partial relationships in bourgeois society, the total relationships of slave society can be seen in more concrete forms. Thus, when slaves live in close proximity to the master, the master will almost automatically become informed about and concerned with the development of families among the slaves. Similarly, slave religion will become a matter for consideration by the masters, not simply because religion can be a source of both slave compliance and slave rebellion,[51] but because the spiritual life of the slave is part of the world that the master must interpret.

For reasons that I will discuss shortly, the ideological consequences of the totalistic relationships of slave society were not developed with any detail in Southern slave law. Professor Genovese has argued that they were best stated in the apparently idiosyncratic works of George Fitzhugh. As summarized by Professor Genovese, the assumptions that slaveowners used to interpret their world were:

(i) What makes a man human is his dependence on the wills of others and his existence as a being in society.

(ii) The need to rely on others implies the sacrifice of individual freedom in return for protection and support.

(iii) Being unable to live apart, man owes everything to society.

(iv) The individual can alienate the whole of his property in his own person, not merely his capacity to labor, and must do so if he expects the protection and support of another. The other must have a property in his person to guarantee protection and support, for the necessary sentiment can only arise from interest.

(v) Human society consists of a series of organic relationships in which man holds property in man.

(vi) Since dependence on the wills of others is what makes a man human, each individual's freedom must be limited by his position as the property or propertyholder of another; since the propertyholder acquires a trust and responsibility in this relationship, his freedom must be limited by the general will of propertyholders as a class.

(vii) Political society is a human contrivance for the protection of man's property in man and therefore for the maintenance of orderly relations of production between individuals regarded as owners or owned.[52]

We will hear echoes of some of these themes in the cases to be discussed, but the assumptions are scarcely elaborated in the cases. The fact that the assumptions of slave society were submerged in the cases is what is interesting at this stage of the argument.

Several reasons may be given for this submerged status. First, as Professor Genovese argued, one finds the assumptions most clearly stated in the apparently eccentric work of George Fitzhugh precisely because he was an irresponsible intellectual who could afford to work out the logic of slave society no matter how abhorrent the consequences might seem to those who had not thought the problems through. Most people, including most irresponsible intellectuals, surely found the disparity between the morality of slave society, when fully displayed, and the morality of Western society, in which they were enmeshed, too great for comfort. The logic of slave society might then be both the only set of assumptions that made sense of their entire range of experience and simultaneously a set of assumptions that could not readily be confronted explicitly. For this reason, perhaps, we must talk about the "latent" structure of slave law.

Further reasons may have forms specific to the legal system, although they are examples of general social processes. Working out the logic of a society is difficult intellectual work, and most judges, like most occupants of any social position, do not have the intellectual capacity to push that logic to its limits. The tradition of adherence to precedent, too, impeded the emergence of a law embodying a detailed elaboration of the assumptions of slave society, for the precedents that were closest at hand involved decisions by bourgeois courts or at best by courts grappling with the emergence of bourgeois institutions. Thus, difficult legal reasoning was needed to manipulate the bourgeois concepts made available by the precedents into forms that could have become the precedents for a new slave law. In light of the suppleness of the law over extended periods, there is little doubt that such a law would have been created. But Southern law as a whole was not given the time needed for that process to take effect. The closest it came were the isolated expressions by judges who, in terms of talent within their own sphere, ranked with George Fitzhugh as intellectuals with insight into the logic of slave society.

So far I have suggested reasons why slave law lacked open expressions of the assumptions that people in slave society needed in order to interpret their world. But the structure of slave law had another, more important component: the latent dichotomy between law and sentiment. If law truly embodied the interpretive assumptions of a society, then slave law would have been a law shaped by sentiment. The preceding discussion indicates why sentiment could not give the entire shape to the law, but it does not indicate the bases for the law/sentiment dichotomy. Once again reference to the need to interpret the world clarifies the issue. Slaveowners participated in a nascent slave society, it is true, but they also participated in a mature bourgeois society. Their cotton was shipped north and to England, and they purchased goods made in commodity production. Perhaps more constraining were the political ties imposed by the federal union: whenever Southerners tried to articulate the premises of slave society, they were forced to explain to Northerners why those premises could be accommodated within the union; Northerners, because of their own assumptions, could only understand arguments stated in bourgeois, individualistic terms; and it is not surprising that slave owners found it difficult to explain paternalism in the language of individualism. Finally, slaveowners were engaged in market dealings among themselves, as the hiring out of slaves in *Gorman* v. *Campbell* shows in the context of a legal proceeding.

The world the slaveowners had to interpret, then, had a dual aspect: it was simultaneously a world of totalistic relationships and of partial ones. It is perhaps possible that some synthetic interpretation of the slaveowners' world could have arisen, but it is hard to imagine what that interpretation would have looked like or how it could have been attractive enough to become a widespread ideology; we are concerned, after all, with a self-contradictory world. The solution seems obvious once the problem has been stated in this way: because the world is bifurcated, similarly bifurcate the intepretations of the world. Slave law recognized regulation by law rather than by sentiment more readily the closer the circumstances came to involve purely commercial dealings. In a sense slave law asserted jurisdiction only over market transactions, leaving other relationships to be regulated by sentiment. Thus, the law/sentiment dichotomy was not coincidentally related to the market relations/slave relations dichotomy, but was rather structurally derived from it.

There is one final part of the structure of slave law that must be explored. Just as the assumptions of slave society were submerged even in the part of the law that purported to respond to those assumptions, so the law/sentiment dichotomy was rarely stated openly. The courts' failure to speak directly about the allocation of law and sentiment to different spheres of activity in slave society can be explained by many of the same factors that were invoked to explain their failure to articulate the consequences of the premises of slave society; thus, the difficulty of the endeavor and the mediocrity of the judges had some effect. Still, a Southern judge could, in appropriate cases, explain clearly that the dichotomy between law and sentiment was sensible. The reason for the absence of such overt expressions in the general law of slavery is the primary subject of Chapter III.

E. The Origins of Categorization, and Its Failure

Southern slave law had two primary characteristics. First, it attempted to allocate control over slaves to the sentiment of the master class. But a complete allocation along those lines would have removed the regulation of slavery from the sphere of law. If there was to be a "law" of slavery beyond the simple jurisdictional allocation, Southern courts had to give it substantive content. The second characteristic of slave law was the effort, repeated in various forms, to confine the content of slave law to the situation of slaves alone. Yet the effort to categorize slave law as a distinct subject matter repeatedly failed. The previous section provided an explanation for the failure of Southern law to reach the simple jurisdictional allocation. Here I address the two facets of the failure of categorization: that it was attempted, and that the effort failed.

By definition, slavery established a hierarchy of subordinate slaves and superordinate masters. But those two classes did not exhaust the social groups in the society; there was of course a large group of free white nonslaveowners. If the classifications of slave and master were the only ones available, nonslaveowners could reasonably fear that they would be treated as a subordinate class. To secure the allegiance of non-slaveowners to the political interests of the master class, they had to be assured that they would not be as subordinated as slaves. Law could provide such assurances by drawing rigid lines around the class of slaves, thereby guaranteeing that the lesser protections that the law gave to slaves would not seep into the law governing nonslaveowners. As many scholars have noted, the categorizing effect of race had the additional attraction of inserting nonslaveowners into the highest class in the hierarchy instead of creating an intermediate category for them.[53] But it was enough for these political purposes to bracket slaves off from nonslaveowners by *some* categorizing device.

Of course we should not overestimate the role of the law generally, or of such details as categorization, in securing the political allegiance of nonslaveowners. The depth to which consciousness of the law and its details penetrated any but the most advanced segments of the ruling class is problematic and is probably impossible to determine now.[54] From the point of view of legal history, that difficulty may not be important, for we can understand the political aspects of law as expressions of aspiration; it would be enough that lawmakers assumed, or hoped, that the law penetrated deeply. From the point of view of Southern history, what can be said is that the categorizing effort in the law is consistent with a range of maneuvers what are visible in such areas as politics and literature, and that all the maneuvers taken together are likely to have penetrated deeply enough. Categorization in the law could support other elements of a general structure of thought even though it rarely had to be called on directly in the effort to secure political allegiance.

Categorization also simplified the judges' job by reducing the number of cases they had to consider when deciding a new case. Without some limit on the range of analogy, judges would have to address in an articulate way every analogy offered by ingenious litigants. When a firm category becomes established, judges can reject proposed analogies, and lawyers will not think of them, on the simple ground that, for example, the present case involves slaves, whereas the suggested precedent involved free persons, without having to consider whether the rationale of the precedent is equally applicable to slaves. It is worth emphasizing that the need to simplify the task of judgment varies with the ability of the judges. A judge like Thomas Ruffin, aware of and comfortable with the suppleness of common-law reasoning, could present cases that others might view as different without any sense that the cases were discontinuous; he could develop an appropriate accommodation of humanity and interest within the ordinary framework of common law. Others seeking the same goal were forced to use analytically indefensible distinctions or rigid categories as their preferred device. The next chapter provides some detailed studies of these variations.

The process that I have called the development of categories resembles a process that could explain the development of what Max Weber called formal rationality. Weber defined formal rationality as a method of reasoning in which "only unambiguous general characteristics of the facts are taken into account" in formulating and applying legal rules.[55] But just as a case becomes a precedent only when a judge chooses to treat it as one, so too are facts general and unambiguous only when we say so. Formal rationalization may then be seen as a process in which judges decide to identify more and more facts as the basis for particularized rules. The rules simultaneously become narrower, for a rule that can be invoked only when a number of specified facts are present covers fewer cases than one that hinges on a single fact. Although formal rationalization presses in the direction of complete fragmentation, Weber's reference to "general characteristics" suggests its limit. If judges are to have a manageable body of law, some synthesis of the rules must be accomplished, by developing what I have called categories.

Weber was concerned with the external implications of the process of formal rationalization that was internal to the law. For his material, those implications were that the process tended to support the interests of the capitalist class.[56] As I have argued, categorization similarly served the interests of the Southern slaveowning class. Perhaps, then, formal rationalization should be understood as a process that is rooted in the inducement toward simplifying the job given to judges who, taken as a group, are almost necessarily mediocre, and that at the same time serves the interests of the politically dominant class.

But Southern slave law was characterized by a failed attempt to develop rigid categories, and the failure is perhaps more interesting than the attempt. I can suggest three reasons for that failure: the intractability of the social reality with which the law dealt, the inevitable openness of reasoning by analogy, and the structural incompatibility of a "law" of slavery in a slave society.

Every legal rule imposes an artificial order upon social reality by ignoring the complexity of that reality and focusing instead on some elements that can be identified and manipulated without too much conceptual or practical difficulty. In the main, this artificiality is accepted as a necessary, if sometimes regrettable, side effect of having a system of law.[57] But there are limits to acceptable artifice, set by the importance of these aspects of social reality that are treated artifically. The difficulty for slave law was that categorization forced the law to disregard the reality of the very institution that defined slave society. The vacillation between race and status as the ground for classifying illustrates the problems, for whichever ground was chosen, the rules would have to ignore the actual interplay between race and status. It is not inconceivable that some acceptable classification might have evolved over a long period. For example, a hierarchy that incorporated free whites and "colored" slaves might have developed, perhaps ultimately in the Brazilian direction. But there were both political and conceptual barriers to such developments. Overcoming those barriers would have required a fair amount of judicial ingenuity, a commodity that is always in scarce supply. Southern law was not given the time to accumulate the contributions that talented individual judges could make.

In addition, the nature of legal rules leads to difficulties in maintaining rigid categories. The courts repeatedly face novel situations, that is, those in which the fact patterns are thought to be significantly different from those that can properly be disposed of by invoking settled rules. The only way to handle such novel cases is by analogy, by isolating those aspects that most closely resemble familiar ones to settle upon the rule, which is then to be adjusted in light of the other significant facts in the case. But that immediately breaks the bounds of the established categories and introduces an instability that can be eliminated only when enough novel cases have accumulated to allow a reorganization of the subject into new categories.[58]

Novelty and its impact can, however, be resisted. For example, institutional arrangements may conceal the way in which facts affect the application of rules, as when juries decide the important questions. But the institutional arrangements may change for reasons unrelated to the problem of categorization. Even more important, legal rules tend to place limits on the degree to which issues can be concealed. As the North Carolina cases on assault examined in Chapter II show, problems of one sort were avoided by committing the question of provocation to the jury, but problems of another sort arose as lawyers tried to test the limits of provocation. In general, even though a court might define a narrow and clear rule for some subject, there will inevitably be other rules the relevance of which can be made apparent by persuasive advocacy and the application of which will blur the categories defined by the clear rule. A rule may establish a category, but a legal system taken as a whole provides the opportunity to destroy, blend, and otherwise modify that category.

Another form of resistance to novelty is cognitive. Judges

can insist that the fact pattern of the assertedly novel case is not significantly different from that in some earlier case. The ability of judges to deny differences that are apparent to others cannot be underestimated. But because this form of resistance is cognitive, its impact will vary with the judges' ability. A Judge Gaston might refuse to see differences that a Judge Ruffin found apparent. Once Judge Ruffin was given the opportunity to speak, though, the coherence of the categories used by judges of lesser ability was destroyed. The less capable judges had to deal with Ruffin's opinions as precedents to be fit into an overall structure, and that was very difficult. Categorization, then, may have been attractive to mediocre judges, but their efforts were undermined by their inability to keep more talented judges, few though the talented might be, from having their say.

Finally, categorization failed because of the contradictions of Southern slave society. The fundamental structure of slave society required the allocation of law to market relations, but because Southern slavery was part of a world capitalist system, the concept of law inevitably shaped the ideology of master-slave relations. Thus, Southern judges were trying to develop a law of slavery when only social control through sentiment could have yielded a stable result. Categorization attempted to confine slave law to the slave setting, but the enterprise was incompatible with the logic of slavery, which entirely denied the relevance of law to that setting.

F. Conclusion

The concern for theory that Elkins brought to the study of slavery has also characterized recent work in legal history. This book uses the model of relative autonomy developed above to discuss the law of slavery. The next chapter draws on a detailed examination of four cases to present a description of the basic structures of Southern slave law. The third chapter describes the major form that the attempt to contain the competing structures took. Again it draws on detailed presentations of cases and concludes with an argument based on theory that links the effort to the sources of relative autonomy. The final chapter then examines a number of areas of civil law that affected the ability to deal in the market for slaves and the masters' power to exercise their choice to free their slaves and argues that limitations on freedom of will, a major component in bourgeois law, were imposed in the interest of the master class as a whole and subverted the bourgeois elements in slave law.

My presentation of the cases includes substantial quotations and some fairly technical analyses. They are needed in order to convey the richness of the structures of slave law and to identify those structures through what was and was not said. I believe that the material will enrich the study of both Southern and legal history.

II. THE STRUCTURE OF THE LAW OF SLAVERY:
SOME CASE STUDIES

I HAVE ARGUED that slave law is used most productively to illuminate the ideological underpinnings of Southern society. This chapter develops that argument through a series of concrete analyses. I have selected four cases for detailed study. They were decided by the supreme courts of Louisiana in 1818, of North Carolina in 1829 and 1858, and of Georgia in 1853, and thus span the antebellum South geographically and temporally. In addition, I have deliberately chosen subject-matter areas of substantial diversity. One case involves criminal prosecution, a typical subject matter of previous studies; the others involve industrial and nonindustrial accidents and implicate questions of contract law as well.

I have arranged the cases so that the analysis moves from a nearly pure market setting to a nearly pure plantation setting. In the first case, the fundamental social relations at issue are those between master and master, dealing in the market for slaves; in the last case, the fundamental relations are those between master and slave, living together in the master's domain. The case studies show how these different sorts of relations gave rise to different ways of thinking about slavery. Specifically, the cases attempt to draw a sharp line between regulation of the institution according to law, appropriate in market settings, and regulation according to sentiment, appropriate on the plantation. However, this effort was doomed to failure because ways of thinking generated by market transactions in slaves, which were a necessary part of Southern slave society, inevitably infected problems arising in pure master-slave settings, and because, once the cases were framed as presenting legal problems, the pressure to analogize from nonslave areas of law was intense. The structural parallelism, market/plantation and law/sentiment, then, lurks beneath the surface of the cases. It occasionally emerges, but in the end it cannot sustain itself. The following chapter discusses the way in which Southern slave law ultimately moved toward a resolution of the problems posed by the failure to develop a well-supported dichotomy between law and sentiment.

A. SLAVERY AND THE FELLOW-SERVANT RULE

One night in the mid-1850s, a freight train owned by the Wilmington and Weldon Railroad passed Joyner's Station, North Carolina.[1] Because it was to be followed shortly by a passenger train, the freight train was shunted off onto a siding. The railroad employed a switchman whose job was to adjust the rails so that the passenger train would continue on the main track. However, the switchman failed to return the rails to their proper position and the passenger train too was shunted to the siding, where it collided with the freight train. A brakeman, a slave owned by Mungo Ponton and leased by the railroad, was crushed between the trains. Ponton sued the railroad but, although the jury awarded him the value of his dead slave, the North Carolina Supreme Court held that the railroad was not liable for any damages.

When the supreme court decided the case in 1858, it noted that the question of the railroad's liability for injury inflicted by one of its employees on another was "not new to the profession," although *Ponton* v. *Wilmington Railroad Co.* posed it for the first time in North Carolina. The rule of nonliability was firmly established in relatively recent but universally approved precedents; Judge Thomas Ruffin, writing the court's opinion, noted that the rule had been adopted throughout New England, in New York, South Carolina, Georgia, Alabama, and Louisiana, and had been rejected only by a divided Ohio court. The rationale for the fellow-servant rule was given classic statement by Chief Justice Lemuel Shaw of the Massachusetts Supreme Judicial Court.[2] It was a "great principle of social duty, that every man, in the management of his own affairs, whether by himself or by his agents or servants, shall so conduct them as not to injure another . . . ," and if a stranger is injured, the employer will be liable for the resulting damage. But, according to Chief Justice Shaw, the case was different where the injured person was another employee. For there the employer and employee had a contractual relation, and "in legal presumption, the compensation is adjusted" to take account of "the natural and ordinary risks and perils," including the risk of negligence by a coemployee, that attended the work. In addition to the presumption that the contract price reflected compensation in the nature of an insurance premium against injury, the fellow-servant rule rested on "considerations as well of justice as of policy." Each employee was in a better position to know and guard against dangers caused by the carelessness of other employees than was the employer, whose managerial responsibilities required diffusion of attention throughout the enterprise. When one employee found himself working beside a careless coemployee, the careful one could notify the employer, who could then devote attention to remedying a particular risk without increasing the general burden of supervision. If the employer then failed to act, the endangered employee could "leave the service." "By these means, the safety of each will be much more effectually secured, than could be done by a resort to the common employer for indemnity in case of loss by the negligence of each other." Thus, the fellow-servant rule was justified by the ability of employer and employee to adjust wages in accordance with risk and by the need to develop loss-distribution rules that maximized safety in a cost-effective way. These are modern terms, but Chief Justice Shaw relied on the concepts they express.

Perhaps Chief Justice Shaw unnecessarily provided both a contract and a tort rationale for the fellow-servant rule. It is nonetheless striking that Judge Ruffin's opinion in *Ponton*, which rested so heavily on established authority, relied solely on the contract theory. Ponton had conceded the general validity of the fellow-servant rule, but tried to distinguish his case on the ground that the injured employee was a slave. A free person, Ponton argued, could negotiate a contract on whatever terms he chose and could leave the job if it proved dangerous, where as a slave, when hired out, "becomes the property, temporarily, of the hirer, with no will of his own, and is beyond the control of the owner." Judge Ruffin rejected the proferred distinction, without mentioning anything about the slave's will or ability to leave a dangerous job, because the action for damages was not for the slave's benefit but for that of the owner, who could have drafted the contract of hire to shift loss from injury to the railroad.

Ponton thus departed from the twofold rationale of Chief Justice Shaw's opinion by abandoning reference to the tort theory. Judge Ruffin's opinion provides a clue that must be developed. He argued that the lawsuit was for the owner's benefit and not for the slave's. In the sense that recovery would flow to the owner, that is true, but the point must be elaborated. Suppose first that the hired slave was simply injured. Then, although the owner would be the direct beneficiary of the damage award, the slave would be an indirect beneficiary: the amount of the award would be that which was needed to compensate the master for the loss in the slave's value, and, if the process of ascertaining damages and the market for slaves worked reasonably well, a part of the award would be designed to allow the slave to be maintained—given food, shelter, and clothing—at the level for uninjured slaves. If, as in *Ponton*, the hired slave died, the analysis is only slightly more complex, but it is important to note the shift that occurs. It can no longer be argued that the particular slave is the beneficiary, even indirectly, of the damage award. Of course, that is true even where free persons are killed, and in both situations attention must shift from individual to group. Where the slave is killed, the goal of compensation is to benefit the owner and, by imposing costs on the railroad, to provide protection to the class of hired slaves.

Chief Justice Shaw's tort rationale was designed to show that employers could be induced to maintain safe workplaces by a cheaper means than provision of a broad tort remedy. By refusing to shift the loss where the employee failed to notify the employer of danger, the law transformed the entire workforce into a corps of police at the workplace, thus reducing the need for a special corps of supervisors. Ultimately, the tort and contract rationales merge, because in theory the workers, assuming greater responsibility, can command higher wages, which when added together would equal the salary of the now useless supervisors. But, by shifting attention from individual to group, we can understand why Judge Ruffin refrained from mentioning the tort rationale. For efficient policing to occur, the employee had to be able, not to leave an unsafe workplace, which on Chief Justice Shaw's theory was only the ultimate step, but to notify the employer of the problem. But in a slave setting, that kind of communication posed difficulties. It would require either that the hired slave initiate contact with the employer or that the slave communicate through his owner to the employer. Each method would breach a basic assumption of slave society: that slave owners or persons in the position of owners had complete control over the lives of their slaves. It is surely true that slaves did initiate contact with owners, but a society that absorbs behavior that deviates from fundamental assumptions need not tolerate legal rules that are explained in an articulate way by referring to those deviations.

In this connection, the one case Judge Ruffin distinguished takes on a new importance. Ponton had cited an earlier case, *Jones* v. *Glass*, as imposing liability on a master for a coemployee's negligence.[3] There, however, the negligent employee was an overseer and had the employer's authority. Since the employer would be liable to the owner for the employer's personal negligence, liability should follow from the overseer's negligence. In the framework of Chief Justice Shaw's tort approach, there was here no need for the employee to act as the watch over the workplace in order to relieve the employer of the burden of supervision. The employer necessarily would supervise the overseer, and, on the tort theory, forcing the employee to bear the loss was senseless. This result could be justified only by a tort rationale, for in both a free and a slave setting, the wage could reflect a premium for the risk that the employer or the overseer would be personally negligent. But the tort rationale was acceptable in a slave setting because it did not require that the slave employee do anything to disrupt the normal hierarchy of communication.

The analysis of *Ponton* can be translated into terms I have already used. As a matter of social reality, it was likely that a slave working in a dangerous place would in fact communicate that danger to someone in authority, the employer or the owner. Communication with the owner, indeed, seems likely to have been more common than policing by free persons in northern industrial settings, because the nature of master-slave relations is likely to have generated relations of reciprocity that are absent in purely market relations. Thus, Judge Ruffin could have relied on these ties of sentiment to bolster the tort theory that attracted Chief Justice Shaw, in a setting where Judge Ruffin could have made a more persuasive case. But he did not rely on the tort theory. The opinion in *Ponton* thus achieves the division between law and sentiment by developing a rule of law and abjuring reliance on sentiment that would actually have strengthened the argument. To use a structuralist way of putting it, the opinion in *Ponton* reveals the following: contract is to tort as law is to sentiment, as market relations are to slave relations. In the North, where slave relations of course played no part in developing the law, Chief Justice Shaw could assimilate contract and tort rationales because bourgeois social relations identified the personality, the sphere in which ties of sentiment might have played a role, with pure will, the basis for contractual arrangements, which could be controlled only by law.[4] In the South, law and sentiment could not be so readily merged because the social relations of slavery generated a totalistic view of personality.

Ponton, then, treats law and sentiment as separate spheres of regulation. I will argue that this result was what all Southern law was aiming for, but that the effort ordinarily failed. *Ponton*'s success, which was a qualified one, rests on three elements. It was decided in 1858, after Southern law had grappled with slavery for an extremely long time, and when, as I will show, it had come as close to solving the intellectual problems as it ever would. In addition, the underlying transaction was as purely commercial as any that slave law was likely to confront. There was, of course, the market transaction involved in renting slaves, just as other items of capital could be rented, but even more, *Ponton* involved a rental to a railroad, the model industrial enterprise of the time, which would transport the slave employee to places some distance from his owner's residence and would thus weaken the social basis for master-slave relations. Finally, the opinion was written by Judge Ruffin, an extraordinarily able judge who, as the distinction drawn in *Ponton* between *Jones* v. *Glass* and the case at hand showed, was able to translate subtle differences in social settings into acceptable legal forms. Although assessing judicial ability is difficult, it is worth noting that Roscoe Pound considered Ruffin one of the ten greatest American judges.[5] When judges were less able, as they were bound to be in general, they could not maintain the clear dichotomy between law and sentiment that slave law required and that Judge Ruffin could develop. Yet it must also be said that Judge Ruffin's accomplishment was qualified by the fact that the dichotomy between law and sentiment remained implicit in *Ponton*, to be disclosed only upon a careful comparison of what Judge Ruffin said with what other judges were saying about the same problem. In the next chapter, we will see why Judge Ruffin's success was necessarily a qualified one.

B. Legal Control of the "Improvident Slave"

When conditions that allowed a court to separate market relations and slave relations were less forceful than in *Ponton*— when the judges were less talented than Judge Ruffin, or the fact setting less obviously market oriented—the line between law and sentiment blurred. *Gorman* v. *Campbell*, described in the Introduction, is a good illustration. The slave there had been hired out to work on a steamboat, had done work not usually done by slaves, and was killed in an accident.[6] The defendant, who had hired the slave, argued that because slaves were persons, with autonomous wills, one who employed a slave could not fairly be expected to supervise so closely as to guarantee that the slave did what he or she was hired to do, no more and no less.

Gorman v. *Campbell* is interesting because of the court's response to the employer's argument. Judge Lumpkin began by noting that the relations between slaveowner and slave user were contractual. A fellow-servantlike approach could have been developed from that insight. The price of hiring a slave, it could be said, necessarily reflected the various risks inherent in the enterprise. In particular, although the contract might have specified the owner's intention that the slave would be used for enumerated purposes, as a boathand for example, the price would reflect the unavoidable fact that the cost of confining the slave, a person with a mind and a will, to those purposes would be great.

As we will see, the court in *Gorman* did not deny the premise that the cost of close supervision would be high. Instead, it relied on an equally valid contractual argument, that the contract price was set in light of the express purposes to which the slave was to be put. The courts, Judge Lumpkin implicitly held, would not invoke general perceptions about social reality to alter the explicit terms of an agreement, no matter how obviously true those perceptions were.

But the analysis of *Gorman* v. *Campbell* is incomplete if it focuses only on the contractual relations between lessee and lessor. The contractual arguments are inconclusive: the rule the court adopted had the effect of forcing the person hiring slaves to bargain for a price reduction because the risk of accidental loss fell on the lessee; the contrary rule would have forced owners to negotiate for price increases for the opposite reason; and there is no reason to think that owners of slaves were in a stronger bargaining position than were employers. Thus we can come to no conclusions about the distributive impact of the rule adopted.

What we can see, though, is the basis upon which the court rested its choice, and that basis had nothing to do with contractual relations. Judge Lumpkin's opinion is strikingly confused after it establishes the contractual framework. It first suggested that the limited purposes for which the slave was hired require the employer to use due diligence to guarantee that no deviation from those purposes occurred, and later the opinion invoked a Louisiana case relying on a similar negligence standard. Unfortunately for Judge Lumpkin, the slave's supervisor, after observing the slave attempting to free the boat from the place where it was grounded, ordered the slave to stop. At that point, no harm to the slave had occurred. Only after the slave had defied his supervisor's order did the log on which the slave was standing give way. Although the facts as stated in the opinion are ambiguous, they suggest that a jury could have concluded that the supervisor gave the order in time for the slave to have escaped injury. The supervisor then might not have exercised the proper level of care for the half-hour before he gave the order to stop, but that failure would not have a sufficiently close causal connection to the injury to make the employer liable.

Judge Lumpkin was extremely skeptical about the testimony that supported the supervisor, stating that two witnesses, "to their credit," did not testify that the supervisor had no knowledge that the slave was in the water, and noted that "their testimony is significantly silent" on another point that might have favored the supervisor. But he did not conclude that the jury erroneously found that the supervisor had exercised due care. Instead, he argued that the employer had to exercise a higher degree of care; relying on prior decisions, he said that the employer was bound "to prevent [the slave] from being in danger." The slave had to be supervised very closely. "[The employer] not only *may* use coercion even to chains, if necessary, for the protection of the property from peril, but it is his duty to do so."

Why, finally, was that the employer's duty? "Humanity to the slave, as well as a proper regard for the interest of the owner, alike demand that the rules of law, regulating this contract, should not be relaxed. We must enforce the obligations which this contract imposes, by making it the interest of all who employ slaves, to watch over their lives and safety. Their improvidence demands it. They are incapable of self-preservation, either in danger or in disease." The counterposing of humanity and interest as both supporting the results is, of course, of great significance, but I have shown that interest could in fact have been served by the opposite result. Thus, the rule adopted in *Gorman* can be justified in the end only because humanity demands it. It is a peculiar humanity that protects slaves from their own improvidence by authorizing their confinement in chains; that is not hypocrisy, however, but the result of the need in a slave society to recognize the slave's humanity in ways that authorized continued repression.

In *Ponton*, the rules of law could be stated without referring to sentiment; Judge Ruffin suppressed arguments made available in the precedents on which he relied, when those arguments would have injected aspects of the slave as person into the law. In *Gorman*, the rules of law were rhetorically justified by reference to contract and sentiment, and were analytically justifiable only by reference to sentiment. The separation of law and sentiment was not achieved, even in a relatively pure market setting very similar to that in *Ponton*. The primary reason was that Judge Lumpkin was not as talented as Judge Ruffin. Lumpkin's limitations can be seen in several parts of his opinion. For example, Judge Lumpkin unnecessarily discredited testimony favoring the employer, and in decidedly unjudicial tones: "It was an accidental omission, no doubt, that the witnesses for the defendant failed to state how London [the slave] came to be on the floating log! Did he jump on it, from the shore? Their testimony is significantly silent upon this material point!" Further, Judge Lumpkin did not weave precedent and the case at hand together with any facility. Rather, he stated the conclusion, with his supporting rationale, and then simply listed and summarized three similar cases. Finally, the cases Judge Lumpkin cited did not in fact all make the employer the guarantor of safety; at least one was, on Judge Lumpkin's account, a simple case of negligence.

In *Gorman*, then, we find a confused blend of contract and slavery-based rationales, embedded in an opinion that could not retain a focus on any single element for very long. This was the general state of Southern slave law, incorporating in legal form the contradictions of a slave society in a bourgeois world.

C. The Classic Case of *State v. Mann*

The structure discovered in *Ponton* and *Gorman* also appears in *State v. Mann*,[7] one of the cases regarded by contemporary scholars as particularly revealing of the core of Southern slave law. To Stanley Elkins, *State v. Mann* illustrated "the completeness with which . . . questions, even extending to life and limb, were in fact under the master's dominion."[8] Eugene Genovese found in it the most faithful expression of the logic of slavery.[9] These judgments, although correct as far as they go, are seriously incomplete, because they ignore the complementary role of sentiment as a regulator of master-slave relations. This failure is especially suprising in Professor Genovese's case, for the entire thrust of his work is toward recognizing the mutual dependency of master and slave. Yet in his discussion of *State v. Mann* he truncated his quotations and concluded by counterposing court and legislature and by discussing a later superficial "reconsideration" of the attitude expressed in *State v. Mann*. I will take up the sequels in the next chapter; here my aim is to show that *State v. Mann* rested on the law/sentiment dichotomy, that the dichotomy was forced into the open by the way the North Carolina Supreme

Court, again through Judge Ruffin, framed the problem, and that the court's way of framing the problem resulted from the mixed slavery-market setting in which the case arose.

It is striking that, giving the passion we will see in the opinion, the facts of the case are barely stated by the court. Elizabeth Jones hired her slave Lydia out to John Mann for a year. "During the term, the slave . . . committed some small offense, for which [Mann] undertook to chastise her; . . . the slave ran off, whereupon the defendant called upon her to stop, which being refused, he shot at and wounded her." Mann was indicted for assault and battery, and the jury was charged that it could convict Mann if it found that the punishment was "cruel and unwarrantable, and disproportionate to the offense committed by the slave." The jury did convict, and Mann appealed. The North Carolina Supreme Court reversed the conviction, with an opinion that must be quoted extensively.

The first sentences of Judge Ruffin's opinion signal that the case is a special one:

A judge cannot but lament when such cases as the present one are brought into judgment. It is impossible that the reasons on which they go can be appreciated, but where institutions similar to our own exist and are thoroughly understood. The struggle, too, in the judge's own breast between the feelings of the man and the duty of the magistrate is a severe one, presenting strong temptation to put aside such questions, if it be possible. It is useless, however, to complain of things inherent in our political state. And it is criminal in a Court to avoid any responsibility which the laws impose. With whatever reluctance, therefore, it is done, the Court is compelled to express an opinion upon the extent of the dominion of the master over the slave in North Carolina.

Even this single paragraph reveals much. It is elegantly constructed to build tension before the reader is told what the problem is, and then to resolve the tension by a flat statement of the issue. Judge Ruffin's frame of reference can be seen behind the first sentence: it is not that such cases—assaults by hirers or masters on slaves—arise that causes difficulties; it is that they "are brought into judgment." That is, slave society is, for reasons that I will go into in a moment, uncomfortable with the use of the courts to handle problems of relations between hirers and slaves. Yet, as we have already seen, the courts handled such problems regularly in suits by owners for damages. And Judge Ruffin acknowledged in the next paragraph of his opinion in *State* v. *Mann* that the court did not "intend to interfere" with the liability of hirer to owner. Thus, a criminal prosecution by state authorities had to be different from a civil suit by an owner. The difference is obvious: although both actions call upon the courts, themselves part of the state, the civil action enforces private arrangements made by owner and hirer, whereas the criminal prosecution imposes an external standard on the transaction. An owner might rent out a slave, at a very high price, if the contract provided that the owner waived all rights to recover for injury to the slave, but the possibility of criminal prosecution would, in practical effect, override such contractual terms. It is market transactions that are regulated by law, and when law attempted to regulate other relations, the judges were disturbed.

The second sentence of the opinion suggests that Judge Ruffin was concerned that the opinion would be read and misunderstood by those unfamiliar with the requirements of a slave system. The natural impulse is to think that Judge Ruffin had Northern abolitionists in mind. That impulse is fed on reaching the later portions of the opinion, where Judge Ruffin criticized "rash expositions of abstract truths by a judiciary tainted with a false and fanatical philanthropy." And, indeed, William Goodell cited the opinion as one that would "repay profound study . . . betraying a consciousness that [the rights of the master] would not abide the test of the first principles of legal science."[10] Harriet Beecher Stowe read the opinion with "deep respect for the man and horror for the system."[11] However, both Goodell and Stowe wrote in 1853 of a case decided in 1829, and Goodell himself noted that "this decision [was] made in 1829, before there was any excitement raised on the slave question."[12] It is unlikely, then, that Judge Ruffin consciously referred to the contemporaneous North, although, given his sophistication, he may perhaps have anticipated the rise of "excitement" on the issue. Further, I have already argued that, in general, the audience for opinions on slavery was internal. In this light, Judge Ruffin's appeal to the knowledgeable can be understood as an attempt to induce sympathetic readers to suspend the repugnance they may initially feel so that, on reflection, they may appreciate how the apparently inhumane doctrine to be announced is compatible with true humanity.

The third sentence of the opinion counterposes "the feelings of the man and the duty of the magistrate." Here too we must resist the temptation of anachronism fed by the recent brilliant work of Robert Cover. Professor Cover identified—in opinions written by judges who, outside of their role as "magistrate," opposed slavery—what he called a "moral-formal dilemma."[13] Their moral opposition to slavery conflicted with their dedication to positivist approaches to law, which required them to defer to positive declarations of law by the legislature that supported slavery. One response to this dilemma was the "elevation of formal stakes," statements arguing that failure to adhere to formal restraints would lead to concrete social disaster.[14] This framework can be imposed on Judge Ruffin's opinion in *State v. Mann*, for, as we shall see, the opinion did conclude that the "public tranquility" required the complete subordination of slave to master. But it would be misleading to see in Judge Ruffin's "feelings/duty" opposition a parallel to Cover's "moral/formal" dilemma, and the fact that some elements of what Cover identified as a problem faced by antislavery judges can be found in Judge Ruffin's opinion casts some doubt on the accuracy of Cover's attribution of the source of the "elevation of formal stakes." Judge Ruffin's problem was not that of an antislavery judge enforcing proslavery law; it was that of a proslavery judge looking into the heart of the law of slavery, and doing so unflinchingly despite what he saw there. In addition, Cover's description of the "escalation of stakes" suggests that it was a rhetorical maneuver designed to alleviate internal decisional difficulties for the judge, but Judge Ruffin, and others who used the device, were probably doing no more than correctly describing what was actually at stake.[15]

Nonetheless, the opposition that Judge Ruffin draws is plainly an important one. It adds another parallel to the opposition between market and slave relations. Judge Ruffin's formulation is: man is to magistrate (or state official) as feelings are to duty. This fits well with the proposition developed earlier in this chapter that Southern slave law treated the opposition between sentiment and law as corresponding to a division between slave relations and market relations. To use once again a structuralist form of presentation, we can array the underlying concepts:

Market relations	Slave relations
Law	Sentiment
Duty	Feelings
Magistrate	Man

What is striking about *State* v. *Mann*, if these formulations are correct, is the decision to treat the case as one involving slave relations. For, although the case involved an assault by a hirer upon a slave, the court thought that it was "compelled" to analyze "the extent of the dominion of the master over the slave." Had the court been willing to distinguish between hirers and owners, its way out would have been obvious. The remedy of a civil suit by a master against the hirer, which would augment price increases that took account of the risk of injury, might not be effective. The master might not be in a position to evaluate the injury potential of the hirer, particularly if the latter were a stranger, and so could not properly set the risk increment to the price. The civil action, depending on the hirer's solvency beyond the rental price, might on occasion be ineffective. Masters therefore would want to have the threat of criminal prosecution as an additional deterrent to misuse of the hired slave, at least if masters could guarantee that criminal prosecution would supplement and not displace the civil action. Masters were in fact in a position to do that, because their control over the slave made it unlikely that prosecution would occur without the master's consent. This line of argument would have allowed the court to support criminal prosecution of the abusive hirer, to avoid the distasteful chore of appearing heartless, and to preserve the underlying structure by assimilating the case to those of market relations.

Judge Ruffin chose not to follow this line. In part this may have resulted from the arguments presented to the court. The attorney general relied on an earlier case upholding a prosecution for an assault on a slave committed by a person with no contractual relations with the master.[16] Judge Ruffin properly put that case aside; in the absence of contractual relations, the owner's interest could be protected only by a civil remedy, which was more likely to be inadequate in cases involving strangers than in those involving persons with enough assets to hire a slave. This remedy would have to be augmented by the state. The other analogy the court rejected was between slavery and "the other domestic relations" of parent to child, or master to apprentice, where the superior in the relation could be held criminally liable for assaults on the inferior. It was Judge Ruffin's rejection of that analogy that led to his anguished statement of the harshness of slavery:

> The difference is that which exists between freedom and slavery—and a greater cannot be imagined. In the one, the end in view is the happiness of the youth, born to equal rights with that governor, on whom the duty devolves of training the young to usefulness in a station which he is afterwards to assume among freemen. To such an end, and with such a subject, moral and intellectual instruction seem the natural means; and for the most part they are found to suffice. Moderate force is superadded only to make the

others effectual. If that fails it is better to leave the party to his own headstrong passions and the ultimate correction of the law than to allow it to be immoderately inflicted by a private person. With slavery it is far otherwise. The end is the profit of the master, his security and the public safety; the subject, one doomed in his own person and his posterity, to live without knowledge and without the capacity to make anything his own, and to toil that another may reap the fruits. What moral considerations shall be addressed to such a being to convince him what it is impossible but that the most stupid must feel and know can never be true—that he is thus to labor upon a principle of natural duty, or for the sake of his own personal happiness. Such services can only be expected from one who has no will of his own; who surrenders his will in implicit obedience to that of another. Such obedience is the consequence only of uncontrolled authority over the body. There is nothing else which can operate to produce the effect. The power of the master must be absolute to render the submission of the slave perfect. I most freely confess my sense of the harshness of this proposition; I feel it as deeply as any man can; and as a principal of moral right every person in his retirement must repudiate it. But in the actual condition of things it must be so. There is no remedy. This discipline belongs to the state of slavery. They cannot be disunited without abrogating at once the rights of the master and absolving the slave from his subjection. It constitutes the curse of slavery to both the bond and free portion of our population. But it is inherent in the relation of master and slave.

The analogy to other domestic relations was rejected, then, because children and apprentices could learn from the consequences of "headstrong passions" and because society would not suffer if parents were punished for using excessive force to discipline their children, whereas slaves would understandably rebel if their "passions" went unchecked and the relation of master to slave would be undermined if the state intervened. Judge Ruffin relied on a court's inability to draw lines between proper and excessive discipline to show just how disruptive it would be to allow criminal prosecutions under any circumstances:

> That there may be particular instances of cruelty and deliberate barbarity where, in conscience, the law might properly interfere is most probable. The difficulty is to determine where a Court may properly begin. Merely in the abstract it may well be asked, which power of the master accords with right? The answer will probably sweep away all of them. But we cannot look at the matter in that light. The truth is that we are forbidden to enter upon a train of general reasoning on the subject. We cannot allow the right of the master to be brought into discussion in the courts of justice. The slave, to remain a slave, must be made sensible that there is no appeal from his master; that his power is in no instance usurped; but is conferred by the laws of man at least, if not by the law of God. The danger would be great, indeed, if the tribunals of justice should be called on to graduate the punishment appropriate to every temper and every dereliction of menial duty. No man can anticipate the many and aggravated provocations of the master which the slave would be constantly stimulated by his own passions or the instigation of others to give; or the consequent wrath of the master, prompting him to bloody vengeance upon the turbulent traitor—a vengeance generally practiced with impunity by reason of its privacy. The Court, therefore, disclaims the power of changing the relation in which these parts of our people stand to each other.

Professors Genovese and Elkins ended their quotations from *State* v. *Mann* even before this point, and Professor Cover used these passages to note that "Ruffin articulated better than any other judge the position that . . . the law must reflect the cruel origins of the relationship."[17] But, if the law "reflected" those origins, it did so by not speaking of them at all, by removing cruelty from the ambit of legal regulation altogether. Ruffin's strategy is clarified by his next paragraph, in which he explicitly relied on sentiment as a deterrent to cruelty:

> We are happy to see that there is daily less and less occasion for the interposition of the Courts. The protection already afforded by several statutes, that all-powerful motive, the private interest of the owner, the benevolences towards each other, seated in the hearts of those who have been born and bred together, the frowns and deep execrations of the community upon the barbarian who is guilty of excessive and brutal cruelty to his unprotected slave, all combined, have produced a mildness of treatment and attention to the comforts of the unfortunate class of slaves, greatly mitigating the rigors of servitude and ameliorating the condition of the slaves. The same causes are operating and will continue to operate with increased action until the disparity in numbers between the whites and blacks shall have rendered the latter in no degree dangerous to the former, when the police [sic] now existing may be further relaxed. This result, greatly to be desired, may be much more rationally expected from the events above alluded to, and now in progress, than from any rash expositions of abstract truths by a judiciary trained with a false and fanatical philanthropy, seeking to redress an acknowledged evil by means still more wicked and appalling than that evil.

Cruelty thus was not tolerated in slave society, nor was the relationship of master and slave truly founded upon force alone. Rather, it was simply that *courts* could recognize no foundation other than force, and that control of cruelty must, and did, occur outside of the law.

I have argued in the opening sections of this chapter that Southern slave law strove to suppress overt recognition of the dichotomy of sentiment and law. *State* v. *Mann* shows why: to talk about the dichotomy was, given the nature of Southern slave law, to force the law to appear abhorrent. As I have indicated, Judge Ruffin could have avoided the result had he treated the case as one involving state remedies designed to supplement the master's private, market-related remedies, which he acknowledged would be available anyway. *Ponton* shows that Judge Ruffin could develop market-oriented arguments when he chose to. Why did he not do so in *Mann* and avoid anguish?

Although no conclusive answer can be given, the fact that *Mann* was decided in 1829 and *Ponton* in 1853 is suggestive. The report does not reveal the precise reason for hiring out Lydia, the slave who was assaulted by Mann, but it seems likely that the image of hiring out that dominated the court's thought at that time was one of transactions between an owner and a renter, perhaps an acquaintance, who needed skilled hands to work under close supervision in an essentially plantationlike setting. In contrast, *Ponton* involved hiring out for purely industrial labor. *Mann*, then, may have generated an image of the relation between hirer and slave that resembled the image of the relation between owner and slave rather than that of the one between employer and employee. Judge Ruffin's opinion suggests another reason for his failure to use market-oriented analyses. He wrote, "Our laws uniformly treat the master or other person having the possession and command of a slave as entitled to the same extent of authority. The object is the same—the services of the slave; and the same powers must be confided. In a criminal proceeding, and indeed in reference to all other persons but the general owner, the hirer and possessor of a slave, in relation to both rights and duties, is, for the time being, the owner." This passage indicates that Southern slave law did not at that time support a differentiated analysis of the various relationships among members of slave society. As I argue in the next chapter, this absence of differentiation had two effects: as *Mann* shows, it left judges in the position of either drawing the necessary analogies and articulating what they would have preferred to leave unstated or suppressing entirely the dichotomy between sentiment and law that shaped their legal universe; and it threatened the rights of whites who might find the law developed in slave cases applied to their own.

The conclusion of Judge Ruffin's opinion indicates the path out of these difficulties:

> I repeat that I would gladly have avoided this ungrateful question. But being brought to it the court is compelled to declare that while slavery exists amongst us in its present state, or until it shall seem fit to the legislature to interpose express enactments to the contrary, it will be the imperative duty of the judges to recognize the full dominion of the owner over the slave, except where the exercise of it is forbidden by statute. And this we do upon the ground that this dominion is essential to the value of slaves as property, to the security of the master, and the public tranquility, greatly dependent upon their subordination; and, in fine, as most effectually securing the general protection and comfort of the slaves themselves.

Professor Genovese saw in this passage Ruffin's "hope . . . that the legislature would find a way to remove the high court's dilemma."[18] But such a hope would be decidedly odd, for if absolute control by owner over slave was "essential" to the preservation of the institution, it is hard to understand the basis upon which the legislature could modify that control without destroying the institution. To understand Judge Ruffin's appeal to the legislature, we must return to a passage quoted earlier. The opinion argued that a court could not "determine where [it] may properly begin." The circumstances of the slave's provocation and the degree of the master's wrath varied so much that courts could not be expected to draw intelligible lines. "The truth is that we are forbidden to enter upon a train of general reasoning upon the subject. We cannot allow the right of the master to be brought into discussion in the courts of justice."

The linkage apparent in these two sentences, between "general reasoning" and the impossibility of judicial consideration of the master's rights, is crucial. It shows that Judge Ruffin's concern lay with an institutional problem peculiar to the courts, the need for courts to develop limitations on the master's rights that could be defended by "general reasoning." His appeal to the legislature was a call to an institution that faced no such constraints; the legislature could draw arbitrary lines, outlawing some kinds of punishment while permitting others that a court might find difficult to distinguish, imposing duties on renters that were not imposed on owners, and so on. Arbitrary categories might allow some weakening of the institution of slavery, but the weaknesses could be confined by the lines that defined the categories. To Judge Ruffin, who could see no lines that were analytically defensible, a weakness anywhere would spread by the force of analogical reasoning from decided cases to every part of the institution.

In the end, Judge Ruffin's fears were not realized, largely because judges throughout the South were not as adept at legal reasoning as he was. In *State* v. *Mann* Judge Ruffin's facility was demonstrated in his ingenious use of the opposition between "the feelings of the man and the duty of the magistrate," between "a principal of moral right" and "the actual conditions of things." The emerging rhetoric of judicial opinions in the 1820s developed a distinction between law and morality in order to make irrelevant challenges to new rules as immoral.[19] Judge Ruffin invoked that rhetoric but transformed its goal; rather than simply denying that law was connected with morality, he asserted that law had a restricted jurisdiction, within which *its* morality could be honored while the morality of sentiment could be respected in the situation presented by *State* v. *Mann*. The main line of legal development was precisely toward the use of artificial categories, developed by the courts and encouraged by what legislatures had done, that served to isolate slave law from the general law and to carve up slave law into discrete packages. That development is the subject of the next chapter; it will be useful to preface that analysis with an examination of a final case in which the law/sentiment and market/slavery dichotomies can be seen.

D. Humanity and a "Miserable, Blind Slave"

That case was decided by the Louisiana Supreme Court in 1818.[20] The plaintiff had owned a slave for many years when the slave was injured by a slave owned by the defendant. The injury was a very serious one, because the slave's only good eye was put out, thereby, according to the court, rendering the slave wholly useless. The plaintiff successfully sued for damages. The trial court's order had three elements, first, the plaintiff was to recover $1,200, the value of the slave, plus the amount of the bill for medical care already given the slave. Second, the defendant was to pay $25 a month, plus a lump sum of $200, for the maintenance of the slave. Finally, the court ordered that the slave "should remain forever in the possession of the plaintiff." The Louisiana Supreme Court reversed, holding that once the full value of the slave had been paid, title to him should pass to the defendant. Thus, the award for maintaining the slave was also erroneous.

This is a simple enough case, and yet it is quite revealing. We must notice first the ground for the trial court's action. The defendant's slave had made the plaintiff's slave "wholly useless." The defendant's liability was predicated on some theory analogous to failure to supervise his own slaves, which suggests some indifference to the harm they might do. That indifference, the trial court surely concluded, might well carry over to the maintenance of a useless slave. It then made sense to leave the injured slave with his longtime owner and to force the defendant to assume only the costs of maintenance, but not the actual care. The latter course would, it seems, have been dangerous to the slave.

In a single paragraph, the supreme court rejected this implicit justification for the trial court's action. It first stated the general rule of its slave law, that when full payment has been made for causing a total loss, title is transferred to the defendant. Then it expressly put aside the premises of the trial court's action, refusing to modify the general rule in light of the particular facts: "The principles of humanity, which would lead us to suppose that the mistress, whom he had long served, would treat her miserable, blind slave with more kindness than the defendant, to whom the judgment ought to transfer him, cannot be taken into consideration, in deciding this case." The structure of this sentence deserves close attention. The court did not deny that the mistress would treat the slave with more kindness; indeed, it stated rather sympathetically the principle of humanity that supported such a supposition. But, conceding that principle, it reverted to the general rule regarding transfer of title. Only after stating that the judgment "ought" to work a change in title, did the court conclude that it could not take the principle of humanity into consideration.

The court thus demonstrated its appreciation of the ties of sentiment that slavery could generate between master and slave and simultaneously denied that those ties were relevant in the law. The separation of the spheres of social relations and of the law is close to the surface and can be discerned without difficult analysis, but it was not openly acknowledged as it was in *State v. Mann*. The reason for the submergence of the separation, as I argue in the next chapter, was the civil-law system of Louisiana, which led to a categorical approach to the law generally: questions arising in one sphere were in that system unrelated to those arising in another. The civil-law system of Louisiana showed what a mature system of slave law would have looked like: a system with a rigid separation of sentiment and law, each recognized as important but each confined to its own sphere.

And yet that would have been a morally intolerable situation, unless the judges were as resolute as Judge Ruffin. No legal system can sustain itself unless participants in the legal process believe that its operations are somehow connected to doing justice—in a slave society, to protecting harmonious, and largely paternalistic, relations between masters and slaves. The Louisiana Supreme Court did not treat its own law so rigidly. It followed the sentence I have quoted with two more: "Cruelty and inhumanity ought not to be presumed against any person. A remedy for them can only be applied, when they are legally proven." These sentences compress some very complex judgments into small compass.

It turns out that the principle of humanity is a bit weaker than the court's reference to the "miserable, blind slave" might suggest. The plaintiff might treat the slave with more kindness, but the defendant would not be assumed to treat him with cruelty. Thus, the court assumed that most slave-owners would treat their slaves at least without cruelty. Ordinarily that assumption might be justified on the ground that the master's desire to preserve slave productivity and his previous social relations with his slaves would constrain his cruelty. But of course neither was available here, for the slave was new to the master and was wholly useless. The court's view therefore rested on the premise that a very strong ideology of the responsibility of the master class was extremely effective at every level of the society.

This can be seen again in the court's reference to remedies for cruelty and inhumanity. Plainly this referred to the possibility that a cruel master would be prosecuted for abusing his slaves.[21] The court's assumptions look in two directions. First, social controls on masters are thought to be effective; cruelty will come to the attention of neighbors, and public officials will move against it. Second, and more interesting, the court assumed that the law should not intervene before cruelty occurred; the remedy could "*only* be applied" when cruelty had been proven. Here we see one strategy for keeping the realms of social relations and of the law apart; doctrines were developed that minimized the occasions for legal intervention and that at the same time assumed the efficacy of noncoercive, ideological controls on the behavior of masters.

Another tension, here between slave society and bourgeois society, can be seen in this case by examining the damage award. Twelve hundred dollars, the court said, represented the full value of the slave. And yet the plaintiff sought more than that; she sought to retain possession of her slave. One can understand this as a case where the owner placed a sentimental value on a slave that was not captured in the market's judgment of value. But the court refused to take this sentimental value into account in determining what relief was appropriate. The difficulty arose from embedding slave relations within a market framework, for market relations disregard the peculiarities of individuals, whereas slave relations rest on the mutual recognition of the humanity of master and slave. That is, relations of personal dependence are incompatible with the premises of market relationships. But the general law of Western society, from which Southern law could not easily depart, rested on market relations.[22] Slave law could not fit comfortably within this framework, and, as I have argued, there was constant pressure to break out of it.

A final point illustrates the same tension. Ordinarily, when the value of a piece of equipment is totally destroyed, title to it would remain with the original owner. The defendant would pay for the loss of value, and the plaintiff would sell the equipment for scrap.[23] Or, to come closer to the slave situation, if the worthless equipment constituted a pure drain on its owner, as when the owner of a vacant building must pay taxes on it, we ordinarily would allow the owner to abandon it. But this solution, which is sensible where ordinary commodities are involved, is unavailable where slaves are. Abandonment would disrupt the social harmony of slave society, by creating a class of unattached, unproductive former slaves; it would open the society to charges of inhumanity; and, what is most important, those charges would be regarded by slaveowners themselves as justified. Just because slaves were human beings, then, an accommodation that was difficult to justify in market terms had to be reached. The only anomaly is that title was held to be transferred. Here my guess is that the court thought in only fair that someone who paid full value for a slave take possession; it was the same case that would arise if the defendant had purchased the slave for full value and then accidentally put out his eye. The notion of fairness on which the transfer rests, that is, seems to be a market-oriented one even though the problem the court faced could not sensibly arise in a market concerned only with ordinary commodities. Conjoined with this, though, may have been a complicated interaction between market- and slave-oriented assumptions. The transfer would destroy the ties of sentiment between master and slave that might lead the original owner to maintain the disabled slave at a higher level than was thought socially necessary, whereas the new owner, imbued with an ideology of master-slave harmony, would confine the maintenance to the necessary level.[24]

E. CONCLUSION

The cases analyzed in this chapter reveal a characteristic underlying structure despite their diverse subject matters and times of decision. That structure treated law as the method of regulating market relations, and sentiment as the method of regulating slave relations. These associations are understandable in light of the Marxist psychology of ideology developed in Chapter I. But the structure was latent rather than openly displayed for several reasons. The articulate defense of the separation of law and sentiment would have forced the judges to confront the contradictions between bourgeois and slave society or, put in a way that emphasizes the problem, the contradictions within slave society in a bourgeois world. This too was developed in detail in the previous chapter.

There is a final point, whose consideration must be postponed. The dichotomy between law and sentiment was as visible in *State* v. *Mann* and *Jourdan* v. *Patton* as it would ever be. In both cases sentiment was invoked as a ground for denying relief through the legal system. But judges found it difficult consistently to reject the use of law to regulate central aspects of their society. The difficulty then was to insert rules sensitive to sentiment into a system of law, in the face of the structural incompatibility of sentiment and law. The next chapters argue that the solution was found in elaborating a sharply defined system of slave law with a distinctive structure that could then be transferred wholesale into the legal system. .

III. THE EMERGENCE OF A LAW OF SLAVERY

SOUTHERN COURTS rarely made explicit the law/sentiment and market relations/slave relations structure that can be found in what they did. In part, that resulted from the difficulty of the endeavor. For example, a suit by an owner against a hirer whose failure to provide medical assistance injured the rented slave and so diminished his or her value involved both market relations, between the owner and the renter, and slave relations, between the slave and both the owner and the renter. If slave law were defined in jurisdictional terms, it is unclear to which arena, law or sentiment, such a case should be allocated. But bifurcation was dangerous as well as difficult. Suppose a stranger assaulted a slave. To hold that remedying the offense through a criminal prosecution fell within the sphere of slave relations would be to acknowledge the authority of slaveowners, not just over their slaves, but over nonslaveowners who interacted with slaves. In a region that had not broken with traditions of equality at least among white people, such an acknowledgment was ideologically impossible. Once again, however, this danger was not alluded to directly. Rather, Southern courts typically argued that certain, usually lenient, rules had to be applied in cases involving slaves because more stringent rules would, by the force of analogy in a precedent system, readily be extended to cases involving whites. The perception of danger, that is, can be found in the cases, but it takes the form of adopting uniform rules because bifurcation seemed inconsistent with the entire system of justice.

The courts slowly worked out an explicit solution that came close to respecting the dichotomous structure implicit in their decisions, although the lines of division in the explicit structure were shifted somewhat from those in the implicit one. Over time, they distinguished sharply between slave cases, a category that included commercial cases involving slaves, and other cases. The courts thus avoided the troublesome implications of a pure slave/market relations distinction, but at the cost of forcing into the slave-law category cases that could not be readily handled using the premises of slave society. The emergence of a law of slavery, distinct from a law of crimes, torts, and contracts where slaves were involved, was facilitated by the increasing codification of the law, especially the criminal law, because the theory of the common law adopted by Southern courts made it possible for them to accept lines between slaves and whites, when drawn by legislatures, that would have seemed arbitrary if drawn by courts. Codification can be seen as a manifestation of the process labeled "formal rationalization" by Max Weber, the product of the cognitive and institutional inability of judges to process the always increasing number of cases that had to be accommodated in a precedent system.

A. The Role of Codification: The Substantive Law of Slave Crimes in Mississippi

One line of decisions in Mississippi illustrates rather dramatically the transformation in legal method that was used to separate slave law from the general law. In 1821, the Mississippi Supreme Court held that under the common law a person could be convicted for killing a slave. In reaching that result, the court relied on the theory that slaves were, at least in this regard, just like all other people. In 1859, the court repudiated that theory and held that because slaves were not proper subjects for treatment through the common law, one slave could not be prosecuted for raping another. The different contexts of the decisions are of course important. The murder case was thought of as involving strangers, whereas the rape case involved relations between slaves on neighboring plantations, where internal discipline by the owners might be sufficient as punishment and deterrent. Thus the results may be accounted for, in part, by invoking the analyses of the previous chapter.

But something more was going on. The courts reached different results in the two cases because the later case refused to adopt the analytic premises of the earlier one. The shift in premises occurred for a number of reasons. A confusing set of cases had muddied the theoretical waters; a significant body of legal commentary was available for the later court, but not the earlier one, to draw upon; and, most important, by 1859, the law regarding slavery was in large measure statutory. The codification of the law of slavery appeared to relieve the judges of responsibility for developing the law, but even more significant, it made it possible for the judges to bracket issues regarding slavery off from the general law. This reduced the threat that repressive decisions in slave cases might have some impact, through their extension by analogy, on nonslave cases and it allowed the courts to work within a system that bifurcated the legal universe in a way that corresponded, although only roughly, to the latent structure of the law.

State v. *Jones* in 1821 held that "murder can be committed on a slave."[1] It is of passing interest that the court, in reaching that result, made no mention whatever of the underlying facts. Because the defendant, who received a death sentence, has a surname and is not identified as a slave, we can conclude that he was a white man, but we do not know what Jones' relation to the slave's master was. The identity of the offender was, however, irrelevant to the court, which proceeded from first principles. The basis for the opinion was the proposition that "because individuals may have been deprived of many of their rights by society, it does not follow that they have been deprived of all their rights." This proposition was established in two steps. First, slaves could be prosecuted for crimes, from which it follows that "they are men and rational beings."

In this state, the Legislature have considered slaves as reasonable and accountable beings and it would be a stigma upon the character of the state, and a reproach to the administration of justice, if the life of a slave could be taken with impunity, or if he could be murdered in cold blood, without subjecting the offender to the highest penalty known to the

criminal jurisprudence of the country. Has the slave no
rights, because he has been deprived of his freedom? He is
still a human being, and possesses all those rights, of which
he is not deprived by the positive provisions of the law, but
in vain shall we look for any law passed by the enlightened
and philanthropic legislature of this state, giving even to
the master, much less to a stranger, power over the life of
a slave. Such a statute would be worthy the age of Draco
or Caligula, and would be condemned by the unanimous
voice of the people of this state, where, even cruelty to
slaves, much less the taking away of life, meets with universal reprobation. By the provisions of our law, a slave
may commit murder, and be punished with death; why
then is it not murder to kill a slave? Can a mere chattel
commit murder, and be subjected to punishment?

Second, murder was defined in the general common law of
crimes as "the taking away the life of a reasonable creature,
under the king's peace, with malice aforethought, express or
implied. . . ."

Is not a slave a reasonable creature, is he not a human being,
and the meaning of this phrase *reasonable creature* is a human
being, for the killing a lunitic [sic], an idiot, or even a child
unborn, is murder, as much as the killing a philosopher,
and has not the slave as much reason as a lunitic [sic], an
idiot, or an unborn child?

The remainder of the court's opinion was devoted to rejecting the defendant's reliance on early Roman law, which
was set aside as the product of "a history written in the blood
of vanquished nations," and which was "extirpated in later
Roman law." The court concluded:

When the northern barbarians overran Southern Europe,
they had no laws but those of conquerors, and conquered,
victors, and captives, yet even by this savage people, no
distinction was recognized between the killing in cold
blood, a slave or a freeman. And shall this court, in the

nineteenth century, establish a principle, too sanguinary for the code even of the Goths and Vandals, and extend to the whole community, the right to murder slaves with impunity?

The tone of righteous indignation, as we will see, became transmuted into a stolid reliance on the facts of life. The most important feature of *State* v. *Jones* is the court's straightforward adoption of common-law rules. Slaves, it said, were people; killing a person was murder; and that was that. The court gave no consideration to the possibility that the social relations between slaves and free persons called for different rules in slave cases, that, for example, the dependence of slaves upon their owners provided them with a protector as good as the criminal law would be against "the whole community." Nor did the court suggest that the delicacy of the subject required that the rules be made by the legislature rather than by a court. It did invoke the prevalent notion that slavery "exists not by the force of the law of nature or of nations, but by virtue only of the positive law of the state," but positive law could be created by judges through common-law reasoning. Finally, the court expressly refused to draw lines within the class of "people," believing that to differentiate slaves from free persons would open the way to distinguishing between philosophers and lunatics. The force of the common-law method of reasoning by analogy from decided cases thus worked in two ways: it impelled the assimilation of slaves into the general category of "people," and it counseled against the creation of subcategories because once one subcategory was approved, the way was open to the creation of more.

In 1829, then, slaves were, for the purposes of legal reasoning, simply people, and rules applicable to the free population were necessarily applicable to slaves. This, of course, had to be qualified, since slaves obviously were a distinct group for purposes of legal regulation. The source of that regulation, however, had to be the legislature, which could draw lines and develop rules that courts, under the twofold pressures of reasoning by analogy, could not. The inevitable legislative intervention then created new difficulties. Under the pure common-law model, legal reasoning and the substance of legal rules were compatible: neither distinguished between slaves and free persons. When legislation took over and special rules for slaves were enacted, the system went out of phase as, in the face of a parallel set of regulations that sharply set off slaves from free persons, the courts strove to maintain a unified set of decisions in which it was permissible to draw upon cases in all areas to resolve problems in any. The outcome was a reconceptualization of the reasoning process: precisely because slaves were so completely dealt with by codified rules, the courts could no longer reason by analogy to regulate the residual areas.

The relation between common-law rules and statutory crimes was explored in a series of cases decided in the 1850s. Jesse, a slave, was indicted in 1854 for "wilfully and feloniously" setting fire to a barn, "contrary to the statute" that provided, "if any slave shall be guilty of burning any dwelling house, stove, cotton-house, gin or outhouse, barn or stable, or shall be accessory thereto, every such slave shall, on conviction, suffer death."[2] Jesse's attorney contended that the indictment was defective and impaired Jesse's conviction, because it failed to allege that he had "maliciously" set fire to the barn. The statute, he argued, assumed that barn burning was already an offense, and simply set the punishment for the crime once it was proved. Because the statute created no new offense, the indictment had to satisfy the requirements needed to state a common-law crime, and one such requirement was an allegation of malice. In contrast, had the statute "create[d] a distinct statutory offense, [by] prescribing a definition of the facts which constitute the crime," the indictment was adequate because it followed the words of the statute. The Mississippi Supreme Court agreed with Jesse's attorney and reversed the conviction. An indictment that tracked the statute would be sufficient it said, where the description of the offence in the statute, taking into consideration its nature and the natural and legal import of the terms used in designating it, is such as to convey a certain, clear, and full idea of the offence intended to be created, and to embrace every ingredient necessary to constitute it, though the words employed be not the same as would be required in indictments for similar offences at common law. . . .

The difference is simply that between offences which are fully and clearly defined in the statute, and such as are described generally. In the former, the description contained in the statute is sufficient; in the latter, the offence must be charged agreeably to the rules of the common law. It depends upon the nature of the offence and the terms in which it is described in the statute, whether the one or the other of these rules will apply to the particular case.

The crime of barn-burning needed more description than that provided by the statute; after all, the court noted in reliance on a part of Jesse's argument, the legislature could not have meant to make it a crime for a slave acting under his master's orders to burn a barn, and yet the statute, by making no reference to "malice or criminal intent," would have that effect. Thus, the court concluded, the statute simply defined the punishment, "leaving the proper description of [the offense] to be supplied, according to the settled rules of law when persons should be charged under the statute." Those settled rules, I must emphasize, were the ordinary common-law rules unmodified by the fact that the case involved a slave.

The easy adoption of common-law rules was even then under some pressure in other cases. The early slave code of Mississippi made an assault by a slave on a white, with intent to kill, a capital offense. This was modified in 1829 so that "malice aforethought express" was needed to subject the slave to capital punishment in cases where death did not occur, with a proviso that "no proof of express malice shall be required where the assault and battery is committed by a slave upon his or her master, employer, or overseer in resistance of legal chastisement."[3] Once again the supreme court confronted questions about the scope of statutory regulation in the context of challenges to the sufficiency of indictments. It is difficult to appreciate the reasons for the court's attention to matters of technical detail in these cases, for modern law has moved from their concerns. Today the courts uphold indictments that are enough to give fair notice to the defendant of the events and the offense at stake.[4] The Mississippi Supreme Court's decisions reflect a similar concern for notice, but, presumably because of difficulties in compiling adequate records that could be used to determine actual notice, that concern was expressed by using the face of the indictment as a measure of actual notice. In addition, precision in framing indictments was one of many requirements imposed on the state generally to guarantee that liberty would be affected only after the most careful consideration by the agents of the state.

Anthony v. *State* involved an indictment for "feloniously, wilfully, and of his malice aforethought" assaulting a white person.[5] The defendant appealed his conviction and death sentence, contending that the indictment was defective because it did not allege that he had assaulted the white person with express malice. The court explained that express malice "is characterized by a sedate, deliberate intention, and formed design, evidenced by external circumstances," whereas implied malice "is the offspring of sudden impulse." It held that the indictment did not follow the rule that "all indictments upon statutes, especially the most penal, must state all the circumstances which constitute the definition of the offence in the act. . . ." Two years later it upheld a conviction under the same statute.[6] The slave was charged with assault "in resistance then and there of legal chastisement, the [victim] being . . . the overseer of" the slave. The court rejected the slave's argument that the indictment did not satisfy the rule followed in *Anthony* v. *State*. Express malice was unnecessary in cases of resistance to punishment, and the indictment left no uncertainty about the circumstances of the assault. The two cases indicate the court's use of the indictment as a surrogate for inquiry into actual notice. In *Anthony* v. *State* the conviction was reversed even though the jury had found express malice; in modern terms, we would say that the lack of notice in the indictment may have led the defense to develop a presentation that ignored the issue of express malice. In the second case, the indictment, by following the language of the statute, provided adequate notice.

The interaction of common law, statute, and concern for precise statements regarding malice appeared in what can in retrospect be seen as a case located at a turning point, as is suggested by the fact that it contains one of the infrequent dissenting opinions on the Mississippi Supreme Court.[7] A statute enacted in 1822 provided that "if any slave, free negro, or mulatto shall prepare, exhibit, or administer to any person or persons in this State any medicine whatsoever, with intent to kill such person or persons, he or she so offending shall be judged guilty to a felony, and shall suffer death." Sarah was indicted in two counts for preparing and administering arsenic in the coffee she served. After disposing of some peripheral issues and upholding the joining of the two counts in a single indictment, Chief Justice Smith moved to the central issue. The indictment concededly did not allege that Sarah had acted with malice aforethought, and her attorney therefore relied on the principle of *Anthony* v. *State*. The court undertook to explain that principle by first distinguishing among statutory offenses. Some statutes described the crimes they created in detail; in such situations, an indictment could use the statutory language and, in particular, need not allege malice aforethought. Other statutes were less detailed; indictments for offenses such statutes created had to be framed "with the same particularity as at common law." The majority drew from this distinction the conclusion that malice must be alleged in all cases where it is "the gist of the offence," whether the crime was a statutory or a common-law offense. The law was thus reconstructed so that the common-law or statutory origins of the crime became irrelevant, to be replaced by a concern for the substance of the offense. With that concern in hand, the court examined the precedents. The statutes involving assault and arson did not make wilful malice an express ingredient, but, according to the court, malice was "the very gist" of the crimes. The antipoisoning statute was indistinguishable, so that malice had to be alleged in the indictment. Because it had not been alleged, Sarah's conviction was reversed.

Justice Handy dissented, emphasizing the distinction that the majority had dismissed between statutory and common-law offenses. "When the legislature have created an offence and clearly described its essential qualities, it is to be presumed that it was intended to dispense with the common law requisites pertaining to offences of a like nature, and to mark out and characterize the crime intended to be punished; and in an indictment for such an offence, it is clear that it is sufficient to describe it in terms of the statute, because the legislature has fully pointed out the nature and description of the crime intended to be punished. They have made both the crime and its punishment." Unlike the majority, Justice Handy regarded it as significant that the statute referred to intent to "kill" rather than intent to "murder." Because the statute used an ordinary, nontechnical word, "the terms used convey the idea clearly and irresistibly to the mind that the act was done from previous malice."

> This necessarily results from the nature of the act; for it is impossible to say that a sane man could administer poison to another wilfully, maliciously, and feloniously with intent to kill him, without conveying the idea irresistibly of previous preparation, deliberation, and malice. There is no room for sudden heat or impulse in such a case, and from the very nature of the act, any idea but that it was done with previous malice, must be excluded as completely as though the vocabulary of technical expletives were exhausted. In the present case, the statute had designated the

offence in a such a manner that both the act and the motive are set forth in the description of it in the act.

Further, the indictment was "plain and not to be mistaken, sufficiently full and comprehensive to bring offenders to punishment, but at the same time sufficiently explicit to give them ample notice of the nature, cause, and extent of the accusation."

It is hard to avoid concluding that, as a matter of technical legal argument, Justice Handy had the better of the exchange. Even on the majority's terms, it is not hard to see why malice had to be alleged where assaults were charged, in light of the substantial possibility that an assault could result from the sudden impulse of the moment and not from a "sedate design." In contrast, administering arsenic in a cup of coffee is not something that usually occurred on "sudden impulse." The more formalistic analysis in *Sarah v. State* led to a result in the particular case favorable to the slave. But I am concerned more with the implications of the way both sides on the court approached the problem than with the merits of their arguments or the moral value of the results they reached. For Justice Handy, the issue was framed in terms of a distinction between statutory law and common law. In particular, common-law principles were simply inapplicable in statutory cases. Thus, if the law of slavery were to be fully codified, it could be confined to its proper sphere. The majority did not disagree substantially with Justice Handy, although they put their position differently. For the majority, the substance or "gist" of the offense was crucial, not its origins in statute or common law. But no substantial argument was provided on the question of what exactly was the substance of the offense; the majority simply asserted that it was "unable to perceive a distinction" between poisoning and assault. Thus, there was not much distance between the majority's concern for the "gist" of the offense and Justice Handy's concern for its "nature." Once the issue was relegated to the judges' intuitions, though, the way was open to advert without serious argument to the difference "in substance" between slaves and free persons, and to leave the matter there.

Five years later, on the eve of the Civil War, exactly that happened. Two cases decided in the supreme court in the April and October terms of 1859 explicitly treated slaves and free persons as simply different; a third case tried to do so but ended with an analytically awkward amalgam of incompatible theories. Before examining the cases, it is worth noting that in 1858 Thomas Cobb's *Inquiry Into the Law of Negro Slavery in the United States* had been published. Cobb, the reporter of opinions for the Georgia Supreme Court and later an active secessionist, presented a more articulate justification of slavery in all its legal aspects than earlier writers had, and the Mississippi Supreme Court found in Cobb's work a presentation that it could adopt nearly without modification. In addition, the court had undergone a transition in 1858 with the appointment of William Harris as a justice.[8] Harris, a virulent proslavery judge, wrote the court's opinion in two of the cases to be examined here and also wrote the 1859 opinion in *Mitchell* v. *Wells*, a case denying power to Mississippi slaveowners to manumit their slaves by will even after the slaves were sent to free states and repudiating earlier, less restrictive rules.[9]

The court expressed its justification for separating slave cases from others in a case raising purely procedural questions. Like most other slave states, Mississippi had a special system of criminal trials for slaves. Under the system in force in 1859, the slave accused of noncapital crime was tried by a court consisting of two justices of the peace and five slaveholders. If convicted, the slave could appeal to the circuit court, the trial level court of general jurisdiction, where the trial would be *de novo*, that is, without regard to the results of the prior proceeding.[10] According to the Mississippi Supreme Court, "it was the object of [the system] to provide a more summary, cheaper, and more expeditious remedy for the trial of minor offenses charged against slaves, and yet to secure to the slave all just protection against the errors of the Inferior Court, established for that purpose."

Bob Minor, a slave, was convicted of grand larceny in the slaveholders' court and was again convicted in the circuit court. He sought review in the supreme court of his conviction, relying on a statutory provision allowing appeals "in all criminal cases."[11] Justice Harris said that the issue had a dual aspect. The right to appeal could be denied if slave cases were "specially excepted by the obvious intent" of the act establishing the special system for slave cases, or if "from their peculiar character and situation, this inferior class of our population are excepted out of our general legislation, and only included therein when specially named." In fact, both criteria were satisfied. The court agreed that if an appeal were allowed, "the whole object and design of the act is defeated, and an act designed to secure a speedy trial will be thereby converted into an instrument of delay, injustice, and oppression, to all parties interested; and, indeed, that by such construction the smallest offences will become, in the mode, and forms, and delays of trial, much more difficult, tedious, and expensive, than offences involving the life of the slave." The court returned to this accommodation of the two statutes in terms of the need to accomplish the purposes of both, in the opinion's conclusion. It referred to the detailed code adopted by the legislature to govern the trial of slaves. "It can hardly be supposed, therefore, that, in the great number, variety, and minute particularity of the provisions, establishing a *system*, having reference to this class alone, it could have escaped the scrutiny of the legislature, if they had so intended, to make provision for [appeals] also. . . ." Allowing an appeal, it said, would introduce "the very delay" that the special system was intended to prevent. Further, such a result would lead to the "absurd" conclusion that slaves would have three levels of judicial consideration, "for the most trivial offences . . . while for capital crimes, involving life, no such provision is made, and while the superior race, the white man, has no such right extended to him, in cases of the greatest magnitude, by our laws."

This purposive analysis rested explicitly on inferences drawn from the existence of a detailed statutory scheme regulating slaves. The court concluded that the legislature intended to make the scheme exhaustive, and thus completely separate from the regulation of free whites. But it was not legislative intent alone that was decisive, for the court relied heavily on the nature of slavery in the South to justify the kind of sharp distinction between slave law and free law that had not been drawn in the earlier cases. The discussion of statutory purpose was interrupted by extensive quotations from Cobb's *Treatise*. Since Judge Harris merely quoted from Cobb, it is unnecessary to elaborate the argument in detail. However, the choice of the subject of the quotation is significant. To determine whether slaves were "excepted out of . . . general legislation" referring to "all criminal cases," Judge Harris asked whether a slave was a person. Cobb addressed this question by examining whether killing a slave was punishable "under the general law prescribing the penalty of murder." He summarized the decisions holding that killing a slave was murder, and listed *State v. Jones* among those cases. But Cobb clearly approved of the tenor of the contrary cases, although he sought a compromise by saying that even without a statute, killing a slave was prohibited but that a statute was needed to provide punishment.[12] And Cobb endorsed the argument of the Georgia Supreme Court that "masters and slaves cannot be governed by the same laws."[13] Thus, general statutory language did not apply to slave cases, and Minor was not entitled to appeal.

As I have noted, this argument was followed immediately by a reference to the detailed statutory regulation of slave trials. Cobb, too, adverted to the role of statutes in "reliev[ing] the slave from . . . absolute dominion" and "from the cruel treatment of his master."[14] The conclusion to be drawn as regards the substantive law of crimes was that slaves could commit and be the victims of only those crimes enumerated in the statutes. The Mississippi Supreme Court therefore held, in another opinion by Judge Harris that contained paragraphs lifted from Cobb, that it was not a capital offense for one slave to rape another.[15] In *George* v. *State*, the court simply repeated the argument that, because slaves had "no rights prior to legislative enactments," only statutes could make slave activity a crime. The analysis of the common law concluded with a remarkable paragraph:

> With the exception of [a Tennessee case and two cases, including *State* v. *Jones*] in our state, and one or two very early cases in North Carolina, founded mainly upon the unmeaning twaddle, in which some humane judges and law writers have indulged, as to the influence of the "natural law," "civilization and Christian enlightenment," in amending, *proprio vigore*, the rigor of the common law, and on a supposed analogy between villanage in England and slavery here, the cases and text-writers are uniform in declaring that slavery, as it exists in this country, was unknown to the common law of England, and hence its provisions are inapplicable to injuries inflicted on the slave here.

Since no statute made slave rape a crime, the defendant who had been charged with that offense was released.

Two points deserve notice. First, the report of the opinion appends a note that "by ch. 62, p. 102 of the Session Acts of 1860, the actual or attempted commission of a rape by a negro or mulatto on a female negro or mulatto, under twelve years of age, is punishable with death or whipping, as the jury may decide." Second, Judge Harris applied the theory that slaves were not subjects of common-law rules in a case where part of the rationale provided by Cobb was unavailable. Cobb had introduced his discussion by noting that assaults on slaves "could be remedied and punished only at the suit of the master for the injury done him in the loss of service or the diminution in value of his slave."[16] Unless the courts constructed an action against the owner of a slave, which they gave no indication of doing, this remedy was unavailable where one slave was the victim of another slave's attack. Thus the distinction between slave law and the general law was even sharper than it might first seem, for the special treatment of slave law occurred where it could be justified only in terms of the nature of slavery, without reference to other policies such as the adequacy of alternative remedies.

Minor v. *State* and *George* v. *State* clearly delineated a sharp distinction between statutory law and common law, but it is misleading to suggest that such a distinction was fully acknowledged. Only Judge Harris' emotion, which allowed him to castigate a prior decision of his own state's court as resting on "unmeaning twaddle," made the distinction clear. An opinion by Chief Justice Smith of the same court, appearing within ten pages of the report of *George* v. *State*, shows a more equivocal response, albeit one that displays the distinction on its surface.

William Ford had been an overseer for John Walker for about one month when he was killed by Wesley, a slave under his supervision.[17] On a Sunday morning, Ford brought Wesley to the smokehouse, where punishment was usually administered. Wesley was tied up, and Ford went in for breakfast. His wife, wanting some meat, went with Ford to the smokehouse. Suddenly Wesley sprang at Ford and, avoiding the knife Ford was sharpening, hit Ford on the head with a large piece of wood. Wesley ran to Walker's house, left when he did not find Walker at home, and returned shortly, after the dogs had started hunting him. At the trial, evidence was introduced that Ford was a violent and cruel overseer. His former employer testified that Ford had been fired for being cruel to the slaves, and three slaves testified that just before Wesley was taken to the smokehouse, Ford had become enraged at Wesley's failure to curry a mule properly and had beaten and kicked Wesley. In addition, Walker testified that he had refused to hire Ford at first, because Walker knew that Ford was "a violent, severe, and cruel man," and that he had hired Ford later, after failing to find another overseer and after being assured by Ford that he had brought his temper under control. The trial court refused, however, to allow Walker to testify about Ford's general character, "with reference to violence and cruelty," or about evidence of "specific acts of unmerciful severity during the time he remained with Walker." Wesley was convicted.

The primary issue on appeal related to the exclusion of the evidence about Ford's general behavior. Wesley's attorneys claimed that such evidence would clearly have been admissible in a case involving a white man, because it would help to determine whether the defendant acted reasonably in self-defense. Since self-defense could be asserted by slaves as a response to criminal accusations, the same evidence should be available. Indeed, they argued, the case for admitting the evidence was strengthened by the fact that the defendant was a slave.

He is, it is true, required to submit to the actual or threatened violence of the white man, far beyond the point demanded between equals. That very fact, in the assaults of the white man upon him, must inevitably awaken and keep in alarm his fears, as to what the unresisted violence of the white man will wreak upon him. As his hope lessens, his fear strengthens. He knows he must yield to great personal suffering, ere he do aught but supplicate. He feels that, at some point, he may strike to save life or limb; and when submission has been yielded, and the suffering endured, and he sees the "end is not yet," but that the violence increases, and threats and preparations for deadlier assaults are made and extended about him, a sense of danger seizes on his soul; his fear, till that time repressed by the hope of cessation, now fills his mind with dread imaginings of the evils to come; and he is then infinitely less able rationally to calculate the degree of danger which threatens him, than the white man, under circumstances of similar, or even much greater hazard. Escape and life, are the unreasoned, resistless motives which nerve his action; and he wildly, madly struggles for refuge and safety, whether angels or devils oppose, under the mere instinct of the frightened brute fettered in the toil. . . . If the slave can allege apprehended danger, every cause of apprehension, incident to the white man, applies to the negro. It is a principle involved in the constitution of the human mind, and uniform in its development and operation among all races.

I have quoted this argument at such length, not only to display its rhetoric, but to emphasize the essential linkage between the claim that slave cases should be governed by common-law rules and the principle, noted in the final sentence, that whites and blacks were subject to the same laws of psychology.

Chief Justice Smith rejected these arguments in an opinion that had two components. It began with a statement of the law of evidence, which denied the admissibility of evidence relating to the general character or specific acts by the victim because ordinarily such evidence did not sufficiently demonstrate that the defendant acted reasonably in self-defense in the specific circumstances of the case. There were exceptions, but they were inapplicable to Wesley's claim. At this point, the opinion switched from the general law of evidence to the law of slavery: "[T]he real question . . . is not whether, in prosecution for murder, it is competent, under any circumstances, for the defendant to prove the general revengeful and dangerous character of the deceased. It is whether the general management of slaves, on a plantation, by the deceased, as characterized by violence and cruelty, . . . may be proved as circumstances going to justify a homicide, by a slave, committed upon him while acting as such overseer." The court rejected Wesley's claim because it rested on a principle that "if recognized by the courts, would produce the most disastrous consequences."

> If the slave, when he is about to be chastised, or has just reason to apprehend that he will be subjected to cruel and unmerited punishment, be informed, that in order to escape, he may innocently slay his master or overseer if he

really believes that by the apprehended punishment his own life will be taken or greatly endangered; and that to make good his defence in a court of justice, it will be sufficient to prove the general violent and cruel conduct of the deceased in the government of slaves; the slave population of the State will be incited to insubordination and murder, and the life of the master exposed to destruction, either through the fears or by the malice of his slaves.

The opinion then returned to the general law, holding that the proferred evidence would not go to establish that the defendant, whether white or black, acted in self-defense.

Unlike Judge Harris, Chief Justice Smith was unable to set aside nonslave cases as simply irrelevant to the problem he faced. Instead, he equivocated, by explaining why the rule in slave cases had to be adapted to their special circumstances, but also by denying that a white, having acted as Wesley had, would have been entitled to introduce the evidence in question. The situation resembles that discussed in the last chapter: the courts strive for, and occasionally reach, the goal of a sharp distinction, here between slave law and nonslave law, which they assimilate to another distinction, between statutory and common law, but the distinctions are extremely difficult to sustain in practice. We can now augment one of the lists from the last chapter.

Market relations	Slave relations
Law	Sentiment
Nonslave law	Slave law
Common law	Statutory law

This array suggests some interesting possibilities. Most obviously, the unitary category of law is here broken down so that some state intervention in slave relations is authorized. Of course, because the material used in this study is a set of judicial opinions, it is unlikely that a pure law/sentiment dichotomy would have been revealed. But it is interesting that when courts act, their intervention takes the form of legislative decision implemented by the courts, rather than the form of direct judicial construction of the law.

The prior chapter revealed a structural relation between the law/sentiment and market/slave dichotomies. A similar relation between the law/sentiment and common-law/statutory-law ones can also be developed. The next sections of this chapter describe three components of that relation. First, the experience in North Carolina is examined. It reveals that the essential distinction is between disposition of cases on the ground that they fall within a particular category and disposition based on a broader search for relevant analogies. The function of codification, in this light, was to establish the set of categories. Thus, a further modification of the array would be:

| Statutory law | Common law |
| Categories | Analogies |

Next, an examination of the law of criminal procedure in slave cases reveals a rather explicit concern that relaxation of general rules because slaves were involved threatened the rights of whites accused of crime. Codification, or the development of a detailed set of categories, served to reduce that threat by confining the implications of any decision to the precise category or statute involved. They therefore were an attempt to resolve the tension between market and slave relations by defining precisely the circumstances under which sentiment was to be a principle for ordering social relations. Third, the largely implicit role of race as a categorizing principle will be discussed.

B. Categorization in the Absence of Codification: The Substantive Law of Slave Crimes in North Carolina

For the Mississippi court, the existence of comprehensive legislative action regarding slave crimes established the categories for considering legal problems in the area. The North Carolina

Supreme Court could not rely on similar legislative action, for the law of slave crimes in North Carolina was the product of judicial development through the common law. Professor Genovese, comparing *State* v. *Mann* with later developments in North Carolina, found a "reconsideration" of the earlier case, which had "followed . . . faithfully" the logic of slavery, by a "liberal" judge whose opinion was "infinitely more humane and considerably less logical."[18] If this judgment were correct, the structure that I have been describing would be undermined. Indeed, if the statutory-law/common-law dichotomy were fundamental, the course of North Carolina law would not fit into the structure. However, close examination of the cases reveals the parallels between North Carolina and Mississippi law.

A quick review of the history of codification is needed to provide the basis for understanding the position of the North Carolina court. Although that history is complex, for present purposes it can be divided into two phases. The first occupied the early years of the Republic, when a significant political controversy developed over the ability of the national courts to create nonstatutory, common-law offenses.[19] The controversy was at heart a dispute about the power of the national government, whether acting through its courts or through Congress, to supplant state law. But this dispute about federalism took the form of a dispute about the separation of powers at the national level between national courts and Congress. Opponents of national power found themselves in an unusual position. During the 1790s, they could influence Congress and bar the enactment of some statutes that they regarded as overreaching and could make legal arguments to the national courts that were sometimes received with sympathy. But because they lacked control over the executive branch and over some portions of the judiciary, some prosecutors were able to grasp power by bringing indictments for common-law crimes. Thus, the configurations of political power led opponents of national power to present their arguments as separation of powers objections. This tendency was augmented after 1800, when Jeffersonian views about federalism gained a majority in Congress and secured the presidency but lost hold of the courts with the last minute appointments of federalist judges to newly created positions. By around 1810, a consensus had emerged that the federal law of crimes had to be entirely statutory, the national courts being disabled from developing a common law of crimes.

The first phase of the codification issue thus had no direct implications for state law; it was primarily concerned with centralization of power at the national level. But the national controversy left an ideological residue, for opponents of national power had framed their arguments in terms of fear of the exercise of power by judges. The arguments therefore had an important "democratic" undertone that moved to the fore when the question of codification was once again placed on the legal agenda. During the 1820s a significant body of legal commentary challenged the power of judges to create law of any sort.[20] Like the earlier one, this new codification movement had its political connotations, for criticism of elite judges and of obfuscating lawyers was part of the rhetoric of Jacksonian democracy. At the outset of the movement, reformers were willing to accept the principles of the common law, but they rejected its particular rules and modes of procedure as resting on a feudal inheritance that was absent in the United States. Later developments began to challenge the common law as a whole. Its rules were said to be socially regressive and, perhaps more important, its heavy reliance on precedent made it impossible for the law to adapt to the rapidly changing circumstances presented by American economic development. Further, the rules were so arcane that they could be understood only by lawyers trained in a guild that was concerned more with its own than with the public interest. At the same time, and somewhat inconsistently, reformers argued that the rules of the common law were so manipulable that skillful, and unscrupulous, lawyers could secure results from befuddled courts that outraged common sense.

During the second phase of the codification movement,

reformers sought a radical simplification of substantive rules of law, the elimination of the arcana of common-law reasoning, and changes in the rules of law in a direction more responsive to American conditions. Codification, they thought, would result in a simple, clear set of rules written in an accessible manner that any citizen could consult when seeking to know what his legal rights and duties were in a complex situation. Elite lawyers responded to the codification movement in a number of ways. Justice Joseph Story, for example, headed a Massachusetts commission on codification whose report urged the legislature to adopt a code that restated broad principles but that would not restrict judges' use of the common-law method of precedent and analogy. Others sought to pass off reorganization and systematic restatement of existing law as a sort of codification. Ultimately, though, the codification impulse passed, leaving its mark on the reform of pleading and procedure and having little impact on substantive law.

Some lawyers tried, as I have indicated, to domesticate the codification movement. Judges in North Carolina, in contrast, presented an articulate defense of the common law as it existed. Their response to attacks on the common law had two facets. First, to rebut the claim that common-law rules were in fact incompatible with American conditions, they showed how court-made law expressed the proper response to those conditions, including, notably, the conditions of a slave society that were entirely lacking in the home of the common law, Great Britain. Although the legislature might in a formal sense be more representative of the people, its intervention could not improve on the results that the judges produced. Second, the judges contrasted the rigidity of legislative solutions, which could not accommodate unforeseen developments, with the flexibility of the common-law method, by which new problems could be solved by drawing solutions by analogy from related areas.

The power of the first argument can be seen in the two extended case studies that follow. The second argument was made explicit in a brief opinion by Judge Leonard Pearson in 1850.[21] Atlas Jowers, a white man, and Bob Douglass, a free black, got into a quarrel when Jowers asked Douglass why Douglass had said to another that Jowers had told a lie. When Douglass responded that he had said so because Jowers had done so, the fight began. Douglass hit Jowers with the end of a whip, and Jowers hit back with a tree limb. Jowers was charged with battery. At his trial, Jowers' attorney pointed to cases, which will be examined in detail below, holding that insulting language used by a slave could justify a white person's striking the slave. The trial judge refused to instruct the jury that that principle extended to free blacks, and Jowers was convicted.

On his appeal, a new trial was ordered because, according to Judge Pearson, "the same reasons, by which a blow from a white man upon a slave, is excusable on account of insolent language, apply to the case of a free negro who is insolent." The court thought it "insufferable" that a free black's insolence could go unpunished, yet insolence was not itself a crime, nor did the free black have a master who could punish him for insolence. What was left was to allow an "extra judicial remedy" by the target of the insolence. The court noted the possible dangers to free blacks from such a rule, for their ownership of, and contracts regarding, property might well cause differences of opinion between them and white persons, "and if a free negro disputes the accounts of a white man," the latter would regard it as insolence. A sufficient safeguard, the court said, existed in the power of a court to decide what was insolence justifying an assault. These rules were a way of making the class of the free blacks, whose existence was "unfortunate," "accommodate itself to the permanent rights of free white men." The opinion concluded:

> Such a being as a slave or a free negro did not exist when the ancient common law was in force. But the excellence of that "perfection of reason" consists in the fact that it is flexible and its principles expand, so as to accommodate it

to any new exigence or condition of society, like the bark of a tree, which opens and enlarges itself, according to the growth thereof, always maintaining its own uniformity and consistency.

The implicit contrast was with a legislative code, which could not readily adapt to the growth of a new class such as that of free blacks. The accuracy of this contrast can of course be questioned, as the Mississippi legislature's immediate response to the decision denying that the rape of one slave by another was a crime suggests. But that the contrast underlay the opinion is unquestionable.

Two important lines of cases illustrate the court's development of a coherent, reasonably well-differentiated set of rules to deal with the conditions of slave crime. The cases dealt with assaults by whites on blacks, as in *Jowers* and *State v. Mann*, and with assaults by blacks on whites. The basic common-law rule was that an assasult was a crime unless it was justified. Rules of justification were developed in light of the psychological assumption that all persons subject to the common law were responsive to the sometimes conflicting dictates of conscience and imperatives of passion, and that passion sometimes understandably overrode respect for other people. The social arrangements of slave society made it impossible simply to transfer the common-law rules of justification to assaults involving slaves, for slaves almost by definition, and certainly by psychological assumption, had to stifle their passions toward whites. Common-law rules thus had to be "accommodated" to the "condition of society." The North Carolina court struggled toward a solution that differentiated justifications according to a set of variables that responded to slave conditions. They inquired into the relationship between the victim and assailant, the severity of the blow, and the degree to which the victim provoked the assault. The outcome, not reached without strain, was a set of rules that sorted the cases into a group of pigeon holes defined by the interaction of the broad variables. Then, just by identifying the correct pigeon hole, the courts could decide the case. As in Mississippi, the result was a rather narrowly confined inquiry. The North Carolina court attained a certain stability, but it is not clear that the stability could have been maintained permanently. For, unlike the Mississippi courts, which could look to the statutes and ultimately to the legislature for guidance, the North Carolina courts had no obvious ways to reject the intrusion of new variables, and the creation of new pigeon holes, into a system of rules. *Jowers* indicates that it was possible, by referring to the reasons for special rules in slave cases, to reject suggested distinctions, and I have argued in Chapter I that cognitive limitations on the ability of ordinary judges to manipulate a complex system of pigeon holes set the bounds on the North Carolina approach. The common-law method praised in *Jowers*, although flexible enough, ultimately approached a rigidity that did not differ significantly from the method of reasoning used in Mississippi law: the law developed categories to handle slave cases, and those categories could not be expanded through reasoning by analogy.

The need to adapt common-law rules regarding justification to slave society was noted by the North Carolina courts as early as 1798. Weaver had hired Smith's slave Lewis for a year and was indicted for murdering Lewis during that time.[22] In charging the jury, Judge Haywood first distinguished among murder, manslaughter, and justifiable homicide. Then he turned to the situation of servants who refuse to obey their masters' orders. A hierarchy of justifications existed. Killing a free servant who disobeyed and "offer[ed] to resist by force" was justifiable homicide; "much more is it justifiable if the slave actually uses force and combats with a master." This invocation of varying standards was not, however, tied to slavery; with respect to both free servants and slaves, actual attempts to kill, forcible resistance, or offering to resist by force provided justification for a homicide. Thus, although the judge mentioned slavery as a differentiating condition, the law he stated to the jury did not in fact place slaves and free servants in different categories.[23]

The hint in *State v. Weaver* that standards of liability had to take account of the special circumstances of slaves was developed a few years later in *State v. Boon*, where the North Carolina Superior Court held "too uncertain" a statute imposing on those who murdered slaves "the same punishment" that was imposed on those who murdered free persons.[24] This statute, enacted in 1791, was the third stage in North Carolina's attempt to control what Judge Johnson called "a crime of the most atrocious and barbarous nature," killing a slave "so much in your power, that he is incapable of making resistance, even in his own defence." Prior to 1774, it appears to have been thought that the malicious killing of slaves was a felony at common law, punishable in theory at least by death, although one of the judges in *Boon* noted that he had heard of no convictions or capital penalties for the crime before 1774. In that year, the legislature enacted a statute to "eliminate doubts . . . as to the punishment proper to be inflicted," which transformed the crime from a capital offense to one punishable by one year's imprisonment for the first offense.[25] By 1791, this penalty appeared to be too mild, and the legislature enacted the statute invalidated in *Boon*. The preamble stated that the prior "distinction of criminality between the murder of a white person, and one who is equally a human creature . . . is disgraceful to humanity. . . ."

As was common in the early 1800s, each of the judges in *Boon* wrote an opinion, and each relied on the maxims that criminal statutes should be construed strictly and that "punishments must be plainly defined and easy to be understood," for "they ought not to depend upon construction or arbitrary discretion." The primary difficulty was this: if killing a slave was a felony at common law, then the increased punishment that the legislature apparently intended to impose could have been guaranteed simply by repealing the 1774 statute. Since the legislature did not do that, it must have had some other purpose in mind, but that other purpose could not be discerned from the statute.

The maxims regarding criminal statutes were clearly necessary to bolster such a weak argument. The judges did add another argument. The statute said that the offender should suffer the same punishment as if he had killed a free man. But the judges noted the varying situations of homicide that had been mentioned in *Weaver*.

> In case the person had killed a free man what punishment would the law have inflicted upon him? Before this question can be solved another must be asked; because upon that, the solution of the first depends. What sort of a killing was it? or what circumstances of aggravation or mitigation attended it? did the act bespeak such depravity of heart, as would stamp it with the name of murder? or were they such as justified it? If of the former sort, capital punishment should be inflicted upon the author of it; if of the latter sort, he is guiltless. That to which the Legislature referred us for the purpose of ascertaining the punishment proper to be inflicted is, in itself, so doubtful and uncertain that I think no punishment whatever can be inflicted; without using a discretion and indulging a latitude, which in criminal cases, ought never to be allowed a Judge.

Even the statute's reference to "wilful and malicious" killing could not be construed to specify the circumstances of appropriate punishment, again because of the maxims of construction. Thus, even though, as one judge put it, "there remain[ed] no doubt in [his] mind respecting the intention of the legislature," the statute could not be enforced. Nothing in these arguments, however, turned on the special conditions of a slave society.

The prosecution in *Boon* had also argued that, without regard to the statute, killing a slave was a common-law felony. In rejecting this argument, the judges did talk about the distinctive qualities of slave society, but in an uninspired way. Judge Hall, for example, argued that it was incongruous to treat killing a slave as a crime, when the offense was also the basis for a civil action by the owner for the slave's value. There could be double "recovery," or even worse, execution of the murderer before he paid civil compensation. Judge Hall concluded, "these are consequences I cannot be led to believe the Legislature intended to give rise to." This dichotomy between criminal and civil law did not settle into the law, although we have seen similar efforts to allocate jurisdiction over slave issues in cases like *State* v. *Mann*. However, the other judges rejected Judge Hall's position, asserting that, although killing a slave was a common-law felony, that crime had been superseded by the 1791 statute which was, unfortunately, too uncertain to be enforced. Judge Taylor rejected the master's claim "to an absolute dominion over the life of his slave":

> The authority for it, is not to be found in the law of nature, for that will authorize a man to take away the life of another, only from the unavoidable necessity of saving his own; and of this code, the cardinal duty is, to abstain from injury, and do all the good we can. It is not the necessary consequence of the state of slavery, for that may exist without it; and its natural inconveniences ought not to be aggravated by an evil, at which reason, religion, humanity and policy equally revolt. Policy may occasionally dictate the propriety of enhancing or mitigating the punishment; may at one time subject the offender to a year's imprisonment, and at another to death; yet amidst all these mutations the crime is unchanged in its essence, undiminished in its enormity.

The law after 1801 was clear enough, even though it was at odds with the expressed wishes of the judges for criminal punishment of masters who killed their slaves. Not until 1817, however, did the legislature respond. It then enacted a statute providing that killing a slave "shall partake of the same degree of guilt, when accompanied with the like circumstances, that homicide now does at common law."[26] This closed one loophole, by incorporating into the statute the varying circumstances that affected criminality, and opened another, by allowing defendants to argue that the conditions of slave society made it impossible to identify "like circumstances" when a white person killed a slave.

The North Carolina court first considered an indictment under the statute in *State v. Tackett*, decided in 1820.[27] The evidence in the case showed that Tackett and Daniel, the victim, had quarrelled repeatedly over the weeks preceding the killing. Daniel, though owned by a Mr. Ruffin, spent most nights with his wife, a free black, who lived in a house on the land of Richardson. Tackett was an apprentice who lived with Richardson, and the dispute between Tackett and Daniel apparently arose when Tackett molested Daniel's wife. As a result, Tackett was fired by Richardson, although he was rehired within a few days, and Tackett and Daniel got into a number of fights. Several witnesses testified that Daniel had threatened Tackett before and after those fights. On the night that Daniel was killed, Tackett returned to Richardson's house and, Tackett said, found Daniel lying under Tackett's window. Tackett testified that he asked what Daniel was doing there, to which Daniel replied by asking what Tackett was doing there. Tackett then went into the house and got the gun with which he shot Daniel. The trial judge refused to allow Tackett to present evidence that Daniel "was a turbulent man, and that he was insolent and impudent to white people," because the evidence would not show that Daniel had been insolent to Tackett. The trial judge charged the jury that words would not justify homicide, nor would a blow that did not threaten death or great bodily harm. Tackett was convicted and on appeal challenged the judge's evidentiary ruling and charge to the jury.

Chief Justice Taylor's opinion for the court first noted that there was no direct proof of the immediate provocation on the night of the killing. Because the evidence as to provocation was circumstantial, the court should have admitted all evidence that would have assisted the jury in determining the probability that Daniel had provoked Tackett. Evidence regarding Daniel's general behavior should therefore have been admitted. The opinion then turned to the charge. The 1817 act was intended to authorize convictions for manslaughter rather than murder, or in reality acquittals, where the defendant was provoked. But, according to Chief Justice Taylor, the legislature

> did not mean to declare that homicide, where a slave is killed, could be only extenuated by such a provocation as would have the same effect where a white person was killed. The different degrees of homicide they left to be ascertained by the Common Law of the country—a system which adapts itself to the habits, institutions and actual conditions of the citizens, and which is not the result of the wisdom of any one man, or society of men, in any one age, but of the wisdom and experience of many ages of wise and discreet men. It exists in the nature of things, that where slavery prevails, the relation between a white man and a slave differs from that, which subsists between free persons; and every individual in the community feels and understands, that the homicide of a slave may be extenuated by acts, which would not produce a legal provocation if done by a white person. To define and limit these acts, would be impossible, but the sense and feelings of Jurors, and the grave discretion of Courts, can never be at a loss in estimating their force as they arise, and applying them to each particular case, with a due regard to the rights respectively belonging to the slave and white man—to the just claims of humanity, and to the supreme law, the safety of the citizens. An example may illustrate what is meant. It is a rule of law, that neither words of reproach, insulting gestures, nor a trespass against goods or land, are provocations sufficient to free the party killing from the guilt of murder, where he made use of a deadly weapon. But it cannot be laid down as a rule that some of these provocations, if offered by a slave, well known to be turbulent and disor-

derly, would not extenuate the killing, if it were instantly done under the heat of passion, and without circumstances of cruelty.

Thus, the court praised the adaptability of the common law, indicating that it could take account of the "actual conditions" of slave society, where, as Tackett's attorney had argued, a white person expecting to receive obedience from slaves would be "degrad[ed]" by submitting to "words of reproach" from a slave. As the Mississippi cases show, however, it was not easy to sustain arguments resting solely on the special characteristics of slave society, and the opinion in *Tackett* concluded with an analysis of the general common law showing that the jury charge was erroneous in stating that the provocation of a slight blow could not convert murder into manslaughter.

With *Tackett* and the 1817 statute at hand, it became possible to decide the question not reached in *Boon*, and in 1823 the court, with Judge Hall dissenting on the basis of his opinion in *Boon*, held that killing a slave was indeed a felony at common law.[28] Only Judge Henderson wrote an extended opinion, whose central argument must be brought out in order to develop the contrast with *State* v. *Mann*. Judge Henderson focused on the claim that the state lacked jurisdiction over slaves, who were solely the concern of their owners.

Murder is the killing any reasonable creature within the protection of the law, with malice prepense, that is, with design and without excuse. That a slave is a reasonable, or, more properly, a human being, is not, I suppose, denied. But it is said that, being property, he is not within the protections of the law, and therefore the law regards not the manner of his death; that the owner alone is interested and the State no more concerned, independently of the Acts of the Legislature on that subject, than in the death of a horse. This is argument the force of which I cannot feel, and leads to consequences abhorrent to my nature. . . .

The law, indeed, should acknowledge a sphere of total autonomy for slaveowners:

> With the services and labours of the slave the law has nothing to do; they are the master's by the law; the government and control of them being exclusively to him. Nor will the law interfere upon the ground that the State's rights, and not the master's, have been violated.
>
> In establishing slavery, then, the law vested in the master the absolute and uncontrolled right to the services of the slave, and the means of enforcing those services follow as necessary consequences; nor will the law weigh with the most scrupulous nicety his acts in relation thereto. But the life of a slave being in no ways necessary to be placed in the power of the owner for the full employment of his services, the law takes care of that. . . .

The line dividing the owner's authority from the state's was thus drawn on the basis of necessity. The common law was "cut down . . . so as to tolerate slavery, yielding to the owner the services of the slave, and any right incident thereto as necessary for its full enjoyment, but protecting the life and limbs of the human being. . . ."

The use of necessity as the measure of authority was developed by Chief Justice Ruffin himself, when ten years after *State* v. *Mann* he wrote an opinion for the court affirming the conviction and death sentence of a master for murdering his own slave.[29] Mira, the slave, was in the late stages of pregnancy when John Hoover began to whip her severely because she did not obey his orders; witnesses testified that when she did not obey, the reason was her physical inability due to pregnancy. The jury was charged that Hoover was guilty of murder if he intended to kill Mira and if he had no provocation for killing her, and of manslaughter if he killed upon the immediate influence of provocation. Citing *State* v. *Mann*, Ruffin said that the law generally left the degree of punishment to the master's "judgment and humanity." "But the master's authority is not altogether unlimited. He must not kill. There is, at the least, this restriction upon his power: he must stop short of taking life." Indeed, the "horrid enormities" of the case, which Ruffin recited in some detail, made the trial judge's charge regarding provocation far too favorable to Hoover.

> They are barbarities which could only be prompted by a heart in which every humane feeling had long been stifled; and indeed there can scarcely be a savage of the wilderness so ferocious as not to shudder at the recital of them. Such acts cannot be fairly attributed to an intention to correct or to chastise.

State v. *Mann* now appears in a different light. Judge Ruffin there may have been following the logic of slave society to its ultimate conclusion in denying the state authority to intervene in a master's punishment of his slaves. But that logic was confined to cases where death did not result. An unprovoked assault resulting in death was murder, as in *Hoover*; provocation, according to *Tackett*, reduced the offense to manslaughter, but the state retained its power to punish the master. If the logic of domination had no internal limits, it was nonetheless constrained by what Judge Henderson called "the influence of the mild precepts of Christianity"[30] and by the recognition that pervades the cases that slaves were, after all, human beings.

The accommodation of necessity by humanity, by using the flexible modes of common-law reasoning, led to a set of results that can be readily described after the final case involving injuries inflicted by whites on blacks is considered. *State* v. *Hale* involved a white man who beat a slave.[31] Hale had no prior relation to the slave, and Chief Justice Taylor noted that offenses like his were

> usually committed by men of dissolute habits, hanging loose upon society, who, being repelled from association with well-disposed citizens, take refuge in the company of coloured persons and slaves, whom they deprave by their example, embolden by their familiarity, and then beat, un-

der the expectation that a slave dare not resent a blow from a white man.

The court's opinion began by arguing that common law produced the "result which is best adapted to general expedience," and that long usage and even the trend of legislation could inform judgment regarding expedience. As usual, the opinion referred to the adaptability of the common law:

> But though neither the common law, nor any other code yet devised by man, could foresee and specify every case that might arise, and thus supersede the use of reason in the ordinary affairs of life, yet it furnishes the principles of justice adapted to every state and condition of society. It contains general rules fitted to meet the diversified relations and various conditions of social man.

An important consideration in this was "the march of benignant policy and provident humanity" embodied in legislation promoted by "the mild diffusion of [the] light and influence" of Christianity.

> The wisdom of this course of legislation has not exhausted itself on the specific objects to which it was directed, but has produced wider and happier consequences in securing to this class of persons milder treatment and more attention to their safety; for the very circumstance of their being brought within the pale of legal protection has had a corresponding influence upon the tone of public feeling towards them; has rendered them of more value to their masters, and suppressed many outrages, which were before but too frequent.

Chief Justice Taylor denied that the master's civil remedy against the assailant was exclusive, because the assault excited alarm and might provoke a "contagious example." Further,

> the instinct of a slave may, and generally is, tamed into subservience to his master's will, and from him he receives chastisement, whether it be merited or not, with perfect

submission; for he knows the extent of the dominion assumed over him, and that the law ratifies the claim. But when the same authority is wantonly usurped by a stranger, nature is disposed to assert her rights, and to prompt the slave to a resistance, often momentarily successful, sometimes fatally so.

This was one of those happy instances where "even domestic safety and interest equally enjoin" a result. The assault damaged the master's property, and yet, given the type of person likely to get involved in disputes with slaves, the assailants would rarely be able to make reparation.

For all purposes necessary to enforce the obedience of the slave, and to render him useful as property, the law secures to the master a complete authority over him, and it will not lightly interfere with the relation thus established. It is a more effectual guarantee of his right of property when the slave is protected from wanton abuse from those who have no power over him; for it cannot be disputed that a slave is rendered less capable of performing his master's service when he finds himself exposed by the law to the capricious violence of every turbulent man in the community.

This series of cases can be analyzed along three dimensions: whether the assault resulted in death or in injury only, whether the assailant was the slave's owner (or was the equivalent of an owner, as for example an overseer was) or a stranger, and whether there was provocation or not. The chart below summarizes the results.

		Injury	*Death*
Owner	Provocation	No (a fortiori)	No (*Boon*)
			Yes (*Tackett*)
	No provocation	No (*Mann*)	Yes (*Hoover*)
Stranger	Provocation	No (*Jowers*)	No?
	No provocation	Yes (*Hale*)	Yes (a fortiori)

These results were the product of common law adaptation to existing circumstances, as the cases repeatedly emphasized. They represented an accommodation of what these cases referred to as humanity and necessity, or, in terms that have been used elsewhere in this study, humanity and interest. Even Judge Ruffin, who in *State* v. *Mann* developed the notion of interest as far as it could be taken, limited interest in *Hoover* because it was barbarous to close one's eyes and to allow the law to tolerate unnecessary inhumanity.

But the use of common-law reasoning contained a threat to the accommodation that the cases worked out. Most dramatically, it was always open to argue that the press of interest, even in a case like *Mann*, should be given less weight than prior cases had given it, not because circumstances in general had changed, but because the case at hand presented an array of facts that showed why and how the prior cases should be limited. On one view the shift between *Boon* and *Tackett* resulted from the acceptance of just such an argument.

The North Carolina court used two strategies to reduce the threatened instability. The first dealt with the obvious point of pressure on the system: the important role that provocation played. As the chart indicates, the absence of provocation was largely dispositive in cases involving strangers and was clearly dispositive in cases where the owner killed a slave. Yet the court never specified what constituted provocation. Rather, it explicitly kept that issue from becoming an element of articulated law, by emphasizing the role of the jury in assessing the facts of particular cases. For example, in *Hale*, Chief Justice Taylor said:

From this difference [between white men and slaves] it arises that many circumstances which would not constitute a legal provocation for a battery committed by one white man on another would justify it if committed on a slave, provided the battery were not excessive. It is impossible to draw the line with precision or lay down the rule in the abstract; but, as was said in Tackett's case, the circumstances

must be judged of by the court and jury with a due regard
to the habits and feelings of society.

The stability of the structure of articulated law was thus preserved by allowing adaptation to occur by the action of juries
that were not required to specify what facts led them to conclude that there had or had not been provocation. It is unclear,
however, that this strategy could have worked in the long
run, for at some point a convicted assailant would have presented to the court the claim that the facts in his case showed
conduct by the slave that the law had to recognize as provocation. The response to that claim would, in a common-law
system, set the stage for further delineation of the notion of
provocation, as later defendants sought to analogize or distinguish the court's opinion accepting or rejecting the claim.
As the next set of cases to be discussed shows, the North
Carolina court resisted the temptation to open the way to
such arguments, and slavery was abolished before the courts
were forced to face them.

The North Carolina court's second strategy is perhaps best
shown in *Jowers*. That strategy involved treating prior decisions as developing a set of rules that had to be followed. In
Jowers the court stated without elaboration that the conditions
of slaves and of free blacks were identical for the purposes at
hand, and the strategy of flat statements drawing analogies
from existing cases could be generalized. The effect of that
strategy, however, was to convert the suppleness of common-
law reasoning into the more rigid reasoning of codelike sys-
tems, where the only question for the court was the selection
of the category into which the case at hand fit. The court's
second strategy, then, implicitly denied what its opinions explicitly celebrated, and the tension would have had to have
been resolved by abandoning either the strategy or the flexibility of common law reasoning.

Another set of cases, involving assaults by slaves on whites,
illustrates in another way the emergence of rigid categories
from common-law analogizing. The sensitivity of the issues

is shown by the extensive reporting of the arguments in *State v. Will*, the first of the set to reach the North Carolina Supreme Court.[32] On January 22, 1834, Allen, a slave foreman, directed another slave to use a hoe that Will claimed as his own because he had made it on his own time. Will broke the hoe and went to work packing cotton, while Allen went to tell Richard Baxter, the overseer, what had happened. Baxter took his gun, and directed Allen to take a whip, and confronted Will. Will "took off his hat in an humble manner." Baxter said something that caused Will to run off, and Baxter shot him in the back. Will continued to flee, and a pursuit was organized. Baxter "collared" Will about five minutes later and ordered other slaves to hold Will. However, Will had a knife and, in a scuffle, wounded Baxter in the arm and thigh. That evening Baxter died from loss of blood. On the next day, Will turned himself in to his owner. The issue raised by the case was whether the killing was murder or manslaughter, which could be resolved only by considering whether a slave could respond to an assault by his overseer with force, and if so, what sorts of threat and response could be allowed. The supreme court, in an opinion by Judge William Gaston, reversed Will's conviction for murder, holding that he had committed only manslaughter.

Judge Gaston's opinion made token gestures toward the absolutism of *State v. Mann*, but it typically undercut that deference with immediate concessions to the demands of "reason and humanity." In fact, the opinion can almost be spelled out from the first use of that rhetorical ploy. After describing the facts and stating that the offense would have been only manslaughter if Will had been an apprentice, Judge Gaston "admitted" that slavery was "strikingly dissimilar" to apprenticeship. The key passage followed:

> Unconditional submission is the *general* duty of the slave; unlimited power, is in general, the *legal* right of the master. Unquestionably there are exceptions to this rule. It is certain that the master has not the right to slay his slave, and I hold

it to be equally certain that the slave has a right to defend himself against the unlawful attempt of his master to deprive him of life.

If the slave could defend himself, the reason had to be that slaves were subject to the same imperatives of passion that free persons were. But, Judge Gaston continued, the reduction of offenses from murder to manslaughter was premised precisely on the judgment that threats to life produced understandable, and less culpable, feelings on which all people could be expected to act. Will's flight from "menaced punishment" was not resistance or rebellion, which would justify inflicting a mortal wound. Rather, it was the expression of "passion springing from human infirmity."

[A]fter the gun was fired, all must see that a vast change was effected in the situation of the prisoner; and that new and strong impulses to action must have been impressed upon his mind. Suffering under the torture of a wound likely to terminate in death, and inflicted by a person, having indeed authority over him, but wielding power with the extravagance and madness of fury; chased in hot pursuit; baited and hemmed in like a crippled beast of prey that cannot run far; it became instinct, almost uncontrollable instinct, to fly; it was human infirmity to struggle; it was terror or resentment, the strongest of human passions, or both combined, which gave to the struggle its fatal result; and this terror, this resentment, could not but have been excited in anyone who had the ordinary feelings and frailties of human nature.

The conclusion followed almost directly from this passage, but *State* v. *Mann* remained to be accounted for. Judge Gaston first proposed a general framework for common-law analysis. A primary rule, for example, that "passion springing from ordinary frailty, is not malice," was given more precision in secondary rules stated in later cases. But only the primary rule could be applied "until in a vast majority of the cases that can occur, the existing tribunals of justice find a safe guide in the undisputed decisions of their predecessors." *State* v. *Mann* was the only precedent that might qualify the primary rule, and, according to Judge Gaston, though it established that a slave's resistance to punishment could not free the slave of criminal liability even where the punishment was unreasonable, it did not speak to the degree of criminality: "[W]hat emotions of terror or resentment may, without the imputation of fiend-like malignity, be excited in a poor slave by cruelty from his master that does not immediately menace death, that case neither determines, nor professes to determine." Judge Gaston could then revert to the primary rule, which he would not reject "unless [he saw his] way clear as a sunbeam." "The prisoner is a human being, degraded indeed by slavery, but yet having 'organs, dimensions, senses, affections, passions,' like our own," and Will's crime was therefore only man-slaughter.

The rigidification of the common law is implicit in Judge Gaston's approach, for if secondary rules—in this context, rules taking account of the special conditions of slave society—could be applied only after long experience, there is analytically no way for the process to begin. Each time a case presents a novel issue, the judge must apply only the primary rule and no precedents applying secondary rules can ever be established. The cases of white assaults on slaves eventually produced a differentiated set of categories because the courts did not adhere strictly to Judge Gaston's model. In contrast, the cases of slave assaults on whites led to an undifferentiated rule regarding provocation: the issue was to be left to the jury. Where retaliation was the question, the evident humanity of slaves seems to have overpowered the considerations of interest that produced the structure discussed earlier in this section. As I have already suggested, juries were used to mask problems in specifying what retaliation would reduce culpability.

Two cases illustrate these developments. In both, slaves were granted new trials after having been convicted of murdering whites. *State* v. *Jarrott* involved a gambling affray.[33] Thomas Chatham, an eighteen-year-old white man, went to a place where slaves gathered on Saturday nights. He stayed there playing cards, until nearly dawn. During the card game, Chatham and another player, a free black, began to argue and asked Jarrott to hold the stakes. When the game broke up, one of Jarrott's coins disappeared. Jarrott, a slave, accused Chatham of stealing the coin, using vituperative language. He threatened to kill Chatham. Chatham offered to let Jarrott search him, and eventually turned his pockets inside out and took off his shoes to show that he had not hidden the coin. Shortly afterward, the coin was found on the ground. Jarrott continued to curse Chatham, who then threatened Jarrott with a knife. Eventually Jarrott and Chatham fought; Jarrott's blow on Chatham's head with a club killed him.

Judge Gaston's opinion first rejected several of Jarrott's challenges to the instructions. Although, as in *Will*, Jarrott "was entitled to the benefit of all those human principles of the common law, which, in indulgence to the frailties of human nature," would reduce the crime from murder to manslaughter, he was not entitled to a charge that a slave could be convicted only if, on the same evidence, a white man could be. The idea of varying standards was invoked: what was sufficient provocation to a white assailant might not be adequate to reduce a slave's culpability.

This difference in the application of the same principle, arises from the *vast* difference which exists, under our institutions, between the social condition of the white man and of the slave; in consequence of which difference, what might be felt by one as the grossest degradation is considered by the other as but a slight injury. And from the same cause, it must necessarily follow, that some acts, which between white persons are grievous provocations, when proceeding from a white person to a slave—whose passions are, or ought to be tamed down to his lowly condition—will not, and cannot be so regarded. The degrees of homicide are indeed to be ascertained by common law principles; but the principles themselves are necessarily, in their application, accommodated to the actual conditions of human beings in our society.

But here too the opinion gave no concrete examples.

In addition, even if Chatham had taken Jarrott's coin, the slave was not allowed to insult Chatham.

It is the difference of condition between the white man and the slave—as recognized by our legal institutions—and not the difference between personal merit and demerit—which creates a legal distinction between the sufficiency and insufficiency of the alleged provocation. *This* distinction, therefore, must be as broad as *that* difference—or it would not only be unsuited to the state of our society, and incompatible with the subordination of ranks essential to the safety of the State—but would be too vague to be admissible as a legal rule. It may be that the white man who debases himself by a familiar association with a slave, and, in the course of that association, is guilty of acts of meanness like that attributed—whether justly or unjustly—to the unfortunate deceased—has no claims to personal respect equal to those of the slave; but the distinction of castes yet remains, and with it remain all the passions, infirmities, and habits, which grow out of this distinction.

However, Chatham should not have attacked Jarrott in response to the slave's insolence; only the owner and the state had authority to punish the slave. An ambiguity in the evidence suggested, indeed, that the quarrel had stopped and that Chatham attacked Jarrott after a substantial interval. If that were so, Jarrott's actions were even more justifiable. Since the jury had not been instructed to consider these questions, the conviction was reversed. Judge Gaston rejected a suggestion by Jarrott's attorney that at the retrial, the jury should be instructed that the offense would be manslaughter if Jarrott and Chatham had been in "mutual combat." Rules reducing culpability in such situations grew "from a sense of equality, and the horror of personal disgrace. They do not prevail—they ought not to exist—between those who cannot *combat* with each other, without degradation on the one hand, and arrogance on the other." Judge Gaston refused to state that, had Chatham first assaulted Jarrott, the latter would have been provoked within the meaning of the rules. No "precise rule" had previously been developed.

And by whomsoever the attempt to prescribe such a rule shall be made, he will find it no easy task to form a rule which shall consist with the principles of public policy on the one hand, and with the just claims of humanity on the other. The superior rank of the assailant—the habits of humility and obedience which belong to the condition of the slave—habits which are not less indispensable to his own well-being than required by the inveterate usages of our people—clearly forbid that an ordinary assault or battery should be deemed, as it is between white man, a legal provocation. The law will not permit the slave to resist. It is his duty to submit—or flee—or seek the protection of his master; but it is impossible, if it were desirable, to extinguish in him the instinct of self-preservation; and although his passions ought to be tamed down so as to suit his condition, the law would be *savage*, if it made no allowance for passion. He may have been disciplined into perfect obedience to the will of his master, and, therefore, habitually patient under *his* correction; but he cannot but feel a keen sense of wrong when authority is wantonly usurped over him by a stranger, and exercised with cruelty. There is therefore no difficulty in laying it down that a battery which endangers his life or great bodily harm—proceeding from one who has no authority over him—will amount to such a provocation. But between these extremes there are intermediate injuries of various grades. In regard to them, we are obliged to resort to the primary rule which pronounces on the character of provocations, and apply it according to the circumstances of each case. That is a legal provocation of which it can be pronounced, having due regard to the relative condition of the white man and the slave, and the obligation of the latter to conform his instinct and his passions to his condition of inferiority, that it would provoke well disposed slaves into a violent passion. And the application of the principle must be left, until a more precise rule can be formed, to the intelligence and conscience of the triers.

Judge Gaston once again invoked the distinction between primary and secondary rules with the resulting delegation of authority to the jury.

Thomas R. R. Cobb, who disagreed with two Georgia cases that denied slaves the benefit of the reduction in culpability when they killed whites because of "necessity," thought that the North Carolina court went too far in granting that benefit in State v. Caesar, where the slave was provoked by an assault on a friend.[34] In a sense, though, the result was determined by the court's prior reluctance to specify the circumstances that the law would treat as provocation. Kenneth Mizell and a friend named Brickhouse spent the evening of August 14, 1848, getting drunk. Late in the evening, they crossed a field and came across Caesar and Dick, two slaves. They told the slaves that they were patrollers and gave the slaves several slight blows. After Dick refused to get a whip, Mizell and Brickhouse hit him more severely on the head. Caesar grabbed a fence rail and struck the white men. Mizell and Brickhouse then went to a friend's house and fell into a drunken sleep; Brickhouse awoke a few hours later, just before Mizell died. The trial judge charged the jury that Mizell's attack on Dick did not reduce Caesar's culpability from murder to manslaughter. Caesar was convicted of murder and sentenced to death.

Each of the three judges of the supreme court wrote an opinion. Judge Pearson began by relying on a leading case that held that, if the fight had been between white men, the "passion" excited by seeing a friend assaulted would reduce the gravity of the offense. However, because slaves were "accustomed . . . to constant humiliation," the general rule was not applicable; because slaves routinely received slight blows, such blows were "less apt to excite passion." Judge Pearson then asked how far the difference between whites and slaves went. The difference, he said, rested on the differing psychologies of white and slave: when a white was struck, his passions were excited by pain, a feeling of degradation, and a sense of injustice, whereas when a slave was struck, there was no feeling of degradation, because the slave was already degraded. However, if "unusual circumstances of oppression" occurred, the feelings of nature would arise, transforming the blow into provocation. Rather rapidly, Judge Pearson transferred his analysis from the case of a slave himself struck to the case of a slave seeing a friend struck. Indeed, Judge Pearson noted, "Are we not forced, in spite of stern policy, to admire, even in a slave, the generosity, which incurs danger to save a friend? The law requires a slave to tame down his feelings to suit his lowly condition, but it would be savage, to allow him, under no circumstances, to yield to a generous impulse." The rule allowing Caesar's acts to be treated as provoked by the assault on Dick would "protect slave property from wanton outrages, while, at the same time, due subordination is preserved."

Judge Nash was somewhat more concerned with the court's role in lawmaking. To deny Caesar mitigation would, he thought, be to make a new rule.

> I ask for the authority so to declare. I am referred to the degraded state of slaves; that what would rouse to phrensy a white man, he is brought up from infancy to bow to. I am told, that policy and necessity require that a different rule should exist in the case of a slave. Necessity is the tyrant's plea, and policy never yet stript, successfully, the bandage from the eyes of Justice. It does not belong to the bench, but to the halls of legislation. I fully admit, that the degraded state of our slaves requires laws different from

those applicable to white men, but I see no authority in the courts of justice to make the alteration. The evil is not one which calls upon the Court to abandon their appropriate duty, that of enforcing the law as they find it. The legislature, and only the legislature, can alter the law.

Existing law was clear, and Judge Nash refused "to wander in the mazes of judicial discretion."

To a dedicated adherent of the common law, the opposition that Judge Nash drew between common law and legislation, and correlatively between justice and policy, was repugnant. It is therefore not surprising that Chief Justice Ruffin dissented, confronting the issue of specifying secondary rules that had previously been avoided by delegating that task to juries.

Judges cannot, indeed, be too sensible of the difficulty and delicacy of adjusting the rules of law to new subjects; and therefore they should be and are proportionally cautious against rash expositions, not suited to the actual state of things, and not calculated to promote the security of persons, the stability of national institutions, and the common welfare. It was but an instance of the practical wisdom, which is characteristic of the common law and its judicial ministers as a body, that the courts should, in those cases, have shown themselves so explicit in stating the general principle, on which the rules of law on this subject must ultimately be placed, and yet so guarded in respect to the rules themselves in detail. Yet it is of the utmost importance, nay, of the most pressing necessity, that there should be rules, which, as rules of law, should be known; so that all persons, of whatever race or condition, may understand their rights and responsibilities in respect to acts, by which blood is shed and life taken, and for which the slayer may be called to answer at the peril of his own life.

Ruffin's brilliance as a common lawyer is illustrated in his use of the very cases that had left the issue open. He regarded *Tackett*, *Hale*, and *Jarrott* as having firmly established what

Judge Gaston would have called a secondary rule that could now be followed. What Judge Pearson implicitly treated as dicta and as generalized truisms, Chief Justice Ruffin treated as considered holding, and the bulk of his opinion was devoted to a detailed analysis of *Jarrott*, demonstrating that the court there had indeed held that an "ordinary battery" was not provocation. Even Judge Pearson agreed with that, however; the difference between Pearson and Ruffin is that the former thought that a jury might properly conclude that the facts established unusual circumstances, whereas the latter thought that a jury could find only an ordinary battery from the facts.

Ruffin knew, however, that the strength of the common law lay in its appeal to reason as well as authority, and he therefore devoted some attention to the rationale of the rule he drew from the precedents. "The habits of the country," he said, "necessarily modify the rules of law . . . and suit them to the exigencies arising out of [the fact that slaves and whites were] living together. . . ."

The whites forever feel and assert a superiority, and exact an humble submission from the slaves; and the latter, in all they say and do, not only profess, but plainly exhibit a corresponding deep and abiding sense of legal and personal inferiority. Negroes—at least the great mass of them—born with deference to the white man, take the most contumelious language without answering again, and generally submit tamely to his buffets, though unlawful and unmerited.

In examining the "actual effect on the bulk of one race of certain conduct on the part of those belonging to the other," Chief Justice Ruffin concluded

that many things, which drive a white man to madness, will not have the like effect, if done by a white man to a slave; and, particularly, it is true, that slaves are not ordinarily moved to kill a white man for a common beating. For it is an incontestable fact, that the great mass of slaves— nearly all of them—are the least turbulent of all men; that, when sober, they never attack a white man; and seldom, very seldom, exhibit any temper or sense of provocation at even gross and violent injuries from white men. They sometimes deliberately murder; oftener at the instigation of others, than on their own motive. They sometimes kill each other in heat of blood, being sensible to the dishonor in their own caste of crouching in submission to one of themselves. That, however, is much less frequent than among whites; for they have a duller sensibility to degradation. But hardly such a thing is known, as that a slave turns in retaliation on a white man, and, especially, that he attempts to take life for even a wanton battery, unless it be carried to such extremity as to render resistance proper in defense of his own life. Crowds of negroes in public places are often dispersed with blows by white men, and no one remembers a homicide of a white man on such occasions. The inference is, that the generality of slaves—those who are well disposed towards the whites, as are almost all—do not in truth and fact find themselves impelled to a bloody vengeance, upon the provocation of blows with the fist or a switch from a white man. That is the experience of the whole country.

Ruffin stated that he knew of fewer than half a dozen killings of whites by blacks in a scuffle, from which he concluded that, when a slave did kill a white, the act flowed "not . . . from generous and uncontrollable resentment, but from a bad heart—one, intent upon the assertion of equality, social and personal, with the white. . . ."

The disagreement between the majority and Chief Justice Ruffin rested in part on differing assessments of the actual impulses of generosity in the slave population. Ruffin indicated some of the potential consequences of affording Caesar the defense of provocation:

It seems to me to be dangerous to the last degree to hold the doctrine, that negro slaves may assume to themselves the judgment as to the right or propriety of resistance, by one of his own race, to the authority taken over them by the whites, and, upon the notion of a generous sympathy with their oppressed fellow servants, may step forward to secure them from the hands of a white man, and much less to avenge their wrongs. First denying their general subordination to whites, it may be apprehended that they will end in denouncing the injustice of slavery itself, and, upon that pretext, band together to throw off their common bondage entirely.

It is hard indeed to disagree with Ruffin's assessment, but he was, after all, in dissent. The substantive law of crime in North Carolina embodied an accommodation of humanity and interest that gave humanity more weight than Ruffin would have given it. Ruffin was right in *State* v. *Mann* in attempting to transfer jurisdiction over cases involving slaves to the master, who could without strain acknowledge their humanity, and away from the courts, where the recognition of the slave's humanity gave a special imprimatur to the need to accommodate humanity and interest.

The accommodation in North Carolina was reached, not by preserving in all slave cases the ability to analogize to all cases involving free persons, but by establishing a set of categories based on a few dimensions abstracted from the cases, and remitting to the jury questions raised along other dimensions. As in Mississippi, it proved impossible to achieve complete closure. Just at the point where closure of the system might have been reached, by specifying what was or was not provocation, North Carolina law reverted to the jury and its ability to decide cases without articulating reasons.

This examination of North Carolina's criminal law should conclude with a striking example of the openness to analogizing that existed as late as 1848.[35] John, a slave, was convicted of murdering Ben Shipman, another slave. Flora testified that, during the six years that she had been John's wife, the marriage was punctuated by many quarrels. The final one occurred on the night that John killed Shipman, who lived a few steps away and who, John thought, had been carrying on an "adulterous intercourse" with Flora. The supreme court held that evidence of such an affair was properly excluded, relying on the general common-law principle that extenuation was proper only when a husband found the parties in the act of adultery. The court cited the classic texts and, most notably here, said not a word about the anomaly of a slave relying on a defense involving a wife and adultery. Slave law, that is, was not a subject apart from the general criminal law; it remained, rather, a subdivision of that law.

The North Carolina cases add an important qualification to the argument that, as a result of categorical reasoning, slave law became differentiated from the general law. Perhaps more obviously than in Mississippi, that differentiation was incomplete in North Carolina. I suggest that there were two reasons for the remaining ties between slave law and general law. Slave law was, especially in North Carolina but as we have seen elsewhere too, represented to be an accommodation of humanity and interest. So long as humanity remained a factor, it proved impossible to consider the law affecting slaves without considering as well the law affecting other human beings. But the relations of slave society made it equally impossible to deny the humanity of slaves. The only solution would have been the jurisdictional allocation that, I have already argued, was the logical tendency of slave society but that could not be reached in the American South.

Second, if the argument in the preceding chapter is persuasive, the underlying structure of slave law required that it be no law at all, but only regulation by sentiment. But the courts necessarily were engaged in making law in a traditional sense, and the contradiction embodied in the term "slave law" had to leave its mark.

C. Procedure, Substance, and the Threat to Whites

So long as slave law could be constructed by using analogies to cases involving free whites, Southern courts were under some strain. They may have wished to relax various technicalities in slave cases, but they ran the risk that elimination of concern for technicality in slave cases would reflect back onto cases involving whites, which formed part of the permissible range of analogy. A prosecutor who successfully argued that an indictment of a slave need not be terribly precise might draw on that case in support of a claim that a misdrawn indictment of a white was tolerable too. Technicality did, of course, protect the interests of individual slaveowners, guaranteeing that their property would be taken from them only after great care had been exercised. But concern for slaves as property seems not to have played an explicit role in the attention to technicality, for Southern courts worked toward a separate system of law for slaves, and once that system was set off from the general system, they expressed significantly less concern for technicality.

Slave law used both procedure and substance to separate slave law and general law. Special courts were established for the trial of minor slave crimes, and procedural nicety was not always demanded in those courts. But ordinarily the slave codes did not fully specify procedures in these special tribunals, appeals and full scale retrials were allowed in some situations, and major crimes ultimately came to be tried in the general courts.[36] Thus, the slave courts were not completely insulated from the influence of rules developed in the general courts, and technicality thus had to be maintained to reduce the threat of reciprocal influence. Substantive rules that took account of the special characteristics of master-slave relations might also have separated slave and free law. However, an examination of the rules regarding evidence in slave trials shows that, though slave law did develop a few "secondary" rules, in Judge Gaston's terms, the primary rule was one premised on the proposition that slaves were like free persons in their susceptibility to threats, promises, and influence. Once again, therefore, slave law could not become a closed system, in this instance because the primary rule recognized that slaves were in fact humans with sensibilities just like those of free persons. The categorizing effort was doomed by that recognition, as well as by the threat to the entire system posed by the logic of a separate role for slaves.

A few examples of the enforcement of procedural rigor will suffice, for other illustrations can be found in other studies.[37] Clarissa was indicted for attempting to poison her owner Nelson Parsons and her overseer Hezekiah Bussey by putting a large quantity of jimson weed in the coffee she prepared for them.[38] She was convicted on the basis of a confession and on the testimony of her mother, Chloe, who said that she had seen Clarissa put the poison in the coffee but that she had thrown the poison away to protect Clarissa. It may have affected the court's approach to the case that Chloe's testimony had initially been beaten out of her, and that Clarissa's should not have been admitted. On the way to the latter ruling, however, the Alabama Supreme Court held that Clarissa's indictment was defective, because it did not allege that jimson weed was a deadly poison. The other example comes from the Mississippi Supreme Court in 1853, which reversed a capital sentence imposed on a slave convicted of conspiring to murder a white man.[39] The problem was that the record did not include the indictment that had begun the case. The court agreed that, "from the known and settled practices of the courts," it might infer that there had been an indictment, but it refused to indulge in a presumption to supply the defect. It concluded:

> As much as we regret the impunity of crime arising from the neglect or incapacity of persons engaged in the administration of law, and as little as we feel disposed to regard objections to form, we are nevertheless bound, in cases which, like the present, are of a highly penal character, to enforce with strictness the rules which the laws of the State have imposed.

The slave could have been tried and convicted again, of course,[40] but the important point is that the court refused to develop a rule that "objections to form" could be disregarded in slave cases.

The experience in Louisiana was significantly different,

because, when in 1846 that state established special courts for the trial of slaves accused of capital offenses, it followed the civil-law tradition of providing a great deal of detail in the controlling statutes. The need for the courts to look elsewhere, to the general rules of criminal procedure, was accordingly reduced, as was the fear that procedure in slave cases might affect that in other cases. Thus, in 1853, the Louisiana Supreme Court affirmed the sentence of death given to John Kentuck, a slave convicted of assaulting a white man with a knife.[41] Unlike the Mississippi court, the Louisiana court did not find persuasive a challenge to the indictment, in Kentuck's case on the ground that it failed to allege intent:

> The law . . . does not demand on the trial of slaves, in the tribunals established for that purpose, an observance of the technical rules which regulate criminal proceedings in the higher courts. "A brief statement of the accusation in writing," is all that is required, and the Act of 1846, under which this prosecution was conducted, expressly declares that "no proceedings had in accordance with it, shall be annulled or impeded by any error of form."

The Louisiana court tolerated even a cumulation of procedural irregularities. Jackson, a slave owned by Mrs. Newcomb, was convicted of setting fire to Mrs. Shaw's house.[42] His appeal presented a number of claims. The 1846 law provided for trial by two justices of the peace and ten slaveowners. A justice of the peace from a ward adjoining the one where the complaint was brought was to select the slaveowners. Jackson was tried in the adjoining ward and argued that the statute required trial in the first ward. The court said that the statute did not "expressly require" trial in the first ward, that the benefits of trial in the locality were secured so long as the trial took place in the same parish, and that, in any event, Jackson could hardly complain about a lack of publicity in his trial, since he was tried in the office of the mayor of Baton Rouge. Jackson also objected that he had been tried by a jury that had only nine slaveowners, since one of the panel had been excused because he could not understand English. However, nine slaveowners were a quorum, and so, the court said, could convict. After the trial Jackson discovered that one of the jurors did not own slaves, although his wife did, but the court said that it was too late to object then. Finally, when the verdict and sentence of life imprisonment were reached, the jury signed an "informal" verdict, which the justices of the peace afterward put into proper form. That, too, did not undermine the judgment. "We would disregard the law [about the irrelevance of errors in form], if we permitted an immaterial informality to prevail over a substantial conviction and sentence of a slave, to a very mild punishment for an enormous crime." The court obviously found a great deal of informality tolerable, summarizing its view of its role in an earlier case as "consider[ing] no objections which do not go to the substance of the prosecution."[43]

There were, however, limits to procedural laxity. In *State v. Isaac*, a slave had been tried once for murder and was retried after one of the justices of the peace refused to sign the sentence.[44] A new jury was empaneled, and the charge was read. At that point, the prosecutor asked all nonslaveowners to withdraw from the jury; the four who did were replaced and the trial proceeded to a conviction. That, the court said, was improper; challenges to jurors had to be made before they were sworn. It then disposed of other questions: retrial was not barred because no sentence had been imposed at the first trial; and, more interesting, the convening justice of the peace could participate in the retrial even though he had voted to convict Isaac at the first trial. In another case, the supreme court strained to reverse a conviction and death sentence for committing a crime that had been abolished by the time the court decided the case, even though no counsel had appeared and no formal statement of errors had been filed.[45] The court was surely influenced by the facts that the slave had been convicted of using a knife to wound his master, who ordinarily could be counted on to file the appeal, and that "men do not often voluntarily throw away their lives." As the court noted, "in prosecutions of slaves, only the substance of things is observed and technicalities are disregarded. . . . Shall that be the practice on the part of the State only, and a more rigorous practice be exacted of the prisoner who has so little power to direct his defence?"

Procedural informality did not, therefore, necessarily harm the slave. The court, following the same tendency, rejected a technical argument that only the twelve-person jury and not the two justices of the peace could grant a new trial.[46] The fundamental perception running through the cases, however, was not related to benefit or harm to slaves, or even primarily concerned with technicality or informality. Rather, the court treated the statutes as both complete and self-confined. The clearest expression came when a slave convicted of murder argued that the evidence against him consisted only of his unsupported confession; the purported victims had never been found and indeed might never have existed.[47] However, the state constitution limited the supreme court to considering only questions of law in slave cases. The slave's attorney argued that that limitation caused no difficulty in cases involving whites, because there the judge's instructions to the jury and rulings on evidentiary issues could form the basis upon which questions of law could be raised, but that the special courts for slaves presented a different problem; in such courts, the justices of the peace sat with the lay jurors and never made formal rulings or gave formal instructions to which exception could be taken. The court called the difficulty "serious," but said only that "it results from the defective organization of the inferior tribunal, and can only be remedied by legislative interference." It is fairly easy to see how a court could develop an argument that insufficiency of the evidence was a question of law that could be considered even though there were no opportunities to object at trial. But the legislative specification of procedure, even if "defective," could not be altered by the courts.[48] With complete codification, then, the system of slave law could be closed, but only in Louisiana was the codification, seen there not as a reform movement but as part of the traditional civil-law system, regarded as complete. Elsewhere, the courts thought that they ought to call on common-law reasoning by analogy to fill in gaps in the system of slave law.

Related issues were repeatedly raised in matters of substantive law as well. Here I will present material about admissibility of evidence, primarily confessions, in slave trials. The general structure of law can be described quickly. Confessions by slaves were admissible if they had been made voluntarily, just as other confessions were. The courts recognized, however, that slaves were susceptible to peculiar pressures, and moved in the direction of holding that the fact that a confession was given to a master was relevant to the question of voluntariness. That principle was ultimately subversive of the general rule of voluntariness, for it could be explained only by referring to the inherent coerciveness of the master-slave relation. Given coerciveness, the voluntariness rule could be preserved only if third parties, particularly representatives of the state, were treated as independent of the master class. That, though, was simply impossible. Thus, the development of secondary rules sensitive to the special characteristics of slave society, and confined to slave cases, was thwarted by those very characteristics..

Ordinary voluntariness cases can be found in the reports with no difficulty. *Jordan* v. *State*, decided in 1856, is typical.[49] Mallory was pursuing Jordan, who was a runaway slave. On coming upon Jordan, Mallory ordered Aaron, another slave with whom Mallory had no connection, to assist in the capture. Aaron was killed in the ensuing fight. After Jordan's capture, Mallory and another white man questioned Jordan. When Jordan refused to answer, Mallory threatened to shoot him, and the other white man struck Jordan with a stick. Jordan then told them where he had lost the knife that had killed Aaron. The knife was found and admitted in evidence against Jordan, although it was actually unclear that Aaron had been killed with that knife. The Mississippi Supreme Court invoked the "settled" principle that neither a confession "extorted by violence" nor the fruits of such a confession could be introduced against a defendant and reversed Jordan's conviction. The opinion contained a brief essay on the exclusionary rule, stated in completely general terms making no reference at all to the fact that Mallory was a white and Jordan a slave.[50]

Similarly general principles were invoked in *Stephen v. State*, in which the Georgia Supreme Court affirmed Stephen's conviction for attempted rape.[51] Judge Joseph Lumpkin began by saying that the "indignation" excited when a slave raped "a free white female of immature mind and body" was offset by "the very helplessness of the accused, [which] . . . like infancy and womanhood, appeals to our sympathy. And a controversy between the State of Georgia and *a slave* is so unequal, as of itself to divest the mind of all warmth and prejudice, and enable it to exercise its judgment in the most temperate manner." Notwithstanding, the opinion later indicated that Stephen "richly . . . deserve[d]" the death penalty. Stephen's confession occurred while he was chained near a storehouse; he told the white man who was watching him that another slave caused Stephen to commit the crime. The white man "cautioned [Stephen] to be careful how he talked, for it might cost him his life." There were no threats or promises, the court said, no "flattery of hope or . . . impressions of fear," but only "the pressures of calamity" weighing upon Stephen.

Other cases simply illustrate the circumstances in which coercion or voluntariness would be found. For example, George, Aaron, and Gause were indicted for the "horrid" murder of their master, "committed under circumstances well calculated to excite and alarm the people of the neighborhood."[52] A large crowd gathered after their arrest; one man hit Gause and told him that Aaron and George had said Gause knew all about it and that he would kill Gause if he did not confess; another man told George that the crowd would kill him if he did not confess; several people in the crowd were heard to say that the criminal deserved to be burned. Judge

Pearson said that the confessions of George and Gause "were extracted by means calculated to excite *the fear of present death in the firmest mind.*" Because the confessions might not be true, they should have been excluded. "If such evidence was received, crowds would always assemble when there was a charge of the commission of a horrid crime, in order to extort a confession." Similarly, the Mississippi Supreme Court reversed a slave's conviction for murdering another slave because a coerced confession had been used.[53] A few days before the murder, Hiram, a third slave, had run away, and on the night of the murder Simon, the defendant, ran off too. Simon was captured by pursuing dogs, who bit him. After the dogs were pulled off, the master's brother asked Simon why he had run away. When Simon did not answer, the brother hit him. On the way back home, the brother asked Simon "what he knew of Hiram's killing" the dead slave, and added that "it will be better for you to tell the whole truth about the matter." Simon then confessed. He repeated his confession twice more that day, both times while the dogs were present. Judge Handy wrote that "very slight expressions calculated to convey . . . that he would obtain any benefit, or escape any punishment, if he would confess," made a confession involuntary. When the brother said that it would be better if Simon told the truth, Simon was intimidated by "the appeal to his hopes and fears."[54]

Confessions extracted involuntarily were frequently repeated, as Simon's was, after the immediate coercion had dissipated. Southern courts presumed that the effect of the coercion persisted, and usually found that the presumption was not overcome. Thus, when Peter was prosecuted for murdering a white man, his confession was introduced.[55] Several people had arrested the slave and, at the master's house, prepared to hang him if he did not confess. The slave concocted a partly exculpatory but largely incredible story, whereupon he was taken by the same group to a magistrate, to whom the slave repeated the confession. The Mississippi Supreme Court held that the coercive effects had not been removed, because the time between the confessions was short and the magistrate had not warned Peter of the effect of confessing. More dramatic was *Dinah* v. *State*, involving a slave nurse who poisoned the five year old child she was attending.[56] Dinah had first confessed when she was beaten for refusing to say why she had run away. That confession, and two others made shortly thereafter, were excluded, but a confession made three weeks later while Dinah was in jail was admitted. Dinah's conviction was reversed because the facts did not overcome the presumption of continuing effect: she was a young slave woman who was questioned while in jail.

> A girl of this age, and a slave, having made the [first] confession . . . would always be under the temptation to repeat the same substantially, from a fear that she would be punished for falsehood, if she should materially deviate from the statement she had first made. In such a case, even the presence of her master, and an assurance from him that she should not be punished, if the truth so required, would hardly be sufficient to make a re-confession of her guilt testimony against her. Her previous confession, her status as a prisoner and a slave, and the expectation that, at some time, her master would resume his dominion as a master, would be circumstances still to be considered and it is doubtful whether even such an assurance from him would leave her in a condition to make such a free and voluntary confession as the law will accept.[57]

As *Dinah* indicates, the fact that the defendant was a slave sometimes affected the evaluation of the voluntariness of a confession. By the 1850s, several judges had indicated their discomfort with a rule automatically excluding coerced confessions. For example, the Louisiana Supreme Court upheld murder convictions of two slaves, based on their detailed confessions given under circumstances including questioning by several whites in a field where the slaves were working after their arrests as runaways, some muttered comments about the slaves' guilt, and some trickery in suggesting to one slave that the other had confessed.[58] The "very slight expressions" rule might have been invoked to exclude the confessions, but Judge Isaac Preston observed:

> The true ground upon which confessions, extorted by violence or induced by promises, are excluded as evidence is that the violence and hope destroy all confidence in the confession. In favorem vitae, too much strictness has been observed on this subject as to free persons. Upon true principles, the objections should go rather to the credit of the confessions than to their admission as evidence. We are not prepared to say the same strictness should be observed, so as to exclude the confessions of slaves as evidence; humanity and charity ought to be extended to them; but if their confessions are obtained without a violation of either, and under such circumstances as to force the belief that the confessions are true, they should be received as evidence.[59]

Once the fact of slavery was recognized as relevant, however, a subversive pressure was created. In part, the pressure resulted from some incidents of slavery, such as the assumed ignorance of slaves of their rights.[60] But far more important was the possibility that the subordination inherent in the slave's position would make involuntary any statement that he or she made to a white. The Alabama Supreme Court noted the issue explicitly in saying that slaves' "condition in the scale of society, throws a certain degree of discredit over any confession of guilt they may make, and renders it unsafe if not improper to act upon such evidence alone, without corroborating proof."[61] In that case, the court concluded that the confession was inadmissible because it had been given in response to a question that assumed the slave's guilt. Discrediting all slave confessions as involuntary threatened not only the effective enforcement of the law, but also the slaveowners' sense of their humanity, given their assumption that slavery was a benign institution.

Yet coercion was present in the relationship. *Dinah* v. *State*, for example, noted the slave's susceptibility to punishment

for repudiating a prior confession and stated that her susceptibility could offset the dissipation of coercion as time passed.
The same idea recurred in *Bob* v. *State*, where a slave was
sentenced to death for shooting his owner's son from the
bushes.[62] After suspicion had focused on Bob, he was severely
whipped and his wounds salted. Twice within the next week,
Bob confessed. At his first trial, the confessions were excluded. Six months later, while still in jail and apparently
believing that one of the men who had whipped him before
was present, Bob confessed again. The Alabama Supreme
Court held that even that confession was inadmissible, for the
reasons given in *Dinah* v. *State* and because "an ignorant negro" might "continue to indulge . . . the expectation that the
time would yet come" when his owner would sell rather than
punish him. "An ignorant slave" might not have understood
that punishment was intended when the confessions were
sought to be introduced at the first trial.

There is, however, an even more important aspect of *Bob*
v. *State*. Bob had attracted suspicion when an inspection of
the shoes of the masters' slaves disclosed that Bob's shoes
matched tracks found in the bushes from which the shot had
come. Several people present exclaimed that they were the
shoes, and Bob made no reply. At his trial, the jury heard
testimony about Bob's silence, on the theory that it was an
implied admission of the accusation made. The court held
that the evidence was inadmissible. Judge Walker noted that
the emotional exclamation demanded no reply, but then
turned to Bob's condition:

> His social relation to his master and mistress, and to the
> other white persons present, forbidding the freedom of
> speech allowed among equals, and making a contradiction
> in most cases an insolence, rendered it unnatural and, per-
> haps, improper, under the circumstances for him to inter-
> pose a denial to the accusation implied in the expression
> which he heard. The habitude of thought and feeling, the
> consciousness of inferiority, and the subordination and dis-

cipline belonging to his condition, made it perfectly natural that he should be silent, because he did not feel authorized to speak, or from an apprehension that a contradiction would be deemed an impertinence.

Southern courts rarely modified evidentiary rules in cases where the slave's status was the only basis for the decision. For example, the Florida Supreme Court succinctly described the facts of a case in which a slave's confession to an arson charge was the sole evidence that led to the imposition of a sentence of death. The slave was arrested on suspicion of arson.

He was taken before the mayor of Pensacola, at his office. A large and excited crowd was present, declaring that the accused should be hung, and but for the firmness and determination of the mayor, would have seized upon him. He was informed by the mayor that the crowd was satisfied as to his guilt, that he would be put upon his trial, and would certainly be hung. That if he had accomplices they would be put upon their trial, and not him—that he would become State's evidence. The mayor further testifies "that the accused was greatly alarmed." The city marshal, who was also present, testifies that the accused was under great excitement, was laboring under great terror, and that he never saw any one more terrified. Under these circumstances, he was urged to confess. When asked what he had to say, he replied, "send for my master and I will tell the whole." Upon his master appearing, the previous statements of the mayor were repeated to the accused, and he confessed his guilt. The next morning he was committed to jail, and upon a second interview with the mayor he again confessed his guilt and accused someone as his accomplice, who on being arrested he failed to identify.[63]

The court said that "there are few cases to be found in the books where stronger influences were brought to bear on the mind of the prisoner," and that his fear was bolstered by the mayor's assurance of protection if he confessed. In addition, the prosecution did not overcome the presumption that the same influences continued to have effect the next day, when the slave repeated his confession.

Then the court brought the slave's status into the analysis:

> Independent of these confessions, the fact that the accused is a slave, and the confession to, and at the instance of his master, are circumstances entitled to the most grave consideration; the ease with which this class of our population can be intimidated, and the almost absolute control which the owner does involuntarily exercise over the will of the slave, should induce the courts at all times to receive their confessions with the utmost caution and distrust.

The lack of corroborating evidence, and uncontradicted testimony that parts of the confession were inaccurate, further underlined "the uncertainty and danger of these confessions."

In Louisiana and Alabama, the logic that made the slave's relation to his master relevant to the issue of voluntariness approached its natural conclusion. As the Alabama Supreme Court put it:

> In considering cases of the kind before us, where the master or owner of the slave is introduced to prove his confessions, we must bear in mind the relation existing between them, of ownership and dominion on the part of the master, and subjection and dependence on the part of the slave. This relation, in many cases, may be supposed to exert an influence over the mind of the slave, with respect to such admissions, when considered in connection with declarations made by the master, which might not attach to declarations made by strangers or persons having no connection with the slave in any way. . . . The slave naturally looks to his master for protection: he is accustomed to throw himself upon his leniency and mercy, and, it may be, by honest confessions of his guilt, to mitigate the chastisement which may await him as the punishment for his misconduct.[64]

The Louisiana parallel involved Nelson, who was being held in the stocks for murder when the overseer, his master's son, approached and told him that "it would be better for him to tell what he had done," whereupon Nelson confessed to killing two unidentified men who were never found.[65] Relying on standard treatises on the law of evidence, the Louisiana Supreme Court held the confession inadmissible because it was made after a person having authority over the defendant had offered him an inducement: "The admonition coming from such a source was well calculated to inspire the slave with the hope of protection from the consequences of his act if fully confessed. . . ." The Alabama court followed the same reasoning where the master "dispassionate[ly] and ingenuous[ly]" had said "these denials only make the matter worse."[66]

The master-slave relation thus could lead to finding confessions involuntary largely, though not solely, because they were given to the master.[67] It similarly relaxed other evidentiary rules, most notably the rule that a person with a pecuniary interest in the outcome of a suit could not testify. The Mississippi Supreme Court stated the general rule that the master could testify, in a murder case where the master would have provided an alibi:

> The master has the custody of his slave, and owes to him protection, and it would be a rigorous rule indeed if the master could not be a witness in behalf of his slave. What would be the condition of the slave, if that rule, which binds him to perpetual servitude, should also create such an interest in the master, as to deprive him of the testimony of that master? The hardship of such a rule would illy comport with that humanity which should be extended to that race of people. In prosecutions for offences, negroes are to be treated as other persons; and although the master may have had an interest in his servant, yet the servant had such an interest in the testimony of his master as will out-weigh mere pecuniary consideration; nor could he be deprived of the benefit of that testimony by the mere circumstance that,

in a civil point of view, he was regarded by the law as property.[68]

In 1856, the North Carolina Supreme Court reconsidered earlier decisions and adopted the prevailing rule, expressing misgivings about the general rule of exclusion in capital cases but then turning to the master-slave relation:

> The testimony of the master cannot be excluded without manifest inconsistency. The slave is put on trial as a *human being*; entitled to have his guilt or innocence passed on by a jury. Is it not inconsistent, in the progress of the trial, to treat him as property, like a chattel,—a horse, in the value of which the owner has a pecuniary interest which makes him incompetent as a witness? And as respects the master, is it not enough, that in the exercise of the right of eminent domain, his property should be forfeited to the public without compensation, and he should be made liable for the costs? Must insult be superadded by saying to him, "you have a pecuniary interest, and, therefore, cannot be trusted; so, we must also take from you the poor privilege of being heard in behalf of your slave, and of having your credit passed upon by the jury?"[69]

Southern courts, however, could not follow the lines suggested by these cases without thoroughly undermining the state's ability to prosecute slaves, the master class' ability to regard itself as the primary protection available to slaves, and its sense that the coercion of slavery was morally tolerable. They therefore refused to take the final step: it was inducement plus confession to a master, not the latter alone, that invalidated a confession. The Louisiana court, making the argument explicit, noted:

> As it is alike the interest and the duty of the master to protect and defend his slaves, confessions made to the master and voluntarily deposed to by him, ought to have the highest moral weight as evidence. . . . There may be, no

doubt, cases where the confession having been made in reference to the defence to be made for the slave, it ought to be received and weighed with great caution, but to exclude entirely confessions made to the master on the ground of his relation to the accused, is not required by any motive of justice or humanity to the slave, and is opposed to sound reason and public policy.[70]

This approach had two points that could be developed to limit the subversive effects already noted. Courts could decide that no inducement had been offered, as in *Mose* v. *State*, where the Alabama court found no inducement when, after repeatedly beating a slave who refused to confess and being satisfied of the slave's innocence, the master washed his hands of the slave several weeks later when another slave implicated Mose in the murder.[71] The slave called for two white men to see him a few days later and confessed to them. In addition, courts could resist the generalization of the idea of subordination, as when the Georgia Supreme Court, in an emotion-laden case where a slave murdered his frail young overseer by beating him even as the overseer tried to flee, rejected the "new proposition" that all slave confessions to whites should be excluded because of the slaves' habit of obedience to requests by whites.[72]

A logical rather than a temporal sequence underlies the course of decision presented here. The rules began by applying a general standard of voluntariness. A special law applicable to slaves alone started to emerge when the courts recognized that slave status was relevant to the voluntariness issue. The special law became more firmly defined when slave status became, not simply relevant to a general inquiry into voluntariness, but one of a very few items that were dispositive on the issue. But a special slave law did not become consolidated and clearly set off from the general law because of the threat to public order and self-conception that such a law would have posed. Thus, along with cases making slave status relevant, pure voluntariness cases persisted,[73] even in situations where the alternative line of decisions might readily have been drawn upon. The Mississippi Supreme Court, for example, upheld the admission in a burglary case of a confession that the slave made after hearing another slave being whipped in connection with the same offense.[74] The court indicated that it would take a narrower view of "inducement" than it could have:

> An appeal to the character or circumstances of a party to his family connection and situation in life—to the claims of justice of others whose rights or safety were involved in his declaring the truth—to his responsibility to a tribunal above all earthly courts for his falsification or suppression of the truth—these and others might very naturally be an "inducement" to a party to make a confession. Yet a confession so induced would not necessarily be incompetent; for the inducement would not be illegal.

It is not suprising, then, to find the same court holding that a slave's confession to his master was admissible in *Sam v. State.*[75] Someone set fire to the master's gin and cottonhouse, and several days later the master retrieved Sam in chains from a place sixty miles away. In the stagecoach on the way back, the master asked Sam why he had burned the ginhouse. We have seen that theories were available that would make the chains, the master's assumption that Sam had committed the crime, and the relationship alone enough. But the court rejected Sam's challenge to the admission of his statement that "he did it because he wished to be hung."

> The relation which the slave bears to the master is certainly one of dependence and obedience, but it is not necessarily one of constraint and duress. It is not to be presumed that the master exercises an undue influence over his slave to induce him to make confessions tending to convict him of a capital offence, because besides the feelings of justice and humanity, which would forbid such efforts, it would be against the interest of the master that the slave should make confessions which would forfeit his life; for he would

thereby sustain a loss to the amount of one-half of the value of the slave. Nor is it to be presumed that the slave will make confessions to his master, tending to convict him of a crime for which he would suffer death, with a view of yielding to the wishes of the master, and when he was aware of the consequences of the commission of the crime; for that would be in opposition to all the promptings of self-preservation, the most powerful of all motives. It is rather to be presumed that he would deny his guilt, relying on the protection of the master, in the absence of inculpatory evidence. For the hope of protection from the master, in consequence of the denial, is a much more natural and reasonable motive, and far more just to the humane feelings of the master, than that of self-sacrifice to the master's cruelty. And the force of this motive is illustrated by the humane conduct which constant experience shows to be exhibited by masters, in the just and reasonable defense of their slaves, when charged with the commission of crimes.

The court noted that exclusion would be "impolitic and dangerous": it would reduce the number of confessions and convictions and increase the private punishment of slaves "otherwise than according to the rules and restraints of the law, which should operate, both in its protection and in its punishment, upon them, as well as upon the white man."

Both the procedural and substantive routes to the differentiation of slave and general law thus turned back on themselves. Full codification of procedure was impossible, and distinctive substantive rules could not be developed without excessive cost. Southern courts were unable, here as elsewhere, to close off slave law as a separate subject matter.

D. THE FAILURE OF RACE AS A CLASSIFYING DEVICE

Southern courts did have available an obvious method to define and thereby restrict slave law. Because lines drawn on the basis of race and those drawn on the basis of condition were almost identical, slave law could have been recharacterized as black law. Although the lines did not divide the world in precisely the same way, the small area of overlap and ambiguity might have been tolerable. Opinions in slave cases strongly supported the slave-law/black-law equation, for the rhetorical opposition of slaves and white men, not slaves and free persons, proved nearly impossible to resist.[76] Racist assumptions, too, made it difficult to sustain a law that distinguished three classes: slaves, free blacks, and whites. Yet when a large number of cases are arrayed, it becomes clear that the slave-law/black-law equation failed as a general ordering principle. When Southern courts had to face the implications of their rhetoric for the legal rationales of the cases, they only inconsistently followed that rhetoric. The reasons, though difficult to pry from the cases, seem to have included problems in determining race when it mattered, miscegenation on a scale large enough to complicate line-drawing, and manumission with its concomitant creation of an undesired, but apparently ineradicable, class of free blacks. The failure of categorization on any basis rested ultimately on structural contradictions within slave law; the failure of race as a categorizing rule then can be seen as the result of processes specific to race and of other processes of more general scope.

The supreme court of Louisiana, in a state with a large population of free blacks, was perhaps more conscious than courts elsewhere of the problems of line-drawing, and it explicitly refused to equate slave law with black law when, in 1856, it held unconstitutional a statute entitled, "An Act relative to slaves and free colored persons" because both the title and the body of the act covered two distinct subjects.[77] Like many state constitutions, the Louisiana constitution provided that each law cover only one subject, to be described in the title. Judge Spofford, in dissent, argued that such provisions were designed to assure legislative accountability by making it clear what the legislature did and by inhibiting log-rolling. The Louisiana statute in question was basically a reenactment in a single statute of the various laws regulating slaves and free blacks that were previously scattered in the statute books. Judge Spofford not unreasonably contended that the purposes of the constitutional provision were fully served by "a title which challenges attention." He also would have characterized the statute as one "relative to persons of color, whether bond or free," and noted that the "one subject" rule had to be applied sensibly because "every 'object' is infinitely divisible." The court's majority rejected Judge Spofford's recharacterization, saying that it was "more specious than real." Further, the division between slaves and free blacks was fundamental: "[I]n the eye of the Louisiana law, there is (with the exception of political rights, of certain social privileges, and of the obligations of jury and militia service) all the difference between a free man of color and a slave, that there is between a white man and a slave." Free blacks, unlike slaves, could make contracts, acquire property, testify in civil suits, and be tried in the regular courts.[78] An air of formalism hangs about the majority's opinion, as it must about any opinion dealing with as formal a provision as the "one subject" rule, but the court rejected the assimilation of all blacks into a single category, at least without clearer legislative direction. Indeed, the court refused to follow Judge Spofford's recharacterization in part because it too would have made a distinction between "bond or free," and "in making a distinction, we recognize a difference."

A habeas corpus case in the Georgia Superior Court made the same point.[79] A petition for habeas corpus was filed on behalf of a boy named James, alleging that James was a free person being held by John Philpot. Philpot's response stated only that James was a Negro. The court found that the response was inadequate, and held Philpot in contempt when he failed to produce James in court. Philpot then engaged in what the court called "evasive" maneuvers, and filed affidavits stating that Philpot had sold James shortly before he had responded to the habeas corpus petition, but not demonstrating that, at the time of the response, Philpot could not have produced James. Philpot sought relief from the finding of contempt, arguing, among other things, that blacks, whether slave or free, could not avail themsleves of the writ of habeas corpus. Expressing some indignation at the argument, the court rejected it. The writ could not be confined to whites, "for then the benefit of this salutary writ would be made to depend upon the particular complexion of the individual, and not upon his political and social relations, . . ." which would leave even native Americans "at the mercy of every ruffian who might choose to seize upon their persons." The legislature had replaced habeas corpus with a statutory remedy for persons held as slaves, but Philpot's response did not claim that James was a slave. Finally, Philpot relied on the statutory presumption that blacks were slaves. The court noted that the statute itself refused the presumption to free blacks, although what that might mean is unclear, and made it applicable only in suits for freedom against masters.[80] The court would not carry the presumption that blacks were slaves so far as to bar habeas corpus for a person who, as far as the record showed, was in fact a free black.

> Now it would be a very hard and unreasonable construction of a mere rule of evidence, to make it reduce a whole class of free people to a level with slaves, deprive them of the most effectual means of protecting their personal liberty, and subvert a constitutional provision. There is a very broad and obvious distinction between the rights and conditions of slaves and free persons of color. Slaves, as we have seen, are not mere things, and have many personal rights secured to them by law, but are without the right of personal liberty or any political rights whatever. Free persons of color are equally destitute of political rights, are somewhat abridged of personal rights, but enjoy in its fullest extent personal liberty. To protect this latter right wherever enjoyed, to restore it wherever unlawfully deprived, the *habeas corpus* was designed, and in a state of society just such as now exists among us, was engrafted upon the Constitution. The slave, therefore, without personal liberty, is without the

benefit of the writ: the free person of color enjoying personal liberty has the benefit of the *habeas corpus* secured to him by a constitutional guaranty.

The court supported its conclusion by insisting that adherence to the law also promoted "expediency and policy." "It should never be forgotten, however, by any, that there can be no true and sound policy which is opposed to strict and impartial justice; and that both individual and general happiness and security are best attained by a prompt and cheerful obedience to just and humane laws."

Given the inadequacy of Philpot's response to the writ, the outcome is unremarkable; it was quite clear, for example, that had Philpot claimed that James was a slave, the statutory remedy with its provision for trial by jury, and not habeas corpus before a judge, would have been available to try James' claim to freedom.[81] Yet the presence of the presumption of slavery from color introduced a complication. The two cases examined so far insisted that the relevant lines were between slaves and free persons, not between blacks and whites. The presumption, which was universal in the South,[82] tended to assimilate the lines. *Gary* v. *Stevenson*, decided by the Arkansas Supreme Court in 1858, illustrates how the presumption operated.[83] A sixteen-year-old boy absconded from the custody of Stevenson, because Stevenson was involved in a commercial dispute with Gary that might have resulted in the sale of the boy to "some remote section of the country." The boy filed suit for freedom, alleging that he was the son of Gary and a white woman, and that he had come into Stevenson's custody through some complicated transactions in which his status as an apprentice was distorted into slavery. Three physicians who had known the boy for several years testified that, in appearance, he had no traces of "negro blood"; he was fair, with sandy smooth hair and blue eyes. Stevenson presented witnesses who testified that the boy was reputed to be the child of a slave named Susan, who was herself extremely fair, and that the boy and Susan treated each other as son and mother. The court concluded that the evidence established that the boy belonged to "the negro race," upon which the presumption of slavery attached even though "the admixture of African blood may be small." It suggested that the evidence, even without the presumption, showed that the boy was the child of a slave, and the court rejected his claim to freedom.

Southern courts occasionally evaded the assimilation of the racial and status lines. Not surprisingly, in Louisiana the presumption was much weaker. "Persons of color," but not blacks, were presumed to be free.[84] The court relied on its sense of the social reality of Louisiana:

> [N]egroes brought to this country being generally slaves, their descendants may perhaps fairly be presumed to have continued so, till they show the contrary. Persons of color may have descended from Indians on both sides, from a white parent, or mulatto parents in possession of their freedom. Considering how much probability there is in favor of the liberty of those persons, they ought not to be deprived of it upon mere presumption, more especially as the right of holding them in slavery, if it exists, is in most instances capable of being satisfactorily proved.

More obviously evasive was *Hunter* v. *Shaffer*, a Georgia action involving a dispute over who owned a slave named Sam.[85] Hunter acquired Sam from Judith Lehiffe, the widow of a South Carolinian. Mrs. Lehiffe then remarried, and the second husband sold Sam again. Shaffer traced his title to this second sale. Because the first sale to Hunter had been recorded, however, Shaffer could prevail only by establishing that Mrs. Lehiffe could not enter a valid contract. He attempted to do so by proving that she was the granddaughter of a black woman and was therefore presumed to be a slave incapable of contracting. Perhaps because Mrs. Lehiffe and her mother had always been considered free, Shaffer's claim was rejected. The court refused to invoke the presumption because it was the creation of a statute and therefore, by the principles of conflict of laws, could not extend beyond Georgia, even to South Carolina whose identical policy the court noted.

> There is no one who has a stronger conviction than I have of the necessity which exists in our State, and in every other, where absolute slavery is known, of preserving a clear and broad distinction between the free citizen and the slave, and of preserving within the just limits prescribed by law, those of the slave race who may have obtained their liberty. Without such distinction, the rights of the master cannot be sufficiently protected, nor the public sufficiently guarded against the disorders consequent on an ill governed slave population, and the confusion of ranks and orders in society.

But no question of the rights of masters was implicated in the case, since the issue of race arose only as a remote part of the chain of title. When Mrs. Lehiffe sold Sam, free blacks were allowed to own slaves in Georgia, and there was no evidence that South Carolina had a different rule. Finally, the court refused to extend the rule that "freedom cannot be established by reputation" applicable in suits involving freedom and police regulations, to ordinary property disputes.

Racial distinctions were under some strain for practical as well as conceptual reasons. In North Carolina, *Nichols* v. *Bell* illustrated one problem.[86] Nichols sued Bell on a contract claim. Evidence showed "that he was neither black nor white, but that he was of a brown color, between that of an African and a mulatto, and that neither of his parents could have been a white person," and that he was reputed to be a free person. Bell, attempting to establish that the contract was void because Nichols was a slave, requested a jury instruction that "in the case of persons of a *shade* of color darker than that of a mulatto, the law presumed they were slaves." Chief Justice Nash affirmed the refusal to give that instruction. He reviewed the cases, going back fifty years, involving the presumption and noted that they distinguished "between a black and a yellow complexion."

If we had the power, we certainly have not the disposition to extend the principle further than as recognised in the cases cited. Let the presumption rest upon the African color; that is a decided mark: but to carry it into shades, would lead us into darkness, doubt and uncertainty, for they are as various as the admixture of blood between the races, and against the rule that presumptions are always in favor of liberty.

But if carrying the presumption "into shades" was distasteful, even more unedifying were cases like *Gary v. Stevenson*, where race had to be proved by testimony. The suit for freedom brought by Abby Guy, which ran from 1855 to 1863 in the Arkansas courts, is an extreme but useful illustration. At the first trial, the evidence tended to show that Guy's mother was "a bright mulatto" who had been held as a slave for many years. In 1844, however, Guy and her children began to live apart from the defendant, and were treated by the neighbors as whites. Eleven years later, the defendant took possession of Guy as a slave. Guy and the children were presented to the jury for inspection and observation, and several doctors who "had read physiology" testified as experts on the physical appearance of blacks, stating that "the negro hair never runs out" but may become straight after three generations and that "the flat nose remains observable for several descents." The jury found that Guy was a free person, but the judgment was reversed because the trial judge had mistakenly instructed the jury that if Guy was "less than one fourth negro," she was presumed to be free. The Arkansas Supreme Court held that if a peson held as a slave had "mixed blood," he or she should be "presumed to be a slave, that being the condition generally of such people in this State."[87] Further, if the jury found that Guy's mother was a slave, Guy was a slave "no matter whether the mother was half, fourth, or eighth negro."

The jury at the second trial again found Guy to be free, and the supreme court now affirmed, although it had the "impres-

sion" that the verdict was "against the preponderance of evidence, through reluctance to sanction the enslaving of persons
who, to all appearances, were of the white race, and, for many
years before suit, had acted as free persons and been treated
as such."[88] One issue on the second appeal involved the use
of expert testimony. During the inspection of the plaintiffs
by the jury, they took off their shoes and stockings so that
the jury could examine their feet. The physicians had noted
that the feet "furnish means of distinguishing negro blood or
descent." The supreme court agreed.

> The experience of every intelligent observer of the race,
> whether in the instances of mixed or unmixed negro blood,
> will doubtless attest the truth of the testimony of the profes-
> sional witnesses. No one who is familiar with the peculiar
> formations of the *negro foot* can doubt but that an inspection
> of that member would ordinarily afford some indication
> of the race. . . .[89]

Recognition of the near identity of race and status created
difficulty precisely because the identity was not complete.
Because of the realities of Southen society, it was adminis-
tratively efficient to create presumptions flowing from race,
and, despite the conceptual problems entailed by the need to
adjust those presumptions to the rule that status and not race
was dispositive, the pervasive racism of Southern society supported the move away from status and toward race as a categorizing device. Again, only illustrations are needed. The
North Carolina Supreme Court reversed a conviction for
keeping a disorderly house where the evidence showed that
raucous Christmas parties were held by a master for his slaves,
which some whites and slaves owned by other masters had
attended.[90] Chief Justice Ruffin wrote that this evidence was
insufficient.

> It would really be a source of regret, if, contrary to common
> custom, it were to be denied to slaves, in the intervals
> between their toils, to indulge in mirthful pastimes, or if

it were unlawful for a master to permit them among his slaves, or to admit to the social enjoyment the slaves of others, by their consent. But it is clearly not so. . . . When the law tolerates such merry-makings among these people, it must be expected, in the nature of things, that they will not enter into them with the quiet and composure which distinguish the gaieties of a refined society, but with somewhat of that hearty and boisterous gladsomeness and loud laughs, which are usually displayed in rustic life, even where the peasantry are much in advance of our negroes in the power and habit of restraining the exhibition of a keen sense of such pleasures. One cannot well regard with severity the rude pranks of a laboring race, relaxing itself in frolic, though they may seem to some to be at times somewhat excessive. If slaves would do nothing, tending more to the corruption of their morals or to the annoyance of the whites than seeking the exhilaration of their simple music and romping dances, they might be set down as an innocent and happy class. We may let them make the most of their idle hours, and may well make allowances for the noisy outpourings of glad hearts, which providence bestows as a blessing on corporeal vigor united to a vacant mind. . . . There was nothing contrary to morals or law in all that—adding, as it did, to human enjoyment, without hurt to any one, unless it be that one feel aggrieved that these poor people should for a short space be happy at finding the authority of the master give place to his benignity, and at being freed from care and filled with gladness.[91]

Similar racist condescension, although often lacking the rather overt class condescension displayed by Judge Ruffin, can be seen in a case treating free blacks as "wards" or "infants," on whose death claims against others passed to their guardians, such as a "discreet white citizen" appointed by the courts, rather than to their heirs.[92] Sometimes, as is inevitable in a racist legal system, racism appeared to benefit blacks. Thus, the North Carolina Supreme Court affirmed the acquittal of a free black who had been hired to carry a white man's goods, which included a pistol, to a work site.[93] "Degraded as are these individuals, as a class, by their social position, it is certain that among them are many, worthy of all confidence, and into whose hands these weapons can be safely trusted, either for their own protection, or for the protection of the property of others confided to them." Racist assumptions were of course not always so apparently benign. For example, the Arkansas Supreme Court hinted that a black defendant charged with raping a white woman would find it hard to establish that sexual intercourse had occurred with the woman's consent:

> But surely it may not be unsafe, or unjust to the prisoner to say that, in this State, where sexual intercourse between the white women and negroes is generally regarded with the utmost abhorrence, the presumption that a white woman yielded herself to the embraces of a negro, without force, arising from a want of chastity in her, would not be great, unless she had sunk to the lowest degree of prostitution.[94]

Racism and its associated notions of hierarchy overcame the impulse to draw lines based solely on status when courts in Georgia, Mississippi, and Arkansas held, during the 1850s, that free blacks, although entitled to own certain forms of property, could not own slaves, even in the absence of a statutory bar such as existed in other states. The opinions contain as feverish a rhetoric as can be found in any area of the law, which plainly resulted from the sensitivity of the issue at a time of heightened sectional conflict. The Mississippi Supreme Court's opinion, indeed, consisted in large measure of quotations from Chief Justice Taney's opinion in the *Dred Scott* case, followed by a peculiarly inappropriate essay on the status of aliens in international law.[95] The issue of a free black's right to own slaves arose in a representative form in Georgia.[96] James Nunez owned several slaves, which he left in his will to his sister and then on her death to his son Joseph, a free black. During Joseph's life, Alexander Urquhart was his guardian, authorized to enter transactions for Joseph Nunez's benefit. At the beginning of 1847, Nunez died without leaving any descendants, and Hugh Walton was appointed administrator of Nunez's estate. Walton sued Seaborn Bryan to recover for the estate the slaves originally owned by Nunez's father. Bryan produced a deed showing that Nunez had given the slaves to Urquhart as a gift a week before Nunez died and that Urquhart had sold them to Bryan six weeks after Nunez died. The jury found for Walton, believing that there was some sort of fraud in Urquhart's actions.

On appeal, Judge Joseph Lumpkin first noted several technical defects in Walton's case, including the failure to produce James Nunez's will forty years after his death or to search for it more thoroughly. Then he addressed the "main point," the ability of free blacks to own slaves. Judge Lumpkin stated his "strong inclination . . . to give [his] sentiments pretty fully upon this subject," and he did, in a virulently racist opinion. First he presented his conclusion, that free blacks were "in a state of perpetual pupilage or wardship" and had only those rights expressly granted by the legislature.

> That the act of manumission confers no other right but that of freedom from the dominion of the master, and the limited liberty of locomotion; that it does not and cannot confer *citizenship*, nor any of the powers, civil or political, incident to *citizenship*; that the social and civil degradation, resulting from the taint of blood, adheres to the descendants of Ham in this country, like the poisoned tunic of Nessus; that nothing but an Act of the Assembly can purify, by the salt of its grave, the bitter fountain—the *"darkling sea."*

Although Judge Lumpkin purported to resist the temptation to review the history of slavery, he did examine, among other things, the contrast between villeinage and Roman slavery, Roman law regarding manumission, and colonization schemes. To the extent that he supplied reasons for the result, they are found in the proposition that manumission, being the private act of the master, could convey no public rights on the free black. Nor had the legislature acted to eliminate the "unconquerable prejudice, if it can be so called, of race"; rather the free black was "associated still with the slave in this State, in some of the most humiliating incidents of his degradation. . . ." After enumerating those incidents, Judge Lumpkin continued:

> I do not refer to these severe retrictions, for the purpose of condemning them. They have my hearty and cordial approval. The great principle of self-preservation demands, on the part of the white population, unceasing vigilance and firmness, as well as uniform kindness, justice and humanity. Everything must be interdicted which is calculated to render the slave discontented with his condition, or which would tend to increase his capacity for mischief.

He concluded with a few words on the policy of manumission:

> In no part of this country, whether North or South, East or West, does the free negro stand erect and on a platform of equality with the white man. He does, and must necessarily feel this degradation. To him there is but little in prospect but a life of poverty, of depression, of ignorance, and of decay. He lives amongst us without motive and without hope. His fancied freedom is all a delusion. All practical men must admit that the slave who receives the care and protection of a tolerable master, is superior in comfort to the free negro. Generally, society suffers, and the negro suffers by manumission. I am fully persuaded that the State ought sternly to withhold its assent to domestic emancipation; and that the true policy is not to seek to elevate the black man in our midst, to a condition of equality which it is impossible for him to exercise wisely for himself or the community. Civil freedom among the whites, he can never enjoy. To this isolated class, it will ever be but a name.

We doubt the propriety of ejecting our free negroes upon the free States. They will not only become troublesome allies in the unconstitutional and unholy work of inveigling off our slaves, and assisting them to escape; but their constant effort and aim will be to create discontent among our slaves; and in case of intestine war, which may Heaven in its mercy avert, such a population would be in a situation to do us much mischief. . . .

[T]he Courts of this country should never lean to that construction, which puts the thriftless African upon a footing of civil or political equality with a white population which are characterized by a degree of energy and skill, unknown to any other people or period. Such alone can be *citizens* in this great and growing Republic, which extends already from the Atlantic to the Pacific, and from the St. Lawrence to the Rio Grande.

Bryan v. *Walton* is notable for the clarity with which the identification of race and status appears, as in the paragraph that justifies restrictions on free blacks by referring to slave discontent. There is of course an argument that full liberty for free blacks would, by providing a model for slaves, generate discontent, but it is hard to read that argument into Judge Lumpkin's opinion. Rather, the paragraph demonstrates the ease with which race and status were assimilated. Even when the specific "reasoning" of *Bryan* v. *Walton* was rejected, the same assimilation occurred. A property dispute similar to that in *Bryan* v. *Walton* arose a few years later in Arkansas.[97] The facts, drawn from a more complex situation, that are relevant to this discussion are that Jonathon Koen bequeathed land and a slave named Charles to a free black. The Arkansas Supreme Court rejected the proposition, drawn from *Bryan* v. *Walton*, that manumission conferred no rights to contract or hold land.

The negro, though morally and mentally inferior to the white man, is, nevertheless, an intellectual being, with feelings, necessities and habits common to humanity. By the act of emancipating, the reciprocal obligations and duties between master and slave, by which the slave owes obedience and fidelity to the master, and the master owes to the slave support and protection, are ended. When this takes place, no one is interested in the protection of the negro. If, under such circumstances, he could not make and enforce contracts, it is difficult to understand how he could, with any certainty, supply his commonest necessities. Such a condition would be inconsistent with civilization. And, besides this, the negro, having no power to acquire property, or certain means of gathering the fruits of his labor, every incentive to industry would be at once destroyed; and, sinking into idleness and depravity, he would become an intolerable nuisance.

But the situation was different when a free black sought to own, not land, but a slave.

Without attempting to discuss slavery in the abstract, it may be said that it has its foundation in an *inferiority of race*. There is a striking difference between the *black* and *white* man, in intellect, feelings and principles. In the order of providence, the former was made inferior to the latter; and hence the bondage of the one to the other. For government and protection, the one race is dependent on the other. It is upon this principle alone, that slavery can be maintained as an institution. The bondage of one negro to another has not this solid foundation to rest upon. The free negro finds in the slave his brother in blood, in color, feelings, education and principle. He has but few civil rights, nor can have, consistent with the good order of society; and is amost as dependent on the white race as the slave himself. He is, therefore, civilly and morally disqualified to extend protection, and exercise dominion over the slave.

In 1846, the same court had summarized the general view in upholding the state's requirement that free blacks post a $500 bond against becoming a public charge or injuring any person.[98] The statute did not violate the privileges and immunities of citizens, because free blacks could not be citizens: "The two races, differing as they do in complexion, habits, conformations and intellectual endowments, could not nor ever will live together upon terms of social or political equality. A higher than human power has so ordained it, and a greater than human agency must change the decree."

Despite some deviations, Southern law taken as a whole appears to have moved from insistence on status as the categorizing device to incomplete acceptance of race as that device. That move was supported by the political tensions of the 1850s that are so evident in *Byran v. Walton* and by the racism that all the cases display. It was, in addition, consistent with the general tendency toward developing a categorical approach to slave law. But it was able to reach only an imperfect use of race as the dividing line, because of a structural difficulty with the categorizing effort. The basic problem was that the law attempted to impose a dichotomized pair of conceptual categories on a social reality that was essentially trichotomized.

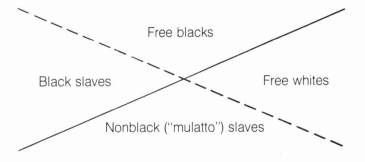

The dichotomy properly used "black slaves" and "free whites" as polar categories. If status was to control, free whites and free blacks had to be treated as a single category, a solution that was politically unacceptable; if race was to control, inevitable problems of "passing" woud have to be

faced. These intermediate categories were probably ineradicable. To transform the society into one in which race was
unequivocally coextensive with slavery, manumission would
have to have been eliminated. But it would have been hard
to suppress the natural inclination of white fathers to free their
slave children, an inclination illustrated in *Bryan* v. *Walton*.
Even more, eliminating manumission would have required
that the master class accept the propriety of social control over
their individual choices. As the next chapter shows, the contradictions of Southern slave society made that almost impossible. Conversely, to transform the society into one in
which race and slavery were only contingently related, the
possibilities illustrated by Abby Guy's case, which were
rooted in widespread miscegenation, would have had to have
been foreclosed. That too was probably impossible. Thus,
even the clearest candidate for the categorizing rule, race,
could not easily be accepted into a stable law for the South
as it was.

This discussion can be summarized by examining a Delaware decision in which the impossibility of using race as the
categorizing device is as evident to the observer as it was
concealed from the judges. *Tindal* v. *Hudson* was a suit for
freedom by Isaac Tindal.[99] His father, a free black, had been
"legally married" to a slave. When Isaac was born, his father
purchased him from the man who owned Isaac's mother.
Instead of freeing Isaac, his father held him as a slave and in
his will bequeathed him to serve until he reached twenty-five.
The suit for freedom from one who bought Isaac from the
estate was said to pose two "novel and interesting" questions:
can a free black own slaves, and "whether a father can hold
his own children in slavery." The court's opinion dealt with
the questions separately. On the first, it argued that slavery
as it existed involved black slaves and white owners and that
it would "not institute a new species of slavery." Further,
free blacks were "almost as helpless and dependent" on whites
as slaves; their limited civil capacity made it impossible for
them to provide the "support and protection" that slave-

owners had to give in a system of "mutual and reciprocal obligations and duties." On the second question, the court said that "humanity revolts at the idea of a parent selling his own children into slavery"; "the natural rights and obligations of a father are paramount to the acquired rights of the master." But of course fathers owned their children throughout the South. Although lawyers' distinctions might be drawn between children born of legal marriages and "illegitimate" children, the Deleware court could say what it did on the second question only by ignoring the reality of race on which its answer to the first question rested.

Race, then, could not provide the categories for separating the law of slavery from the general law. Only a complete codification of slave law would provide the conceptual tools that the intellectually limited could use to handle their problems.

On December 19, 1860, the Georgia legislature adopted a comprehensive codification of state laws, which drew together prior statutes and court decisions.[100] The commission that prepared the code included Thomas R. R. Cobb. The civil code defined "different kinds of persons" and specified the meaning and incidents of slavery. The penal code detailed the crimes and procedures to be followed in cases involving slaves and free blacks. On January 19, 1861, the Georgia secession convention voted 208 to 89 to secede from the union.

IV. SOCIAL CONTROL OF THE MASTER'S WILL: THE CONTRADICTIONS OF SLAVE SOCIETY

THE POLITICAL AND STRUCTURAL contradictions of the idea of a law of slavery gave shape to the subjects examined in the preceding chapter. Those contradictions were not obscured by many of the complexities of Southern slavery, because most of the cases involved criminal law and procedure, where the state intervened after events that had no market connections. By examining subjects that did have such connections, we can explore in more detail the internal contradictions of slave law and can develop the contradictions created by the intermingling of slave and bourgeois society.

The motivating principle of bourgeois law is an undifferentiated individualism. The reduction of human labor to labor power gives rise to concepts of the highest generality, in which, for example, labor power is fungible with money. At the same time, although productive labor is undifferentiated, the power to mobilize productive labor is committed to the unregulated choice of individuals. For political and historical reasons, the pure version of bourgeois law cannot be implemented, but its motivating principle makes both distinctions among forms of property and state intervention to override individual choice anomalous and always needing explanation. In contrast, the motivating principle of slave law is a differentiated communalism. Slavery rests on the fundamental distinction between human labor and those who own it, and the total relations between master and slave generate the idea that all relationships, including those between master and master, should be total. In slave law, then, we should find a reluctance to treat all forms of property, and especially slaves, as reducible to a common measure in money and an acceptance of social control of the master's choices. The insertion of slave law into a bourgeois framework therefore causes new problems, as bourgeois principles must accommodate the incompatible principles of slave law.

This chapter begins with a study of the process of accommodation. Cases in which the courts were called upon to decide whether specific slaves should be transferred from one owner to another show the rapid movement from bourgeois principles, which required that the particular slave have some characteristics that the new owner specially valued, to slave principles, which treated all slaves as categorically distinct from other forms of property. The second section of the chapter examines the law of allocation of risk in transactions involving slaves. Here bourgeois law allocates risks as it is assumed that freely contracting parties would. The principle of individual choice thus exposes what slave society expected of masters, but it does not contradict any assumptions of slave society. Those contradictions appear in the final section of the chapter, which takes up the law of private manumission. There the conflict between the master's individual choice regarding his property and his responsibility to the larger community was sharpest.

A. The Uniqueness of Slaves as a Class

Bourgeois law embodies a strong presumption that all transactions involve completely fungible commodities. Thus, where some transaction goes awry, the law presumes that things can be set right by a monetary award of appropriate damages, for the parties are presumed to be unconcerned about the transaction itself so long as they receive the profits, whether from the transaction or from some other source. Sometimes, however, bourgeois law protects the transaction. In particular, when one party agrees to transfer property to another, bourgeois law allows the courts to compel performance of that agreement where the property is in some sense unique. Given the presumption of fungibility, however, uniqueness has to receive a special definition: property is unique when the damage award is unlikely fully to compensate for the costs to the parties of determining damages.[1] As a general rule, bourgeois courts will not compel the performance of personal service agreements, because the existence of a market in undifferentiated labor power makes evaluation of damages easy and because it is thought that enforcement of an order compelling performance would be difficult.

The law of slavery was different. Beginning with the bourgeois requirement of uniqueness, Southern courts rather quickly developed the rule that courts would direct the transfer of slaves rather than the payment of damages, without regard to the peculiar characteristics of the particular slaves. Labor, not labor power, was being transferred, and enforcement was obviously no problem. Virginia provides an illuminating series of cases. In *Allen* v. *Freeland*, Allen purchased several slaves at an auction in a tavern.[2] Both Fariss and Wright had claims to being the prior owner; Allen paid $1,200 by giving two bonds to Fariss in exchange for bills of sale from Wright to Allen and from Fariss to Allen. However, Fariss believed that Wright actually owned the slaves and that he was holding the bonds as a favor to Wright. All this confusion was important, because Freeland claimed that Wright, whom he had sued two years earlier, had fraudulently concealed his assets. Freeland obtained a judgment for $1,000 and sought to collect the money by having the sheriff seize and sell two of the slaves that Allen had purchased. Allen sought to prohibit the sale. The question, then, was whether, assuming that the initial transfer of the slaves to Allen was valid, he could be protected by an award of damages against Freeland if the slaves were sold by the sheriff.

Judge Carr took what might be called the bourgeois approach. The slaves Allen had bought were not, like those in an earlier case, "family slaves" or in any other way special.

No sacrifice of feeling, no consideration of humanity, are involved. These were not family slaves, but strangers to the plaintiff,—bought from a distance, and casually purchased at a public sale; no statement that they were peculiarly valuable for their character, qualities, or skill in any trade or handicraft; or that the plaintiff bought them cheap, and would be injured by the loss of his bargain. He has paid no money, and never can be forced to pay a cent, if he does not hold the slaves. The money which he intended to vest in this way, he has had the use of; and could now vest it much more advantageously, in the same kind of property. All his legal remedies [for damages] are before him. . . .

He further noted that there was reason to believe that Allen was implicated in Wright's fraudulent scheme to evade Freeland; how else could the transactions involving Fariss be explained? He concluded, therefore, that the sheriff's sale should not be prohibited.

The other judges agreed with this result and in general with both grounds for decision. But Judges Green and Brooke were less confident that slaves were fungible. After reviewing the law of specific performance and uniqueness, Judge Green indicated that

I should incline to think that slaves ought, *prima facie*, to be considered as of peculiar value to their owners, and not properly a subject for adequate compensation in damages, as land is considered to be to a purchaser; but that this presumption may be repelled, as in the case of a person purchasing slaves for the avowed purpose of selling them again.

He was also "incline[d] to think" that the presumption was overcome in this case, but he did note that "slaves are a peculiar species of property. They have moral qualities, and confidence and attachment grow up between master and slave; the value of which cannot be estimated by a jury."

Judge Brooke developed this idea, and indeed concluded that, aside from the fraud, the injunction should have issued.

> Slaves are not only property, but they are rational beings, and entitled to the humanity of the Court, when it can be exercised without invading the right of property; and as regards the owner, their value is much enhanced by the mutual attachment of master and slave; a value which cannot enter into the calculation of damages by a jury. In all such cases, therefore, this Court has exercised a restraining power, except a case in which, whatever may be the decision of it, the property is to be sold, and the only controversy is as to proceeds of the sale. In this case, though *Allen* purchased the property at a public sale, and was but a short time in possession of it, in his opinion, he might have gotten a bargain; he may have set a higher value on the moral qualities of the slave (of which he may have been informed by others) than a jury would have compensated him for.[3]

Judge Brooke thus included bourgeois notions in the analysis—the imperfection of jury determinations, the possibility that Allen had placed a special value on the slaves based on information that he had expended some effort to acquire, the difficulty in persuading a jury that such secret information existed. But he also explicitly relied on the humanity of the slave and the attachments between masters and slaves.

Allen v. *Freeland* set out three positions: slaves were not unique (except for a narrow category of family slaves and the like); slaves were prima facie unique (but the presumption was overcome on the facts); slaves were unique (except for a very narrow category of purely commercial disputes). The Virginia Court of Appeals moved rapidly through the first two positions and ultimately arrived at the third.[4] Eleven months after *Allen*, Judge Carr seemed to get agreement on his nonuniqueness position.[5] In 1816, James Caldwell bought part of White Sulphur Springs from his brother-in-law Bowyer. Four years later, after he had fallen deeply in debt to

others, James Caldwell conveyed all of his property in trust
to John Caldwell, as security for his debt to Bowyer. James
Caldwell's creditors obtained judgment and, as in *Allen*, proposed to sell his property. Bowyer and John Caldwell sued
to enjoin the sale. Once again, issues of fraudulent transfer
lurked in the case. Judge Carr wrote for the entire court that
in the circumstances damages were adequate, especially in
light of the fradulent transfer from James to John Caldwell.
As to the slaves that Caldwell owned, Judge Carr argued that,
Allen aside, all the cases involved injunctions issued on behalf
of owners, not, as in the case at hand, on behalf of those who
simply used the slaves as security.

> It must be obvious to every one, that various causes may
> exist, to give slaves a value in the eye of the master, which
> no estimated damages could reach. The slave may have
> been raised by him, and may possess moral qualities, which,
> to his master, render him invaluable. He may have saved
> the life of the master, or some one of the family, and thus
> have gained with them a value above money and above
> price.

But that could not be true of slaves held as security. *Allen*,
Judge Carr said, did not involve such slaves and, in any event,
would allow an injunction on behalf even of an owner only
"where from the peculiar nature of the property and circumstances of the case," damages would be inadequate.

Less than three years later, the picture had changed.[6] Henry
Randolph purchased some slaves from the estate of Archibald
Cary. He paid with a note on which his brother Brett was
surety. Several years later, Cary's executor sued Brett Randolph, who paid the judgment that the executor obtained.
Then Brett Randolph sued Henry Randolph's estate. As in
the prior cases, when Brett Randolph sought to satisfy the
judgment by selling some slaves, other claimants entered.
Two of Henry Randolph's daughters sought an injunction,
stating that the slaves had been given to them by Randolph's

estate and that they had held the slaves for seventeen years. Judge Carr restated his position and would have required the daughters to allege and show a peculiar value to the slaves.

> We must all agree, that there are many cases, in which a slave has no peculiar value with his owner; some, among the large slave-holders, where he is not even personally known; or he may be vicious or worthless. To these, and other such cases, the principle of equitable interference surely would not apply. . . . Is there any hardship in this? Whether the slave has a peculiar value with his master, none can so well know as the master himself. He can speak from his own feelings, his own knowledge. The simple fact of asking the aid of Equity, will hardly be taken as proof, that he sets a peculiar value on the slave, by those who witness the thousands of applications to that tribunal, in cases wholly unfit and improper.

Judge Green again took the intermediate position.

> I cannot help thinking, that slaves ought, *prima facie*, to be so considered. They have moral qualities, which make them, in some instances, peculiarly valuable to their owners; but which would not be the subject of inquiry in each particular case, without great inconvenience and uncertainty. And whatever may be their qualities, we know that attachments naturally and generally grow up between master and slave, which cannot be the subject of pecuniary estimate by a Jury. This *prima facie* presumption may, however, be repelled by circumstances. As, if the slaves were necessarily to be sold, (as in the case of their being pledged for the payment of debts) and the question is between a creditor claiming under a specific *lien*, and one claiming under execution; or, if they were in the hands of the owner as a subject of traffic; in such cases, the injury done to the owner by seizing and selling them, under an execution against another, would be precisely and accurately measured by their market value.

Judge Coalter gave additional arguments for his agreement with Judge Green:

> The master has only his own *pecuniary interest* to consult, and his own affections and predilections to gratify, in all of which he will be aided by the Courts; but, he owes a *duty* to the slave, as well as the slave does to the master, and which he ought to perform; the duty of protection from a violent seizure and sale, which may terminate in the destruction of his happiness, and in breaking asunder all his family ties and connexions. I have known slaves who could not be sold for $20, and whose masters ought to consider themselves bound by ties of real gratitude to avert such a calamity from them, if able to do so, at the expense of a hundred. Surely, such considerations ought to receive the attention and countenance of the Courts.

Judge Cabell too would not require the claimant of slaves to allege peculiar value.

> Slaves are rational beings, and, as such, have moral qualities, which are calculated to render them of peculiar value in the estimation of their masters. It may be laid down, as a position almost universal, that the master, unless obliged to sell, would think himself poorly compensated for the loss of a slave, by the price which a jury might fix upon him. Moreover, slaves are human beings; and therefore, I do not think that even their attachments and feelings are to be disregarded. The inhumanity of wantonly invading these attachments and feelings, forms with me an additional argument in favor of the interference of a Court of Chancery.

He concluded that the general rule should favor injunctions against the sale of one person's slaves to satisfy the debts of another. If there were exceptions, those who wanted the sale to proceed would have to establish them. Judge Brooke simply referred to his opinion in *Allen,* but three months later he stated the rule that emerged out of the five opinions in

Randolph: "in every case in which the owner of slave property
. . . applies to a Court of Equity, he will be entitled to an
injunction, . . . though he neither alleges, nor proves peculiar
value of the property."[7]

Virginia's course was repeated throughout the South. In
Mississippi, a case in 1840 involved an intrafamily dispute
over two slaves, Mary and Henry.[8] Walker claimed that he
owned Mary based on title that ran back to one brother,
whereas another brother claimed that the transfer that led to
Walker's claim was based on the first brother's misconduct.
The Mississippi Supreme Court held that, on the unchal-
lenged allegations, the second brother was entitled to an order
transferring Mary to him. He had alleged that Mary was a
"family slave," and thereby brought his case within the exception to the general rule, "an indulgence which has long
been extended to the claims of attachment which may have
grown up between the slave and his owner." Interestingly,
the court cited both *Allen*, which supported the narrow view,
and *Randolph*, which supported a much broader position, as
"direct authorities" for the result. It is not surprising, then,
that the Mississippi courts quickly adopted the *Randolph* rule.
In 1843, the chancery court, faced with an attempt by creditors
to execute a judgment by seizing and selling six slaves whom
the debtor had already sold, granted an injunction, noting
that "the importance which has been attached to slave property" had led to the rule of automatic injunction "even without any allegation of peculiar and special value."[9] In the same
year, the state supreme court endorsed that rule, after reviewing Virginia, Tennessee, and South Carolina cases, although
it mischaracterized the Virginia ones, because the very fact
that slaves were sought allowed the court to infer that the
owner preferred them to money damages.[10]

Alabama and Georgia stand in contrast with this otherwise
uniform pattern. *Baker* v. *Rowan* was another of the cases in
which two claimants, one a creditor and the other a purchaser
from the debtor's estate, sought the same slaves.[11] The purchaser sought to prevent the creditor from taking the slaves

out of the state. The slaves, a mother and her two children, were family slaves, and the purchaser was the debtor's son. The Alabama Supreme Court held that the injunction was proper but questoned the *Randolph* rule. An injunction was available if the slaves were "family slaves, to which the owners are attached," but it was insufficient simply to allege that the slaves were family slaves; the complaint also had to specify "the circumstances which could create peculiar value or attachment." This stringency, although dictum in *Baker*, made a difference eight years later in *Hardeman* v. *Sims*.[12] There the injunction was sought to prohibit the transportation of a "family negro" who had been given to Hardeman by his grandfather. The slave was sold to Sims when she was six, nine years before the injunction was sought. The court began with the standard observations about the master-slave relationship.

> It is certainly true, that slaves, although by our law considered property, differ in many respects from other chattels, and many cases may be supposed in which it is not proper that they should be considered as mere chattels. They are intellectual, moral beings, and attachments of the strongest kind, sometimes grow up between master and slave, having its origin not infrequently in early infancy, and strengthened in after life by dutiful service and obedience, on the one hand, and care and protection on the other.

But it concluded that the complaint did not establish that there were those attachments; the slave had been sold many years before, at a very young age.[13]

One notable point about these cases derives from what they did *not* say. Courts uniformly allowed injunctions of specific performance in cases involving land. And in many contexts slaves were regarded as real property. For example, sometimes treating slaves as real property allowed them to descend to the owner's heirs, thus preserving their style of life.[14] Strikingly, however, Southern courts did not resolve the question of specific performance by simple analogy to land. There is a passing reference in Judge Green's opinion in *Allen* and another in an early North Carolina case.[15] But these references meant only that for the same reasons that land was unique, so were slaves. Again, the Virginia court developed the argument in some detail.[16]

> Slaves are not only property but rational beings; and are generally acquired with reference to their moral and intellectual qualities. Therefore damages at law, which are measured by the ordinary market value of the subject, will not generally afford adequate compensation for the breach of a contract for the sale of slaves. There is at least as much reason for enforcing the specific execution of a contract for the sale of slaves, as of a contract for the sale of real estate.

It rejected the Alabama approach, noting that an owner was entitled to an injunction, on the theory that some attachment between master and slave had formed even though the "connection may have existed only for a day. A purchaser of slaves for his own use, looks to their qualities, and generally buys such only as will suit him. In each case, peculiar value will alike be presumed."

Indirect light is thrown on the question of uniqueness by a few cases discussing the proper way to evaluate slave property. For example, in *Bertrand* v. *Arcueil*, the plaintiff bought three slaves, husband, wife, and child, for $1,100.[17] Two days after the purchase, the mother and child became ill, and both died two weeks later. The plaintiff sued to set aside the entire transaction. The defendant claimed that, even if the plaintiff had not known of the illness at the time of purchase, still he should be bound to pay for the father. Louisiana's statutes allowed rescission of an entire transaction if one of "matched" things was destroyed. The court initially held that, although the father's value as a field hand might not have been enormously decreased, "the spirit of the rule is applicable." "Slaves constituting a family would probably labor more cheerfully and harmoniously together, and, by consequence, would be more useful than those not so related; and besides natural justice and humanity would dictate that they should be sold together." On rehearing, however, the court changed its mind. Since the slaves were sold as field hands, there was no "necessary dependence of one member upon another. . . ." Judge Slidell, the author of the original opinion, dissented, noting that most purchasers would pay more for a family than for three equivalent but unrelated slaves. The majority thus treated slaves as fungible, not as unique; it implicitly suggested that the premium paid for a family could be taken into account when reducing the original purchase price, but that the premium alone did not justify the rescission of the entire transaction.

In contrast, cases from Alabama and Virginia emphasized the need to recognize slave identity. The Virginia court held that, if slaves could not be distributed to heirs without separating infants from mothers, "which humanity forbids," compensation in money to equalize slaves was proper.[18] A similar controversy over an estate led to an interesting Alabama decision in this area. Uriah Bass, who died in 1819, left eight slaves to his two married daughters and left a lot "equal in value" to those slaves to each of his five unmarried daughters.[19] The will provided that the slaves would be priced when the younger daughters married or came of age. The problem was that the value of slaves fluctuated, so that when Bass died, perhaps five slaves might be equal in value to the eight given the married daughters, but when a younger daughter came of age, prices for slaves might have dropped so much that twelve slaves would be needed to provide equal value. The court held, sensibly, that the valuation referred to the date of Bass' death. This was to be measured by "those essential qualities which render [slaves] useful and profitable," including age and comeliness. The result, the court said, promoted stability and avoided sales of family slaves, to whom some attachment probably had developed.

In general, Southern courts treated slaves as unique and authorized specific performance or injunctive relief whenever slaves were involved. It is possible to reconstruct this aspect of slave law along bourgeois lines, by noting the difficulties juries might have in determining the value of secret information possessed by purchasers or of the sentimental attachment that could have been thought to be so widespread as to justify a general rule foregoing jury examination of the question. But many of the same points could have been made about ordinary items of property as well. The contrast with the standard rule of bourgeois law is twofold: the courts in the South ordered transfers of labor, and they did so without any showing that the particular slaves were unique. The courts' failure to invoke the real-property analogy provides a key to understanding the general rule, for they instead relied directly upon the totalistic relations between masters and slaves, which generated ties of sentiment and affection that justified special legal treatment of those relations. Equally important, the courts started by requiring some special relationship but ended, except in Alabama and Georgia, by treating all slaves alike. This generalization probably resulted from the confluence of several factors. It supported an ideological view of slavery as always and everywhere implicating ties of sentiment. Although allowing state intervention in transactions between masters, it minimized the intrusion on master-slave relations, by eliminating detailed inquiry into individual relations. For the same reason, it created a broad category subject to special treatment. In all this, Southern courts used the forms of bourgeois law while giving them a specifically slave-oriented content.

B. Allocation of Risk and the Master's Responsibility

The theory of contract law in a market society is straightforward. Contracts are designed to allow exchanges that all participants believe will profit them. Since all exchanges are subject to hazards, contracts also allocate the costs of those hazards. Contract law is designed to give effect to the decisions of the contracting parties. It does so by reducing the costs of negotiating agreements. When a transaction goes awry, the courts must decide which party must, in the absence of a provision allocating the costs of the particular mishap, bear those costs. Courts can promote efficient transactions by allocating the costs as the parties probably would have themselves. This eliminates the need to negotiate contract terms dealing with many contingencies, for most parties would allocate costs as the law does anyway; only those parties who can increase their profit by inserting a different allocation into the contract must negotiate their special provisions. Thus, contract law discloses what judges think about normal behavior by contracting parties.

The clearest examples from Southern slave law are the cases involving the question of responsibility as between owner and hirer for necessary medical care of hired slaves. Three Alabama cases illustrate the general rule. In the first, Childress hired out a slave to Edward Smith, who called in a physician to attend the slave.[20] When the physician sued Childress, the owner, the court held that Smith, the hirer, was liable, unless the owner had requested the services or a contract provision allocated the cost of medical care to the owner.[21] The court later found the owner liable where the hirer had apparently permitted the slave to work on his own.[22] The owner, it said, had "both a moral and legal obligation to supply [the slave's] necessary wants," which could not be discharged by letting the slave go unsupervised either by himself or by a lessor. "The master cannot, by his contract with another, absolve himself from the obligation he is under to the slave and the community to afford him protection and provide for his necessary wants in sickness or old age." The owner's moral obligation was reinforced by rights against the hirer. In *Hogan v. Carr & Anderson*, Hogan leased his slave to Carr for one year.[23] Seven months later, Hogan took the slave back, after discovering that Carr had mistreated him and placed him in danger of losing a leg; Carr had refused to provide medical care. After the slave recovered, Hogan offered him again to Carr, who refused to accept him. Hogan then sued for the unpaid rentals, and won, because Carr had violated the implied contractual requirements of humane treatment and provision of necessary medical care.

Latimer v. Alexander, a Georgia case, summarized the rules comprehensively.[24] Latimer, the owner, hired his slave out to Thompson for a year, to act as a waiter at Thompson's hotel. During that time, Atlanta, where the hotel was located, suffered an outbreak of smallpox, and communications between the city and the surrounding county were obstructed. When the slave caught smallpox, Thompson had Dr. Alexander treat him, without notifying Latimer. Alexander sued Latimer, the owner, for the costs of the medical care. Judge Lumpkin reviewed earlier cases holding the owner liable. In one, the owner had driven the slave away by cruel treatment; he was held liable to the doctor who treated the runaway because no one else stood in the master's position of control and responsibility. Indeed, Judge Lumpkin said, the owner might sometimes be liable even if he hired the slave out, where the hirer had no assets or failed to supervise the slave. But in *Latimer* the hirer should be liable. As we will see, the hirer would have had to pay the entire rental even if the slave died, and he was required to exercise reasonable diligence in discovering illness and guarding against it. Both legal rules gave the hirer an incentive to provide and pay for reasonable medical care. Judge Lumpkin noted that the rental fee was $91 whereas Dr. Alexander's bill was $100. He thought it outrageous that Thompson should have the services of the slave for a year, but that Latimer would lose money because the slave caught smallpox from a guest whom he was required to serve.

These cases show the court's reluctance to force those who provided services to slaves to bear the costs. It was a private obligation of the owner and hirer, to be settled between them on the assumption that hirers generally would bear the costs. That the obligation was private is strikingly illustrated by another Alabama case.[25] After a slave, Rich, was charged with killing his master, he was placed in the county jail, where he became ill. The physician who treated Rich at the jailor's request sued the county for payment, but the court held that the county was not liable. Despite the understandable reluctance of the dead owner's heirs to support Rich, they were indeed required "to provide for his necessary wants in sickness, whilst confined under a criminal charge." There were limits to the master's responsibility, however. John Lingo owned a slave named Jim who was indicted for arson.[26] Lingo refused to hire an attorney to defend Jim, but Miller & Hill stepped in and, by a vigorous defense, secured an acquittal. Lingo sold Jim and refused to pay the attorneys. The Georgia Supreme Court held that the master had no duty to provide counsel when his slave was indicted. It saw no "great need" for such a duty.

> *Every* master has an interest to prevent his slave from being punished, an interest that increases with the increase of the punishment, to which the slave is exposed. *Nearly* every master, together with nearly every member of his family, has also an affection for his slave.
>
> This being so, it may be pretty safely assumed, that if in any case, the master refuses to employ lawyers for his slave, the case is one in which the master ought not be required to employ them. It may be pretty safely assumed that every such case will be a case in which the master, a juror biased, by both interest and affection, to acquit, has convicted.

But, of course, the anomaly of a juror biased in favor of the slave convicting and a jury not so biased acquitting is obvious.

Rules regarding the distribution of costs in the event of total loss were also shaped by policy decisions designed to provide financial incentives for humane treatment. The common-law rule was that the hirer of a slave had to pay the full rental even though the slave died during the term of rental. In Georgia, Judge Lumpkin carefully reviewed the cases before following that rule.[27] He properly rejected the argument that the slave's death was an act of God, whose burden would have fallen on the master if the slave had not been hired. After all, he argued, acts of God come in all shapes, including droughts that reduce the productivity of the hired slaves, and certainly the hirer should bear that risk. Judge Lumpkin recognized, however, that all that was at stake was whether to require the parties to negotiate over the risk; the hirer, for example, could purchase life insurance or, more likely, pay the equivalent of a life insurance premium to the owner in exchange for the owner's assumption of the risk of death. Judge Lumpkin's analytic tools then gave him the proper ground for choice, "motives of public policy."

> Humanity to this dependent and subordinate class of our population requires, that we should remove from the hirer or temporary owner, all temptation to neglect them in sickness, or to expose them to situations of unusual peril and jeopardy. We say to them, go, and they must go; stay, and they must stay; whether it be on the railroads, the mines, the infected districts or any where else. Let us not increase their danger, by making it the interest of the hirer to get rid of his contract, when it proves to be unprofitable. Every safeguard, consistent with the stability of the institution of slavery, should be thrown around the lives of these people. For myself, I verily believe, that the best security for the permanence of slavery, is adequate and ample protection to the slave, at our own hands.[28]

Unlike the specific performance cases, these cases invoked rules involving houses and land that Judge Lumpkin called "strongly analogous."

There is reason to believe that the no-reduction-in-rent rule was unenthusiastically received. Five years later, a similar case came before the Georgia court, but this time the hirer presented some evidence, though not much, that the owner had agreed to assume the risk of death.[29] The jury believed the hirer and awarded only a portion of the rental amount to the owner. Judge Lumpkin noted the owner's argument that he had "lost his case on account of the unpopularity of the law. . . ."

I hope he is mistaken. I am aware that hirers, who constitute a large class, especially in towns, cried out against the decision when it was made. This was natural. But when it was recollected what a large portion of the slaves hired out were the property of women and minor children, and how important it was to hold out to hirers a strong inducement to take care of the negroes entrusted to their care; that the owners, for the time being, lost all control over them; that the hirer became the temporary master in all respects; and that the slave must do his bidding, no matter how hazardous the service; that the same doctrine obtains in most of the slave States; and that it never has been questioned in England, that the tenant is bound for rent, notwithstanding the destruction of the tenement; the clamor subsided, and several sessions of the Legislature have since intervened without changing the Law. It never should be. It is founded upon principles of justice, as well as of humanity. If the hirer does not see fit to protect himself by his contract, and take the negro for the year, why should the owner be considered as having insured his life for the year, and be held responsible for its continuance, when he gets nothing for the risk?

Judge Lumpkin did not indicate his awareness of the possibility that the rental price might have included a risk premium.

The law of contracts involving slaves that has been presented so far seems simple. The rules were straightforward and do not exhibit any of the tensions seen in other areas of slave law. One tension is deeply concealed: Southern courts accepted or rejected analogies to real property depending solely on whether the substantive rules could be supported independently by appeals to humanity. This approach made the law of slavery susceptible to ready separation from general law, as soon as it became important to notice that the analogies to general law played no dispositive role in decision. Another tension must be examined in greater detail and in several contexts. Unlike land or houses, slaves were property with

minds of their own, and just as Southern culture was shaped
by the interaction of slaves and masters, so was Southern law.
One effect appeared in reduction-in-rent cases where the slave
ran away. The Georgia court found cases in conflict about a
hirer's liability on a promise to return property that was lost
by "inevitable casualty."[30] But slaves were a special kind of
property. Although running away might have been "a peril
incident to the very nature of the property," it was not inevitable.

> It is incident, as "running away is a peril incident to the
> very nature of the property" in a horse or mule. But who
> would think of holding that one who had undertaken, by
> special contract, to deliver a horse on a given day, should
> be excused by proving that he had run away. It is true that
> the liability of a slave's escape is much greater: but this is
> only a question of degree, and it cannot be said to be a
> casualty against which no provision could be made. It is
> not necessary to assume, that bolts and bars and chains
> would be necessary, in order to ensure the detention of the
> slave. Good treatment would, in most cases, do it quite as
> effectually. And such a contract as this before us might be
> made by the owner of a slave, for the express purpose of
> endeavoring to assure such good treatment. We would not
> be understood as imputing harsh treatment of this slave to
> the hirer, in this case. There is nothing in the record to
> authorize this—and in what we have said, we are simply
> laying down general principles.[31]

If mistreatment was not an issue in that case, it was in others.
In Arkansas, for example, Berry hired two sisters from Dia-
mond.[32] When Berry beat the slaves, they escaped back to
Diamond's residence. Before returning the slaves to Berry,
Diamond told them to come home again if Berry "hit them
a lick." They did so, and Diamond not only refused to send
them back another time, but sued Berry for breach of contract.
The court hinted that Berry might be liable for a portion of

the rental price, but held that he could not be liable for failing to pay the entire amount.[33]

To explain how slaves shaped other aspects of the law, some preliminary detail is needed. In the runaway cases, the courts emphasized the specific agreement to return the slave at the end of the term of hire, thus demonstrating their awareness that they were engaged in enforcing the parties' intentions and developing rules designed to minimize the need to negotiate contract terms.[34] Similar approaches were taken in cases involving claims that the hirer had used the slave for unauthorized purposes. Unlike horses or lathes, slaves, as capital assets that were also labor inputs, could be used for a large variety of purposes, some more profitable and more risky than others. The rental price would ordinarily be set in light of the proposed use of the slave, but hirers not infrequently were tempted by the returns on alternative uses to divert the rented slave to those uses.

Spencer v. *Pilcher*, where the facts are given in some detail, illustrates the issue.[35] A thirteen-year-old slave, Monroe, was hired out for one year to Spencer, the owner of a nearby farm, for $15. One week before the term ended, Spencer took his farm products on two flatboats down the Ohio River, intending to sell the products, as he had in the past, along the way. Monroe and two other hands went along. On the first evening, the boats were moored separately. Spencer watched one boat, while the hands took care of the second. Shortly after Monroe boarded the second boat, he fell into the river and drowned, despite all efforts made by Spencer and the other hands to save him. When Spencer returned to Virginia from New Orleans the following spring, Monroe's owner sued for breach of contract. He introduced evidence that young slaves like Monroe were hired out for $15 when they were to do agricultural work but were leased at substantially higher prices if they worked on the rivers. The jury awarded $317 in damages against Spencer. The Virginia Court of Appeals affirmed, rejecting Spencer's challenge to the evidence regarding customary prices for alternative uses of slaves. It also rejected his effort to construe the lease as one that gave the hirer of a slave the same degree of control that an owner had, in the absence of a specific contract term limiting the use of the slave.

> The master or owner of a slave is bound to treat him as an intelligent, sentient being, and will not be presumed, without proof, to place him under the dominion of a temporary bailee, to be used how and where he pleases. If he hires him with a reasonable expectation that he will be employed in a business comparatively healthy and free from danger to life, it ought not be permitted to the bailee to immure him in an unhealthy mine, or to subject him to the hazards of distant voyages, and the perils of a business he has never followed. Humanity to the slave requires this, and the security of the rights of property imposes other restrictions on the bailee, for the sake of the owner. A slave hired in a state recognizing the rights of the owner, cannot be taken to *England*, where the moment he touches the soil he is disenthralled, or to one of the nonslaveholding states, where the dangers of seduction and loss are probable and imminent. If the bailee encounters this risk, and the slave is lost, the loss must fall on him who braves the consequences.

It was irrelevant that, having diverted Monroe to unauthorized ends, Spencer acted reasonably once the risk of loss materialized. The rule of contract interpretation could, of course, vary,[36] but *Spencer* v. *Pilcher* once again shows a court presuming how parties would allocate risk, by referring to "humanity to the slave." Like *Berry* v. *Diamond*, it also shows that slaves hired out were given, and could create, a space in which they were freer of control than when they remained with their owners; a slave aware of rules like that in *Spencer* was in a position to refuse some work ordered by the hirer, when he or she could not have refused the same work ordered by an owner.

A hirer was not ordinarily an insurer of the slave's safety, however. In the absence of specific contractual language, the hirer who used the slave for the intended purposes had only to exercise the degree of care "which a kind and humane master would bestow under the circumstances," by providing, for example, timely medical care.[37] The effect of this rule was to make the hired slave no better off for having been let out, except to the extent that the hirer but not the owner could use the slave for limited purposes only. The slave, however, could disrupt the owner-hirer relation, most notably by running away. *Bayon* v. *Prevot*, decided in Louisiana in 1815, provides a glimpse at slave behavior.[38] Bayon's slave ran away and was arrested and jailed in New Orleans, where he became ill with dysentery. Prevot, a neighbor, visited New Orleans and, without a request from Bayon, took the slave from the jail. On the trip back, Prevot let the slave go on shore whenever the boat stopped. Several witnesses testified that the slave was very weak. Sometime during the second night of the trip, the slave ran off again. The court, apparently not noticing the incongruity of severe illness and escape, held that Prevot had acted properly:

> [S]urely, it cannot be required of any one to exercise a species of care and diligence in violation of the plainest dictates of humanity, or to require of an agent to do that which, if done by the principal, would fix on his character the stain of brutality. The taking the slave, diseased as he was, from the confined and unwholesome air of a prison, was certainly an act well intended on the part of Prevot, for the benefit of the master: and on his way up to the parish of Ascension, his state of sickness would not allow him to be confined. His subsequent escape is the misfortune of the owner, for which the agent, under all the circumstances of the case, ought not to be made responsible.

The issue of duty of care arose as well in cases involving overseers. In one, the Louisiana Supreme Court held an overseer who was "attentive . . . and made a good crop for his employer" indefensibly cruel in his treatment of the slaves.[39] The court said that this behavior violated statutes that were "dictated by considerations of humanity, and restrict[ed] the authority of the master." The overseer was "answerable to his employer in damages, and to public justice, which he has offended." But private law and public justice did not always coincide so neatly. The North Carolina Supreme Court held a hirer's overseer liable for damages to the slave's owner when the overseer shot a slave who walked away from justifiable punishment that the overseer was about to inflict.[40] As we have seen, the owner would not have been subject to criminal prosecution in North Carolina for such an assault, but the court thought the situation of an employee's private liability was different: "The act of shooting the slave betrayed passion in the overseer, rather than a desire to promote the true interest of his employers, or to keep up their subordination, which the state of our society demands." The distinction between criminal and private liability, of course, represents another form of the attempt to separate law and sentiment. Not surprisingly, then, if the slave were killed, even while resisting recapture, the pursuer could be liable to the owner.

> The laws for the government of slaves should be enforced firmly and wisely; and of course without unnecessary severity. The law is careful of the safety of the slave within his prescribed sphere. Regarded in the twofold aspect of persons and of property, the same law which protects the master, guards their rights as persons. It would, hence, be no justification of the homicide of a runaway, that he was slain by the captor, in an effort to avoid an arrest, by flight. For the same reason, a person in an attempt to arrest a runaway, who offered resistance, would not be justified in taking the life of the slave, unless by such resistance his own person or life were put in imminent danger.[41]

In the case before the court, there was no indication of such danger. "An act of homicide committed under such circumstances, cannot be justified by any principle of morality, of law, or of policy growing out of the institution of slavery." Even as slaves worked for a hirer, they could force those

who profited from their labor to recognize that they were
people. Again, Judge Ruffin provided a clear expression in
Heathcock v. *Pennington.*[42] Pennington hired a ten-year-old
slave from Heathcock, to drive out the horse hauling gold
from Pennington's mine. On a January evening, the slave was
directed to work through the night. The slave had no coat
and periodically warmed himself at a fire quite near the mine
shaft, which was about 160 feet deep. Near daybreak, the
slave was at the fire when his supervisor called him to start
the horse; the slave, already drowsy, tumbled down the shaft
and was killed. Pennington offered to show that he employed
his son and one of his own slaves in the same manner. The
jury, instructed that Pennington was required to exercise
"ordinary care," found in Pennington's favor, and the supreme court affirmed. Judge Ruffin's opinion dealt with
nearly every aspect of similar cases, and so can usefully be
quoted at length.

> Ordinary care . . . may differ very much according to the
> nature of the thing, the purpose for which it was hired, and
> the particular circumstances of risk, under which a loss
> occurred; a coach, for example, is not kept like a casket of
> jewels. So, a slave, being a moral and intelligent being, is
> usually as capable of self preservation as other persons.
> Hence, the same constant oversight and control are not
> requisite for his preservation, as for that of a lifeless thing,
> or of an irrational animal. Again, if an owner let his slave
> for a particular purpose, it is to be understood that he is fit
> for it; and therefore he may be set to that service and kept
> at it in the way that is usual. If he hires him, for instance,
> as a mariner upon a sea voyage, it is implied that he is to
> do the duty of a sailor. The ship's master, therefore, does
> the owner no wrong and evinces no want of due care by
> sending him for a useful purpose to the mast-head, though
> it happen that from want of experience or a steady head,
> he fall and and be hurt. If, indeed, he were sent aloft in a
> tempest and forbidden to use the common means of security

by lashing himself to the mast or rigging, that would make a difference. But surely the omission to give the slave particular instructions to use those ordinary means of preservation could not render the bailee liable, as for culpable neglect; since every one would confide in his understanding and his position to take care of himself, as a sufficient guarantee for his using the ordinary precautions against the danger, naturally incident to the service. Moreover, the owner must have foreseen those risks and provided for them in the hire. These considerations tend to the conclusion, that the defendant here would not be liable, if the loss had arisen from a cause naturally connected with the employment, for which the slave was hired.

Heathcock "certain[ly] . . . knew" that the slave would be employed near the mine shaft during the night; the dangers were so obvious that Heathcock should have warned his slave if he thought it necessary. Nor was the use of a fire, rather than a coat, for warming unreasonable; the fire was located conveniently for all the workers and served to light the shaft as well. Judge Ruffin repeatedly emphasized that the slave, "possessing the ordinary degree of intelligence and instinct of self preservation," was reasonably used by Pennington.

The obverse of *Heathcock* was presented in *Couch* v. *Jones*.[43] Couch hired his slave Calvin to work on the construction of a railroad. On the night of February 4, 1854, Calvin assisted in preparing some blasting material and was killed by a large fragment of rock thrown on him when the blast was set off. Although Calvin's job involved loading carts, he had worked with blasting material and, indeed, had warned the superintendent at the work site of the dangers of blasting at night. The superintendent testified that the blasting occurred at dusk and that he had warned all of the employees to leave the blasting area. Again, the jury's verdict for the defendants was affirmed. The court agreed that the defendants had exercised ordinary care: "In the care which is to be taken of a slave, he is to be considered an intelligent being, with a strong instinct of self-preservation, and capable of using the proper means for keeping out of, or escaping from, scenes of danger." Judge Pearson dissented, noting his discomfort with the result in *Heathcock*. He would have held that, because the superintendent knew that Calvin frequently worked at the blasting site, he was negligent in issuing only a warning to employees in general.[44]

In some ways the most dramatic instance of slave self-assertion occurred in *Collins v. Hutchins*, a Georgia case.[45] Hutchins rented his slave Henry to Collins for $180. Henry was employed in building a railroad when, in early June 1853, he became sick and was sent back to Hutchins. Two doctors chosen by Collins attended him and thought that he had recovered, but Henry died in late July. The jury awarded Hutchins $1,200, because Collins had taken Henry away from the work site at which Hutchins expected him to be used and had put Henry to work at another site, which was, however, no less healthful than the first. Further, Henry had been seen by Collins' physicians and resided at his owner's house only as Collins' hospital. Collins also claimed that the real cause of death was Henry's failure to follow the doctors' orders, because he imprudently ate peaches and watermelons too soon after his illness. But, said the court,

> [a] negro is an intelligent human being, having the power of thought and volition, and capable of ministering to the cravings of his appetite, and providing for their gratification, but does not generally have judgment to direct him in what is proper for him, or prudence and self-denial to restrain him from the use of what is injurious. He cannot be shut up and controlled and managed as a horse or a cow, but from the necessity of the case, must be left, under orders for the best, with power, if he disobeys, to do wrong. The boy was still under the direction of the physician of the defendant, though he had ceased to visit him. He had told him, when he got stronger, to call at his office, and the overexertion of the boy in going to his office, and his im-

prudence in eating the fruit, were the sole cause of his last relapse.

These last cases obviously intermingle tort and contract notions; indeed, in *Collins* the court came close to stating a contributory-negligence argument, that is, that the owner, by failing to keep Henry from overeating, had caused the death. It is notable, too, that the cases in which tort and contract problems were mixed tended to be ones where the hired slave was used in nonfarm employment such as mining or railroad construction, for it was precisely in those settings that the ideological basis for a law of slavery, the close to-talistic relationship between master and slave, was weakest. The conceptual structure that the courts had developed for these cases therefore lacked strong support from the ideology of slavery. At the same time, however, courts had repeatedly resolved complex risk-allocation questions by indicating that the rule chosen demonstrated slave law's sensitivity to the demands of humanity. With that approach in the background, courts could not readily develop a purely market-oriented set of rules either. Slave law in this area was therefore a confused blend of slave and market notions.

Perhaps the best examples of this confusion are the cases adopting and applying the fellow-servant rule in the South. In most risk-allocation areas, courts throughout the South tended to use similar rules. The fellow-servant rule stands out as a major exception: there was explicit disagreement among the courts over the question of a hirer's liability to an owner for injuries to the hired slave caused by the hirer's other em-ployees, and that disagreement rested precisely on the varying degrees to which the courts were willing to go in treating the owner-hirer-slave relationship as a purely market relationship. As we saw in Chapter II, the fellow-servant rule was given its primary impetus in the United States by Chief Justice Lemuel Shaw of Massachusetts, and every Southern case took his opinion in *Farwell* v. *Boston & Worcester R. Co.* as its focus. But courts in Georgia and Florida refused to apply the rule in cases involving slaves. They could not disentangle the contract rationale from the tort rationale of the fellow-servant rule and instead relied again on humanity to the slave.

Judge Lumpkin wrote the Georgia court's opinion in *Scudder v. Woodbridge*.[46] The slave Ned had been hired as a carpenter on a riverboat traveling from Savannah to St. Mary's. He was killed by the waterwheel, in which he was caught while helping others to get the boat off. Finding Scudder's employee, the ship's captain, negligent, the jury awarded Woodbridge $500. Judge Lumpkin recognized the general fellow-servant rule. Because it is so revealing, most of the opinion following that recognition deserves to be read.

> But interest to the owner, and humanity to the slave, forbid its application to any other than *free white agents*. Indeed, it cannot be extended to slaves, *ex necessitate rei*. The argument upon which the decisions referred to mainly rest is, that public policy requires that each person engaged on steamboats and railroads should see that every other person employed in the same service does his duty with the utmost care and vigilance; that every hand is qualified for his place, and that everything connected with the line is in good order. Moreover, it is urged, that the want of recourse on the principal will not only make each agent more careful himself, but induce him to stimulate others to like diligence. Can any of these considerations apply to slaves? *They* dare not interfere with the business of others. *They* would be instantly chastised for their impertinence. . . .
>
> But can any one doubt that if this unfortunate boy, although shipped as a carpenter, had been ordered by the captain to perform the perilous service in which he lost his life, and he had refused or remonstrated, that he would have received prompt correction? and that *on the trial* of a bill of indictment for a misdemeanor, his conduct would have deemed sufficient justification for the supposed offense? No! slaves dare not intermeddle with those around, embarked in the same enterprise with themselves. Neither

can they exercise the salutary discretion, left to free white agents, of quitting the employment when matters are mismanaged, or portend evil. Whether engaged as carpenters, bricklayers or blacksmiths—as ferrymen, wagoners, patroons or private hands, in boats or vessels in the coasting or river navigation, on railroads, or any other avocation—they have nothing to do but silently serve out their appointed time, and take their lot in the meanwhile in submitting to whatever risks and dangers are incident to the employment. Bound to fidelity themselves, they do not, and cannot act as securities, either for the care or competency of others. And what can the master know of the condition of the vessel, road, work, or machinery, where his servant is employed, or of the skill or prudence of the persons associated with him? No two conditions can be more different than these two classes of agents: namely, slaves and free white citizens; and it would be strange and extraordinary indeed if the same principle should apply to both.

Again: a large portion of the employees at the South are either slaves or free persons of color, wholly irresponsible, *civiliter*, for their neglect or malfeasance. The engineer on the Ivanhoe was a colored man. Had the accident been attributable to his mismanagement, to whom should Woodbridge have looked for redress? But we think it needless to multiply reasons upon a point so palpable. There is one view alone which would be conclusive with the court. The *restriction of this rule is indispensable to the welfare of the slave.* In almost every occupation, requiring combined effort, the employer necessarily entrusts it to a variety of agents. Many of those are destitute of principle, and bankrupt in fortune. Once let it be promulgated that the owner of negroes hired to the numerous navigation, railroad, mining and manufacturing companies which dot the whole country, and are rapidly increasing—I repeat, that for any injury done to this species of property, let it be understood and settled that the *employer* is not liable, but that the owner

must look for compensation to the *co-servant* who occa-
sioned the mischief, and I hesitate not to affirm, that the
life of no *hired* slave would be safe. As it is, the guards
thrown around this class of our population are sufficiently
few and feeble. We are altogether disinclined to lessen their
number or weaken their force.

If Judge Ruffin in North Carolina, whose opinion was examined in Chapter II, treated the case as one of contract only,
Judge Lumpkin in Georgia treated it as one of tort only. The
tort rationale for the rule was that it promoted vigilance and
reduced the costs of superintendence. Both Judge Lumpkin
and Judge Ruffin, the former explicitly and the latter implicitly, acknowledged the impropriety of that rationale in slave
society. But the power of "humanity to the slave" blinded
Judge Lumpkin to the alternative contract rationale, that the
owner, by increasing the rental price or by demanding that
the hirer act as an insurer, could protect his interest and
thereby his slave's.[47]

The Florida Supreme Court, in an almost incoherent opinion, also rejected the fellow-servant rule in slave cases.[48] It
explained that the rule was based on the theory that the negligent employee was not the agent of the employer, who
therefore had no duty to see that other employees were not
injured. But, it said in a very confused passage, the slaveowner
was not the hirer's agent either. Rather, their relation was
contractual. Not realizing the implications of that observation, the court continued by rejecting the assumption of risk
component of the fellow-servant rule.

Unlike white persons, the slave does not, upon entering
into the service of another, voluntarily incur the risks and
dangers incident to such service. He has no power to guard
against them by refusing to incur the peril, or by leaving
the service of his employer. He is but a passive instrument
in the hands of those under whose control he is placed.

It then returned to the contract theory, saying that the hirer had to take ordinary care of the slave both directly and through agents. But it concluded:

> Apart from the views we have presented, considerations of public policy, the interest of the master, and humanity to the slave, require that he should be excluded from the exception to the rule, and that he should be shielded from the unrestricted control and oppression of irresponsible subordinates. The liability of the employer, *civiliter*, for the misconduct of his subordinates, will naturally add to the personal security and protection of the slave. Public policy emphatically demands, that the owners of boats, railroads, and other public conveyances, should employ careful and capable agents in their respective business.

The deep confusion expressed in the Florida court's opinion parallels the difficulties encountered by Judge Ruffin and Judge Lumpkin. The Florida court tried to discuss both tort and contract theories but failed to recognize that both theories subverted important aspects of market transactions in slave society, the tort theory by suggesting that slaves could supervise their supervisors and the contract theory by suggesting that a rental premium would allow the owner to discharge all the duties of humanity that the master-slave relationship imposed on him. Judge Ruffin's silence about the tort theory in the *Ponton* case discussed in Chapter II, like Judge Lumpkin's silence about the contract theory, shows an understanding of the dangers of the pure theory. Yet blending the two proved impossible, because the relationships out of which fellow-servant problems arose were themselves anomalous. They were neither pure market nor pure slave relationships, so that neither bourgeois nor slave law provided the conceptual tools with which to handle them. Again, it deserves noting that the problems arose in quasi-industrial cases, even though, as we have seen, slaves were hired out for plantation work as well. It may be that Southern courts, faced with the

188 ★ The Master's Will

contradictions of leasing slaves for quasi-industrial use, would have found it impossible to develop the kind of stable legal framework that has often been thought necessary for industrial development. But it is enough for our purposes to see that the ideological view of a master's responsibility, based on master-slave relationships, set the framework of assumptions within which risk-allocation decisions were made, and that the ideological view of a master's power as an individual, based on bourgeois individualism, provided the opportunity for the development of social institutions that were incompatible with slave relationships.

C. The Illegality of Individual Choice

So long as individuals are authorized to dispose of their property as they choose, a society runs the risk that an inadequately socialized owner will disrupt the harmonious social relations that should order it. This is particularly true where one element of the approved ideology exalts individual choice as a value in its own right. We have seen one example with the fellow-servant rule, where the power of masters to hire out their slaves created a situation for which slave society could not develop legal rules that were easily rationalized. Southern courts of course enforced limits on the behavior of masters, as the cases regarding a master's liability for killing his own slaves showed. But the issue arose in a variety of other contexts.

For example, when a slave committed a crime, the owner had incentives, both humanitarian and financial, to dispose of the slave by sale rather than risk a partial loss through the slave's imprisonment.[49] Judge Lumpkin of Georgia, in discussing the validity of sale of a slave who was shortly after the sale charged with rape, noted:

> I am fully sensible of the gross impropriety of endeavoring to screen a slave from merited punishment, especially for offenses committed against white females. I am not insen-

sitive to the fact, however, that, prompted by humanity, and from no mercenary motives, masters are sometimes induced to put their slaves out of the way to prevent them from becoming the victims of popular excitement, until the tempest of passion is past and reason has resumed her sway. And while this motive even cannot justify the act, it goes far to mitigate its criminality.[50]

But in the case at hand, the contract was not illegal anyway, because the slave was sold before he was charged and the criminal case, it turned out, was eventually dropped.

The Mississippi Supreme Court explained the reasons for rules prohibiting contracts by which masters transferred their slaves to avoid punishment.[51]

The important question . . . is this: How far the alleged crime of the slave abridged the master's right to dispose of him? As a general rule a man may dispose of his property, and exercise all other rights, to the extent that the law does not restrain him in so doing. This restraint is only imposed to enable the government to discharge its duty to the citizen in protecting him in the enjoyment of certain rights, which might be endangered if individual rights in the particular case were permitted to be exercised. . . .

. . . When a slave commits a crime, the private rights of the master must yield to the superior rights of the State, and he can only be influenced by those considerations which influence all good citizens, a fair and faithful administration of the law. The master can legally exercise no right which will interfere with the State in discharging her duty to society. . . .

. . . Any other rule would place the criminal code as to slaves completely at the mercy of their masters, and society could only be protected against the enormities of this class of our population in those cases in which the private interest of their masters would not be prejudiced by consenting that the law might be administered, and its penalties inflicted on the guilty. The master himself has no such rights or exemptions from punishment if he commits crime. They occupy common ground. They have violated some personal right deemed sacred, which it is the highest duty of the government to protect, and which can only be protected by inflicting the penalty of the law on the offender.

Similar equivocal recognition of the master's power to misbehave occurred in cases where the master ordered a slave to commit a crime or a tort. As the Arkansas Supreme Court said, the slave's duty lay in obedience to the master's direction, but at the same time the slave could act wrongly on his own.[52] After reviewing decisions from other states in the South, the court agreed with the prevailing view that the master was liable in a damage action only for torts committed under his direction, in order to avoid placing masters at the mercy of the miscreant slaves. It did, however, suggest that the legislature consider modifying the law by making the owner liable, "thus removing many causes of jealousy and ill-feeling against the owners of that species of property," but only up to the value of the slave.[53] The same court was not willing to exempt slaves from criminal punishment when the slave acted at the master's command.[54] It adopted the common-law rule of master and servant "by analogy."

> The slave, however, is a human being—he is regarded as a rational creature—a moral agent. He, as well as the master, is the subject of government, and amenable to the laws of God and man. In all things lawful, the slave is absolutely bound to obey his master. But a higher power than his master—*the law of the land*—forbids him to commit crime. The mandate of the law extends to every rational subject of the government. None are high enough to claim exemption from its penal sanctions, and none too low to be reached by them. Where the mandate of the law, and the command of the master come in conflict, the obligation of the slave to obey the law is superior to his duty of obedience to his master.

However, the slave should not, "in justice, be punished so severely, as where the crime is voluntary on his part."

By far the most important area in which legal rules limited the master's power, numerically and ideologically, was that of manumission by will. Studies like those of Professors Nash and Howington[55] have regarded the manumission cases as providing accurate indices of the judges' neutrality or bias on slave issues. As we shall see, they were that, and much more. The cases presented three major issues—the legality of manumission outside the state, the legal effect of a master's direction that slaves choose between slavery and freedom, and whether statuses between slavery and freedom could be tolerated—that interacted in complex ways.

Courts faced these issues with an analytic framework consisting of three elements. First, in the absence of positive legislation, a slaveowner, like all other property owners, was "free to relinquish his right to it, at pleasure." Thus, the Alabama Supreme Court refused to void a sale that was conditioned on the purchaser's agreement to take the slaves to Illinois and to free them there, because the state's constitutional provision giving the legislature power to regulate manumission did not reduce of its own force the master's power to dispose of his property.[56] A few years before, the same court had reviewed the precedents, British and American, in detail and had held that the master could manumit by will as well as by contract, because that power was a necessary incident to the master's absolute property in the slave.[57]

> [S]uch is the genius and expansive nature of the common law, that it adapts itself to the necessities and exigencies of society, and when a new species of property is introduced, and the statute law is silent as to the rules by which it is to be governed, the common law embraces it, and its rules are applied to it, modified, of course, according to the nature of the property thus subjected to its governance. . . .
>
> The master, having an unqualified property in his slaves, may dispose of them in any way he pleases, unless restrained

by some rule of law, or fixed and settled policy of the State. The jus disponendi, or right of disposing of his property, is an inseparable incident to its absolute and unqualified ownership. This general power which the master has over the slave, both in respect to his treatment and manumission, has been controlled and guarded by legislative checks, prompted alike by humanity for the slave and security for the State. In considering the rules which apply to, and regulate this peculiar species of property, we must look upon them in their double capacity of chattels and intelligent beings. Considered in this latter capacity, our law, pervaded as it is by the spirit of christianity, and founded on principles of humanity and benevolence, throws around them its protection. . . .

. . . Subject to these, and other restrictions which we shall presently notice, the right of the master to his slaves is the same with his right to any other chattel. He may sell and dispose of them without writing; may convey, or bequeath them by his last will and testament, absolutely or in trust, precisely as other personal property; and but for the inhibition created by the statute law, he might at pleasure renounce his property in them by manumission.

Chief Justice Chilton therefore objected to limitations on foreign manumission as an interference with a "clear common law right." If there were to be limitations, they should come from the legislature.

However much we might desire the law to be different, however much we might suppose sound policy requires that a restraint should be imposed upon this natural right of causing one's property to be removed to another State where it may be dealt with injuriously to our institutions, still, it is not for us to change or make the law. Our solemn duty is to administer it as we find it. It is not for the court, but for the legislature, to determine whether there is too great a disproportion between the white and slave population of Alabama, or what number of slaves would best contribute to the security of the institution, and to the development of the wealth and agricultural resources of the State. If, influenced by our views as to what is the policy of this state with respect to manumission in another State, we should hold that the personal representative of [the deceased master] shall not take the slaves mentioned out of this State, because it would to this extent lessen the number of slaves and, consequently, the wealth of Alabama, and would be adding to the free negro population of some sister State persons who may contribute to incite our slaves to insubordination or insurrection, upon the same principle we must hold every bequest of a slave to a person residing in a free State void, because, if the executor delivers the slave to the legatee in such State, it works his manumission. Indeed, it is difficult to calculate the results to which such a principle of decision might lead.[58]

The second basic element was the uniform legislative prohibition of domestic manumission, with varying degrees of severity. A master could not free his slaves without specific legislation;[59] in some states, the master could direct that his slaves be freed if they were to be removed from the state within a short period—"free, and then send" provisions—whereas in others only emancipation that took effect elsewhere—"send, and then free" provisions—were allowed. A simple form of the interaction between these first elements is shown in *Bryan* v. *Dennis*, a Florida case decided in 1852.[60] In 1829, the Florida legislature declared that domestic manumission was illegal, that any slave manumitted "shall not be deemed free" and would be forfeited to the state, but that an owner could free his slaves if he gave a bond for the transportation of the slave out of the state within thirty days. Jacob Bryan came to the state in 1830 with two female slaves, one of whom gave birth later to two other slaves. In 1842 he wrote a deed purporting to free all four slaves; when he died in 1847, Bryan left no will. Bryan's heirs secured legislation releasing the state's interest in the slaves, and they then sued to recover the slaves, who had been living as free since 1842. The Florida Supreme Court held that none of the slaves were free. The state's "well defined" policy was "opposed to the settlement of [free blacks] within her borders, and as a consequence, to the unrestricted right of her citizens to manumit their slaves."

> The conviction upon the public mind is settled and unalterable as to the evil necessarily attendant upon this class of population and although treated by our laws humanely, they have ever been regarded with a distrust bordering upon apprehension—a class of people who are neither freemen nor slaves, their presence at all time deleterious and often dangerous to the public welfare.

The third, and perhaps most important, element of the courts' analytic framework flowed from the individualistic premises of the law. They would attempt to carry out the owner's intention, so far as it could fairly be determined. But at this point a great deal of room for maneuver appeared. Suppose, for example, the will was a "free then send" one in a state that refused to allow such manumissions. Should the court try to accomplish the master's goal of emancipation, or should it insist on strict compliance with the law? Or suppose the will said "free and send"; how should it be interpreted in states where the sequence made a real difference? It was here that judges could express their judgments about the comparative weight of the policies favoring individual choice and those opposing emancipation, but they always recognized, first, that the latter policies were in tension with other fundamental analytic elements, and second, that a properly written will could effectuate an intention to emancipate. Thus, the most that even a vigorous antiemancipation judge could do was to develop a set of rules of incredible complexity that could trap the unwary. As a practical matter, of course, that was no small accomplishment, in a society where slaveowners might not consult lawyers even about the transfer of property at death. But it inevitably weakened the ideological impact of purely formal rules.

Two examples of judicial interpretation of wills can introduce the more detailed discussion. In 1804, Virginia's highest court decided *Charles* v. *Hunnicutt*.[61] During the 1770s and 1780s, Virginia's Quakers campaigned for legislation that would relax the existing ban on private manumission. Anticipating the success of that campaign, Gloster Hunnicutt, himself a Quaker, wrote a will on April 13, 1781, the day he died. He stated that "my will and desire is, that [six slaves] should be manumitted on or before the first month next 1782. . . . I give the [slaves] to the monthly meeting, of which I am a member, to be manumitted by such members of the said meeting as the said meeting shall appoint." Unfortunately, Hunnicutt was too optimistic, by a narrow margin, about the imminence of the Quakers' success. It was not until May, 1782, that the Virginia legislature authorized private manumission. Meanwhile, though Hunnicutt's wife and brother, two of his executors, were faithful to his wishes, his son, the third executor, was not. The brother, as the meeting's delegate, signed a deed of emancipation on July 6, 1782, but the son continued to hold the six blacks as slaves. The Virginia Court of Appeals unanimously agreed with the blacks that they were entitled to their freedom.

The case presented two troublesome issues. First, Hunnicutt had directed manumission to occur before it became legal; second, the membership of the Quaker meeting fluctuated and so the will might not have properly identified those to whom the slaves should temporarily pass. Judge Tucker, who wrote the longest opinion, relied on two principles for interpreting wills: that they should be given meaning that is consistent with the law where that could be done, and that they should be interpreted in light of the testator's evident, although perhaps incompletely expressed, intention. A close reading of the "will and desire" clause led Judge Tucker to conclude that Hunnicutt had expressed a preference for manumission, and that the law would "supply the words, [']if the laws will then permit[']." Thus, the slaves were given to the monthly meeting in trust, to be freed as soon as it was lawful for the meeting to do so, either by special legislation or pursuant to the general law that was soon enacted. As to the second issue, Judge Tucker agreed that the meeting could not hold property for its own benefit, but it was allowed to act as a trustee. Judge Roane's opinion added little except a justification, rooted in the need to decide suits for freedom expeditiously but fairly, for relying on equity principles in a common-law suit for freedom. Unlike Judge Tucker, however, Judge Roane did allude indirectly to a principle favoring liberty, when he characterized the meeting's obligation as a trust "for that emphatical species of charity which is infinitely stronger than any of those enumerated" in English statutes. The remaining opinions went over the same ground. For our purposes, what matters is the insistence by each judge that the aim is to effectuate Hunnicutt's real intentions; only Judge Roane made passing reference, in his case favorably, to the value of the goal that Hunnicutt sought to reach.

A contrasting result based, however, on a structurally similar analysis was reached by Judge Lumpkin in the 1857 case of *Drane* v. *Beall*.[62] Thomas Beall wrote a very detailed will making special provision for one slave, Mariah, and seeking to free all of his other slaves. The latter provision stated, "I will that all my negroes shall receive their freedom and be emancipated from slavery. . . . And such negroes so freed and emancipated from slavery shall be sent to Liberia, California, or any free State or Territory . . . as they choose to elect." The will then gave money to the American Colonization Society if the slaves chose Liberia and said that the slaves to whom Beall "ha[d] given their freedom" should be kept on his plantation for four years to raise a stake for their resettlement. Under Georgia law, it was permissible to send slaves out of the state, there to be freed, but a will could not direct that slaves should be freed in Georgia and then sent elsewhere.

Not surprisingly, Judge Lumpkin found that Beall's will fell in the latter category.

> It never occurred to the testator, for a moment, that it was wrong to give his slaves present freedom by his will, provided they were to be carried out of the State, within what he supposed to be a reasonable time, to enjoy it. He did not intend to violate the law. But the mistake he committed was in supposing that a gift of freedom, *in praesenti*, to his slaves, to vest at his death, although it be but for a moment of time, was not unlawful. In whom was the title of these slaves, from the death of the testator to the time contemplated for their removal? Not in themselves, for they were incapable of taking; not in the Executors, although they were clothed with a *quasi* trust or agency respecting them. The title vested, *eo-instanti*, at the death of Beall, in his personal representatives, in trust for the residuary legatees or distributees, and it is not in the power of the Courts to divest it. For myself, I entertain not a doubt but that a testator may by his will direct his Executor to remove his negroes to some other country, where they may acquire, as well as enjoy their freedom, and that the performance of such a trust, will be permitted, if not enforced against such Executor; I am equally well satisfied, that the bequest of freedom to slaves in this case is void, as it was to take effect in this State, and the slaves are made the legatees of their own freedom, a boon they are incapable of taking.

Judge Lumpkin was unwilling to torture clear language to allow the slaves to be freed, even though Beall's obvious wishes were frustrated; there was, after all, no reason to think that Beall would have regarded the sequence "free then send," which he wrote, as different in substance from "send then free," which Judge Lumpkin required. But it is important to note that the sole effect of the court's decision was to emphasize precision in drafting wills; the decision created no insurmountable barriers, only easily overcome technical impediments, to manumission. That Judge Lumpkin was not insensitive to the owner's wishes was shown in his discussion of the provisions involving Mariah, an old house servant who was "liable to severe spells of sickness." Beall had left her to William Satterwhite, a member of the family that had previously owned her. Satterwhite was directed to let Mariah be "as free as the laws of the state will allow her to be," and if Mariah became dissatisfied with him, she could select another trustee. Satterwhite also received property to generate income for Mariah's support and land on which Mariah was to live. The lower court had held that these provisions amounted to a domestic manumission and were void. Although no appeal was taken from that ruling, Judge Lumpkin noted that the supreme court "might feel some hesitation in affirming" that construction. The provisions, he said, seemed "to make a humane provision for a faithful servant who was sickly and superannuated during the remnant of her days, she having spent the prime of her life in his service. . . ." As in *Hunnicutt*, then, the court in *Beall* enforced existing law without reference to this wisdom of manumission and, though it prevented the owner's intention from being effectuated in the present case, it indicated its willingness to enforce the same intention were it cast in the required form.

Although the richest material comes from cases involving domestic and foreign manumission, the formality of many of the results may convey a false impression. I will begin the detailed examination of the manumission cases, therefore, with the apparently more consequential problem, also illustrated in *Beall*, of what Southern judges called "quasi freedom," in which a slave, not yet freed, was either given substantial present liberty or was promised freedom in the future. Some slaves of course had their owner's permission to live in a state of quasi freedom, but the issue for slave law was the extent to which legal consequences would attach to that permission. In *Stanley v. Nelson*, an Alabama case, a slave named Spencer, who operated his own painting business, negotiated with Nelson to hire Nelson's slave George and delivered a note signed by Stanley in which Stanley promised to pay $140 for the use of George.[63] Actually, Spencer was owned by Madison Thompson and was himself leased to William Hoke, who let Spencer arrange the painting business. The Alabama Supreme Court held that Stanley's note was void and uncollectable, because Thompson and Hoke violated a criminal statute when they allowed Spencer "to go at large and trade as a freeman."

> These statutes had their origin in a wise and conservative legislative policy. Their purpose was, to prevent the demoralization and corruption of slaves, resulting from a withdrawal of discipline and restraint from them, and to prevent the pernicious effect upon the slave community of the anomalous condition of servitude without a master's control. If the owner or hirer of a slave permits him to go at large, to make contracts, and to carry on business as if he were a freeman, notwithstanding the slave may make compensation for this privilege, the law, as it existed in 1852, is not only violated in its letter, but in its wise policy.

As we have seen, however, slaves hired out for particular purposes had a form of freedom, because their employers, unlike their owners, could use them only for those limited purposes. Again, the recognition of the master's basic property rights conflicted with a rule linked to the conditions of slave society.

The issue of quasi freedom arose most often, though, in manumission cases, where the illegality of the intermediate status might be quite consequential: a master who desired to have his slaves live with substantial freedom near their old homes might prefer continued enslavement there to emancipation far away. Several cases from North Carolina and Georgia show the restrictive approach to quasi freedom. In *White* v. *White*, Joshua White executed a deed in 1776 purporting to free his slave Hagar, then ten years old, when she reached eighteen.[64] He then sent Hagar to his son Jacob, who for many years stated that he did not own, but merely protected Hagar and her children. In 1809, Jacob gave the slaves to the Quakers, naming several individuals as trustees. Meanwhile, Joshua had died, giving Jacob all the property that Joshua had "already possessed him with," and giving the rest of his property to his other children. When Jacob died in 1820, his executor sought to recover the slaves from the Quakers, who refused, for the next eleven years, to return them. The executor argued that Joshua's will gave the slaves to Jacob; the Quakers replied that, since Joshua thought he had freed Hagar in 1776, she was not included in the will. Judge Ruffin, writing for the court, held that *Jacob's* gift to the Quakers was void, because he intended that the Quakers treat the slaves as free persons. But that did not establish the executor's claim, for Joshua's 1776 manumission was also void. Judge Ruffin hinted that Hagar then became the property of the state, but escaped from the case by holding that the executor's claim was barred by the statute of limitations.

More straightforward quasi-freedom cases presented the courts with better opportunities to explain what was wrong with quasi freedom. In one, Isaac Thornton signed a document shortly before he died, in which he stated that he freed Jane, a dark twenty-seven-year-old woman, and Amanda, a nineteen-year-old "of yellow complexion," and their children, most described as "yellow" or "very white" and alleged in the lawsuit to be Isaac's children.[65] Thornton said he would retain control of the slaves during his life, and that, when he died, his friends Edwin Thornton and William Chisholm would acquire the slaves in order to send them and all of their children, including those born after the deed was signed, to Liberia or to some free state. John Thornton, Isaac's brother and his only surviving relative, objected. The Georgia Supreme Court agreed. Isaac could not arrange things to make the slaves free "afterwards."

[T]hey would have assumed a condition, in part, that of slaves—in part, that of free persons of color; and this latter part would have been constantly growing to be the whole.

Every successive moment after the execution of the deed, would have brought the negroes nearer and nearer to the confines of freedom. An hour before Thornton's death, they would have got within an hour of liberty. As he died, they would just reach there.

And during the whole term of this condition—a condition to last whilst Thornton's life lasted—they would or might have been residents of the State, seated in the midst of its slave population.

Is it not plain that evils would result from putting slaves in such a condition—the same in kind as those that would result from putting them in a condition of entire freedom? The evils might be a little less in degree; we think that this would be all the difference. And as the case of the deed, if it had conferred entire freedom, would, beyond dispute, be [illegal]. . . , the case of this deed, conferring, as it does, partial freedom, must be considered at least [as illegal]. . . .

The North Carolina Supreme Court took a similar position. It held that the children of a female slave who were born after the owner made a will freeing her but before he died were not freed, unless the will specified that all future issue should be freed too.[66] In 1860, it faced the quasi-freedom question directly. Lewis Williams' will provided that when all his young slaves reached the age of twenty-five, they should be freed and sent to Liberia if they wished.[67] He said that he distinguished between those over and under twenty-five because the younger slaves "might be less sickly, and might make out better in Africa." The money for sending the slaves to Liberia was to be raised by hiring them out for one year. The court held that the manumission clauses were void. It assumed that a grant of freedom to take effect in the future was valid and that slaves could choose between slavery and freedom. But it noted that every will that involved "a trust, open or secret, for a state of qualified slavery," had been held void. Williams had written just such a will.

The grounds upon which this policy is based are manifest. It has a regard, not only to the favored slaves themselves, (being thereby rendered idle and worthless) but also to other slaves who are thereby induced to become discontented with their condition, disobedient to their masters, and unfit for the social state, which is essential to the well being, the happiness and even the very existence of both master and slave. . . . It is true, that the slaves are ultimately to be carried out of the State, but that is not to be done immediately, nor, as to all the slaves, at any one fixed time, as, for instance, at the death of a tenant for life; but it is to be done at constantly recurring periods for perhaps a century to come. The very fact, that the same person who is to have the services of the slaves, until they arrive at the age when they may choose their freedom, is to carry out the trust for emancipation, will have a strong tendency to induce him to relax the reins of a necessary discipline, with the hope of influencing their choice of bondage for the benefit of his children. This will be an evil as long as he may live, operating injuriously, not only to the favored slaves themselves, but, by way of bad example to his other slaves and to those of his neighbors. In our opinion, the policy of allowing the prospective emancipation of slaves, is carried far enough already, and while we do not feel at liberty, or even inclined, to disturb what has been settled by the adjudications of our courts, we do not feel disposed to go further, and support a scheme of emancipation which is likely to be attended with such bad results as the present.

But that approach threatened not only the future manumission wills but even the "send and then free" wills. It was, after all, physically impossible to transport the slaves elsewhere immediately upon the owner's death. As Williams' will shows, it was also financially difficult at times, and wills often provided for a period during which the slaves, already promised freedom, would work to raise the necessary money. Judge Lumpkin in *Beall* addressed the provision for a four year period.

It is said that a reasonable time must be allowed, because some time must elapse, longer or short, according to circumstances, despite the testator, as in case of caveat, suit in chancery, possible insolvency of the estate, etc., and this is certainly true. But the time required for the meeting and overcoming these and other unforeseen contingencies, is one thing; and for the testator to direct by his will, that they shall be kept within the State for a specified period, four, six or ten years, to accumulate funds to defray the expenses of their transportation, and support them in their new home, is quite a different thing. . . .

Suppose it be true then, that the hand of the Executor is upon the slaves, as the hand of the master, until they leave Georgia, and that they are subject to his control, still can it be denied, that during this four years, these slaves are working for themselves? That they are enjoying the profits of their own skill and labor?

In our judgment, principle and policy, not to say positive law, are opposed to this whole scheme of emancipation.

The logic of the rule against domestic emancipation thus induced the courts to question the status of quasi freedom, which in turn raised doubts about even foreign emancipation. Those doubts did not mature into enforceable rules, perhaps because of limitations of time; had the North Carolina court had the "century to come" it mentioned in the 1860 *Williams* case, such rules might have developed. However, as we saw in Chapter III, Southern law was under great pressure to recognize only two statuses and to identify them with race. The miscegenation in *Thornton* indicates why that pressure could not be fully accommodated, but the rule against quasi freedom, and the logic that lay behind it, indicate one direction in which accommodation might be attempted.

It would be misleading to suggest, however, that Southern courts uniformly tended to limit foreign emancipation by notions of quasi freedom. The Virginia Court of Appeals, for example, went quite far in allowing slaves to remain in the state after they had received a promise of freedom. In one case, the owner's will gave the slaves a year to decide between freedom in Liberia and continued enslavement.[68] Unfortunately, the owner died leaving a number of debts, and his executor hired out the slaves to pay off the debts. More than a year passed before the debts were paid, whereupon the testator's brother, who was to receive any slave who did not choose to go to Liberia, claimed them all, arguing that none of them had chosen to go to Liberia within the specified time. All of the judges agreed that the time limit was not a strict condition, and all looked simply to "the meaning, the intention, the will" of the testator, as Judge Carr put it in the first words of his opinion. Indeed, only one judge even mentioned the additional interpretive principle of construing liberally wills conferring freedom. But this case might have fit into Judge Lumpkin's exceptional category in *Beall*. More dramatic was *Nicholas* v. *Burrus*, in which the will emancipated slaves over forty in one year, slaves between thirty and forty when they reached forty, slaves between twenty and thirty when they reached thirty-five, and younger slaves when they became thirty-one.[69] Several of the slaves were freed quickly, but Nicholas, one of the younger slaves, was sold to satisfy a debt owed by the former owner even though the estate had other assets that could have been used to pay the debt. Twenty years later, Nicholas sued for his freedom. The court affirmed the jury's verdict for Nicholas, discussing almost exclusively a technical question regarding the evidence needed in a freedom suit, as distinguished from a suit in equity, to show that the executor had agreed to the terms of the will. No judge mentioned the problem of quasi freedom.

These cases were decided in 1833, and by 1841 dissent began to appear. In *Anderson* v. *Anderson*, the court upheld a will freeing slaves when they reached twenty-one.[70] The case involved children born after the owner's death to a slave under twenty-one at the time of his death. Judge Allen called the testator's intention "the polar star to guide us in the construction of all wills." But Judge Brooke dissented, relying on a parallel line of cases requiring a very clear expression of an intention to emancipate after the testator's death, although even he agreed that the children were to be freed when they became twenty-one.[71] He justified the requirement of a clear expression or "complete provision" by describing the anomalies of prospective emancipation in terms indicating his difficulties with its legality:

> The rights of the master must be controlled, the moral influence that subjects the slave to the master disregarded, and a spirit of hostility engendered while they continue to be slaves, calculated to diminish their value while slaves: the property of the master is to be invaded in a manner subversive of the institution of slavery, and likely to have an influence on those who are slaves for life; and the next step may be to interfere with the master in their case also, if the humanity of the court is to be appealed to.

But foreign emancipation, at least if not preceded by a substantial amount of time before removal, posed no similar threat to the system, and courts throughout the South upheld wills to that effect. The North Carolina Supreme Court found that one will created a lawful trust for a charitable purpose when it created a fund to pay the expenses of removal,[72] and later explained why a bequest of slaves to the American Colonization Society was valid:

> In the nature of things, the owner of a slave may renounce his ownership, and the slave will thereby be manumitted, and that natural right continues until restrained by positive statutes. It was, indeed, early found in this State, as in most of the others, in which there is slavery, that the third class of free negroes was burdensome as a charge on the community, and from its general characteristics of idleness and dishonesty, a common nuisance. Hence the legislative policy, with us, was opposed to emancipation, and restricted it to a particular mode and upon a special consideration— which was by license of the Court and for meritorious services. But that was purely a regulation of police, and for

the promotion of the security and quiet of the people of this State. It sought only to guard against evils arising from free negroes residing here. Except for that purpose of policy, it was not intended to impose any restriction on the natural right of an owner to free his slaves. Emancipation was not prohibited for the sake merely of keeping persons in servitude in this State, and increasing the number of slaves, for the law never restrained their exportation, either for the purpose of servitude abroad, or for that of emancipation there. On the contrary, all our legislative regulations had a reference exclusively to emancipation, within our limits, of slaves, who were intended to remain here.[73]

Even a secret agreement to emancipate slaves was held valid by the North Carolina court, although here Judge Pearson dissented.[74] Sarah Freeman, after many discussions with her friend John Newlin, left only a small apart of her land to her husband; she left the rest of her estate, including thirty slaves and $7,000 in securities, to Newlin, intending that he emancipate the slaves and use the securities for their support. Newlin's efforts to do so were frustrated by the challenge to the will. Judge Ruffin for the court wrote that Newlin was required to free the slaves. Judge Pearson thought that there was no good reason to arrange things in such a secret way rather than by direct manumission in the will and that Freeman must therefore have been attempting to evade the statutory restrictions, such as the requirements that the executor post a bond, imposed on such wills. A few years later, though, Judge Pearson wrote for the court that one who was freed in a will and was preparing to leave the state had the legal capacity to own property, which was often necessary to

enabl[e] the negroes with ease and comfort to provide a home for themselves, and get to it. The object is to make them go away, so as not to add to the number of free negroes, and the law imposes no restriction and continues no incapacity, except so far as it is necessary to accomplish that object. With this saving, the humanity of our laws strikes off his fetters at once, and says, go "enjoy life, liberty, and the pursuit of happiness."[75]

Thus, as late as 1853, the North Carolina court tolerated not only a substantial period during which a slave soon to be freed could remain in the state, but even granted such a slave legal rights that were, in other contexts, regarded as utterly inconsistent with slavery.[76] We have seen that by 1860, the same court took a position that restricted the owner's power to confer such a status in aid of society's interests.

A similar movement occurred elsewhere. In Mississippi, for example, the supreme court in 1846 held valid a will directing that slaves be freed and then sent to Liberia and Indiana.[77] The court had earlier enforced a "send and then free" will in an extremely controversial case,[78] and now said that "the mere collocation of words, if their meaning be the same, cannot vary their construction." A few months later it upheld a bequest of slaves in trust to the American Colonization Society.[79] But in 1856 the court's position changed, when it refused to enforce an identical bequest.[80] The society was established to remove freed slaves from the United States, it said.

> [H]ence the establishment of the society had a tendency to encourage emancipation, if indeed that was not an object within the especial contemplation of the institution. Its operation was calculated strongly to promote emancipation, and it may, therefore, be regarded as founded on a principle not consistent with the growth and permanency of the institution of slavery; for it cannot be supposed that an effect so obvious was not intended as a part of the system.
>
> Such being the principle of its foundation and the tendency of its operation, it is manifest that the holding of slaves, as chattels, with the power of selling them as such, would be directly repugnant to the policy of the institution and subversive of one of the objects which it was designed to accomplish. Such a power is too inconsistent with the general policy of the institution to be derived from general

words in the charter, which under different circumstances would give the right.

The society could therefore not hold slaves as an owner with full powers of ownership. Instead, its charter enabled it only to hold slaves for the limited purpose of emancipating them, and that was prohibited by statute. It is hard to avoid reading the opinion's references to "the policy of the institution" as having a concealed second reference—the problem was that holding slaves was perhaps inconsistent with the policy of the Colonization Society, but also that the society's policy was almost certainly inconsistent with the institution of slavery.

Here too, however, the willful master had a way out, since the decision was at least in terms premised on the provisions of the society's charter. A bequest to an individual, as in *Newlin*, was not subject to that restriction; as we have seen before, Southern law, even as it moved in the direction of restricting a master's choices, left substantial maneuvering room in which the master's desires could be carried out. But by 1860, some courts had developed a very powerful method of restriction, even beyond the development of stringent definitions of quasi freedom. When a master desired to free a slave, it was often out of a blend of moral and personal reasons that derived from the master's recognition of the slave as a human being. It would have been inconsistent with that recognition, though, for a master to force anything, even freedom, on a slave. Thus, wills generally provided that slaves who agreed, or chose, would be freed, and indeed the American Colonization Society's charter required consent from the slaves before they could be sent to Africa. In the 1840s, provisions allowing slaves to choose tended to be upheld without serious attention.[81] The Alabama Supreme Court changed the picture in a very brief opinion in 1848, when it denied effect to a will that gave eight slaves the choice between Liberia and continued enslavement as the property of the estate.[82] After doing so, however, it expressed its aim of "giv[ing] effect to [the testator's] intention" by denying that the executor had to hire out or sell the slaves to pay the monetary legacies contained in the will.

Ten years later, the Virginia Court of Appeals adopted the "no election" rule, in a hotly contested case where the judges divided three to two.[83] As did most similar wills, the one in question gave the slaves a choice, and if they chose freedom, they were to be hired out until they had raised their transportation money. Judge Daniel's majority opinion began with an emphasis on the owner's intention that initially seems unnecessary. But his strategy quickly emerged: if he could establish that the choice was an essential element of the owner's desire—the way in which the owner belatedly recognized the slaves' moral equality with him—Judge Daniel would be able to frame the case as presenting the court with a choice between a clear intention to provide the slaves with an illegal election and an equally clear intention that if choice were impossible, enslavement would continue. The court would not override the owner's recognition of the slaves' moral status by forcing freedom on them, for, as Judge Daniel interpreted the will, the owner had concluded that, if the slaves could make no legally effective choice, they might as well remain enslaved.

> With these views of the will before me, I cannot undertake to say that there would not be as plain a violation of the testator's intentions in forcing emancipation and its consequences on his slaves, against their election to remain here in slavery, as there would be in withholding freedom from them, on their expressing a preference to be emancipated.

He then turned to the question of the legality of the proffered choice and reviewed the descriptions of slavery offered by Kent, Story, and Tucker. He relied on the quasi-freedom cases to show Virginia's hostility to granting legal effect to slave actions and distinguished earlier cases enforcing wills giving slaves a choice on the ground that the precise issue had not been adequately argued. Finally, Judge Daniel addressed the question of principle. To him, the premise that slaves had "no civil or social rights" necessarily led to the conclusion that slaves could not choose freedom. The idea behind the quasi-freedom cases came into play.

> No man can create a new species of property unknown to the law. No man is allowed to introduce anomalies into the ranks under which the population of the state is ranged and classified by its constitution and laws. It is for the master to determine whether to continue to treat his slaves as property, as chattels, or, in the mode prescribed by law, to manumit them, and thus place them in that class of persons to which the freed negroes of the state are assigned. But he cannot impart to his slaves, as such, for any period, the rights of freedmen. He cannot endow, with powers of such import as are claimed for the slaves here, persons whose *status* or condition, in legal definition and intendment, exists in the denial to them of the attributes of any social or civil capacity whatever.

Thus, the ban on quasi freedom prohibited the creation of a situation in which, between the time of the owner's death and that of the slave's election, the slave had more rights than any other slave. It is obvious, though, that the fears of slave subversion that motivated the quasi-freedom cases could not fairly arise in the "election" situation.

Judge Moncure's dissenting opinion emphasized the connection between the case presented and the legislative decision to allow manumission to take effect in the future, which itself created a lawful type of quasi freedom. Further, he could not understand the distinction between a will freeing slaves written after the master consulted them as to their wishes and a will directing that they be freed if they so chose after his death. For the majority, "capacity to choose" was a legal concept; for the dissenters, it was a practical one, for the slaves had a "very weak and imperfect" capacity to choose.

> [They] have certainly feelings and wishes which the master may be willing to consult in regard to their emancipation.

To do so, is not to create that middle state between slavery and freedom, which is unlawful. It is merely to propound a question to a slave requiring a categorical answer. If he wishes to be free, he is made a freeman in an instant; but is made so by the act of his master, whether that act be executed before or after the expression of his wish; provided it be executed according to law. There is not a particle of time intervening between his slavery and his freedom; and so no particle of time in which he occupies a state between the two.

Here too we see the opinion reflecting the fundamental distinction between law and sentiment.

Judge Moncure continued that, although slaves did not have civil rights, when they chose between freedom and slavery they were not exercising a civil right. At this point the opinion became confused; apparently choice was not a civil right because the ultimate mover in the manumission was the owner. Judge Moncure reviewed the cases, as had Judge Daniel, in which wills allowing choice had been enforced, and emphasized masters' reliance on those cases. Indeed, he noted, the will in the present case had been written over twenty years earlier, and only two or three years after the last such case.

If public opinion has undergone any change as to the policy or propriety of authorizing masters to emancipate their slaves, or to emancipate them *in futuro* or upon condition, such chance must develop itself in the action of the legislature, and not of the courts, whose business it is *jus dicere, non jus dare*, to expound the law as it is written and settled, and not as it ought to be, or as it may be supposed that public opinion would have it to be.

The court divided in the same way over a will manumitting ninety-seven slaves, some having families and others being quite old.[84] The slaves were freed directly, but the will provided that they could choose to be sent to Liberia or elsewhere or to choose new masters in Virginia from among the master's relatives. The majority now invoked a very stringent rule of construction. Since manumission "transformed [the slave] into a new being," every connection between master and slave had to be severed.

> If it appears that the will contemplates a continuance of that relation in a certain contingency; that the slave, notwithstanding the provision as to his manumission, is in a certain event to remain in the condition in which he was born, to continue without change a slave of his estate, subject to the control of the representative of the estate, such an intention is inconsistent with the idea of an intention to confer absolute manumission, and tends to throw light on that portion of the will which treats of manumission.

The owner had unconditionally freed "her faithful servant Charles" because she probably knew his wishes. But the ninety-seven others were probably strangers to her.

> There was therefore strong reason why, with the most benevolent feelings towards her slaves, she should not, without consulting their wishes, renounce all property in them, sever the connection between them and her estate, and by the mere exercise of her legal power, banish them from the place of their birth, dissolve the ties connecting them with others in their own condition, and cast the old and helpless, who had labored all their past lives in her service, into a distant country, without any provision for their support. She had no doubt as to their legal capacity to choose between freedom and slavery; and from the consideration before adverted to, it is manifest to my mind she did not intend to coerce them; but to give them, after a fitting time for enquiry and consideration, the right to elect for themselves what should be their future condition.

The majority thus relied on the owner's benevolent desires to thwart her evident intentions, but, as we have repeatedly seen, it used a rule of construction that could be made irrelevant by a differently worded will. However, the majority's approach did exclude from the master's range of choice one understandable method. Again Judge Moncure wrote the dissent, here to much greater effect because the owner's desires were being so obviously overridden: she had written, "free, then let them choose—between the only options available to free blacks in Virginia, emigration or reenslavement." The choice, that is, was illusory, except to the extent that those who chose reenslavement had a restricted choice for their new masters.

Perhaps the most extended discussion of "election" wills came in *Creswell* v. *Walker*, decided by the Alabama Supreme Court in 1861.[85] Faced with cases from six slave states "silently recognizing" such wills, the court adhered to its 1848 views.

> So far as their civil status is concerned, slaves are mere property, and their condition is that of absolute civil incapacity. Being, in respect of all civil rights and relations, not persons, but things, they are incapable of owning property, or of performing any civil legal act, by which the property of others can be alienated, or the relations of property . . . in any wise affected.

The form of the argument is deductive, or, in terms used earlier, categorical: given the nature of slavery, a legally binding election was simply inconceivable.

> According to the legal conception of slavery, as it exists in the southern States, a human being endowed with civil rights cannot be a slave. The possession of these rights is incompatible with the condition of slavery, and any attempt to confer them upon a slave, *durante servitute*, is an effort to accomplish what is legally impossible. Our law recognizes no other status than that of absolute freedom, or absolute slavery; and the courts have uniformly rejected, as a legal solecism, the idea that a slave, while a slave, can be invested with civil rights or legal capacity. Therefore, any attempt of a master to clothe his slave with the power to perform an act, which involves the exercise of civil rights and legal capacity, must, in the nature of things, fall.

An election was a civil act, affecting legal rights, and when given to a slave created an impermissible intermediate status.

The court struggled with the criticism of its analysis that pointed to the pervasive recognition of slave choice in other areas of slave law.

> It is true that slaves are human beings, and are endowed with intellect, conscience, and will. Their moral and intellectual qualities determine, to a considerable extent, their value, and are often looked to in ascertaining the rights and liabilities of others in relation to them as articles of property. Being endowed with intelligence, conscience and volition, they are deemed capable of committing crime; and the same public policy which, so far as the performance of civil acts is concerned, refuses to consider them as persons, gives them a criminal status, and recognizes them as persons in respect of acts involving criminal responsibility. Because they are rational human beings, they are capable of committing crimes; and, in reference to acts which are crimes, are regarded as persons. Because they are slaves, they are necessarily, and, so long as they remain slaves, incurably, incapable of performing civil acts; and, in reference to all such, they are things, not persons.
>
> This obvious distinction is overlooked by Mr. Cobb, in his criticism [of the 1846 case]. So far as civil acts are concerned, the slave, not being a person, has no legal mind, no will which the law can recognize. But, as soon as we pass into the region of crime, he is treated as a person, as having a legal mind, a will, capable of originating acts for which he may be subjected to punishment as criminal. Considered in his relation to this latter class of acts, the theory of a complete annihilation of will in the slave, is wholly unfounded; while in relation to the former class of acts, it is entirely consistent, and, indeed, is the only theory that can be consistent, with the fundamental idea of negro slavery as it exists with us—namely, that in respect of civil rights and legal capacity to perform acts of a civil nature, the slave is not a person, but a thing.

The term "formalism" has been overused in recent writings on American legal history, but it is hard to see anything more than a solution being effected by a completely unrationalized categorization.

As the court in *Creswell* noted, its analysis was not widely adopted. Just when the Virginia court accepted the "no election" rule, the North Carolina court rejected it.[86]

> [I]t is not true in point of fact or law, that slaves have not a mental or a moral capacity to make the election to be free, and, if needful to that end, to go abroad for that purpose. From the nature of slavery, they are denied a legal capacity to make contracts or acquire property while remaining in that state; but they are responsible human beings, having intelligence to know right from wrong, and perceptions of pleasure and pain, and of the difference between bondage and freedom, and thus, by nature, they are competent to give or withhold their assent to things that concern their state. All that is implied, necessarily, as assumed in law, where emancipation is allowed at all; for it changes the relation between the owner and the slave, and that requires the assent of both, and is sanctioned by the law as existing in nature. It may be regulated or even prohibited by the law. But no one ever thought that it required a municipal law to confer the right of manumission on the owner, or the capacity of accepting freedom by the slave. They preexist, and are founded in nature, just as other capacities for dealings between man and man.

Here Judge Ruffin treated choice as the dissenters in Virginia did, regarding it not as a legal but as a practical-moral concept. That approach was entirely consistent with Judge Ruffin's effort in *State* v. *Mann* to treat the legal incidents of the master-slave relationship as determined by sentiment. A year and a half later, the same court upheld a will allowing a slave to select a new master.

> It is certainly the policy of the law to keep the races of white and black distinct from each other, and to maintain

in the governing race, all needful, legal authority, and secure on the part of the governed unconditional subordination and obedience. This is a necessity of the condition of things amongst us, and essential to preserve the civilization that happily exists. But we are unable to understand the force of the objection, that this policy is contravened by the clause of the will in question.

The substance of the arrangement, made for the slave, is, that he shall be sold to a master, of his own selection, at the price of five hundred dollars. . . .

[T]o hold that [this] vitiate[s] the purpose of the testator and make[s] void his will, in respect to that slave, would be to exclude from the system of slavery every indulgence in its management, or at least, so to hedge it about, in this respect, as to make it stiff and harsh, and thus impart to it an aspect it does not now possess.[87]

The "election" cases provide the final elements in the contradictory structure of slave law. Again the use of parallel columns will clarify the analysis.

Market relations	Slave relations
Law	Sentiment
Contract	Tort (fellow-servant cases)
No choice	Choice (election cases)

This array reveals an apparent anomaly, for contract analysis, premised on individual choice, is aligned with the view that the slave is allowed no choice. But the anomaly is only apparent and is readily resolved. Individual choice was to be honored, but only within the master class. The "election" cases clearly draw a line between the master's decision, which could be overridden only by the most pressing social needs, and, in the restrictive states, the slave's decision, which had no effect. The same line was drawn in Judge Ruffin's analysis of the fellow-servant problem, in which the contract argument flowed from the proposition that the slaveowner could adjust the rental price. Thus, the following pattern is found in the cases.

Market relations	Slave relations
Law	Sentiment
Contract	Tort
No choice	Choice
Categories	[Analogies]

Once again an anomaly appears, for the argument in the preceding chapter led to the conclusion that slave law was linked to the development of a categorical approach to the problem:

Market relations	Slave relations
Common law	Statutory law
Analogies	Categories

But the contradiction between slave relations and a law of slavery was there left unresolved. Now we can see that the use of a categorical approach enabled Southern courts to shift one structure of analysis into another.

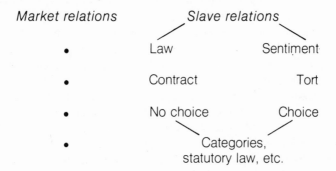

In this way the social contradictions of Southern society were embedded in slave law, which embraced two distinct and inconsistent sets of ideas. This internal contradiction supplied an opportunity and posed a dilemma. Because two structures were available, any judge could choose to work within that structure which conduced to the result he desired to reach, for reasons external to the law. That is how marginal differences in attachment to slavery were expressed. But at the same time, a judge who selected one structure for one case had several problems. He had to close his eyes to the existence of another equally coherent structure that would have yielded a different result. In addition, he had to face up to the consequences of the choice for later cases: either be bound within one structure by the prior choice or be open to the charge of inconsistency. Neither course was an easy one.

The openness of slave law can be summarized by an examination of Georgia manumission law. Professor Nash calls Georgia "ardently pro-slavery,"[88] but he acknowledges that the picture is complicated. The best way to proceed is largely chronologically, for that reveals most clearly the manner in which Georgia law oscillated between the available structures.

In 1801 and 1818 the state legislature regulated manumission. In an offhand opinion in 1830, the superior court held that these statutes prohibited domestic manumission as part of the state's policy against increasing the free black population "to the annoyance and injury of the owners of slaves."[89] Remarkably, the will provided for the emancipation in Liberia of slaves who so desired, and was enforced despite the testator's failure to provide a fund for their transportation; the court thought it "probable that the Colonization Society will pay the expenses, if it be necessary." Shortly after it was created in 1845, the state supreme court adopted the same interpretation of the statutes, although it expressed some misgivings.[90] Marshal Keith had died in 1842, leaving a will that expressed a desire to free his servant Ishmael. The executors were directed to hold a substantial amount of property, including several slaves and some land in Georgia, in trust for Ishmael. Similar grants were made regarding two female slaves. All in all, the will was as close to a quasi-freedom one as can be designed. Judge Lumpkin avoided the hardest questions by finding the next of kin barred by their five-year delay from challenging most of the will. He did, however, address the provision for emancipation; using a standard deductive argument, he noted that Keith could have sent his slaves to Africa while he lived, and could have dedicated any of his property to that purpose, and thought it "equally certain" that he could do the same by will. In a passage quoted in Chapter I, Judge Lumpkin argued that foreign emancipation, because it reduced the black population, was consistent with state policy. He then denounced domestic manumission, which Keith's will might have sought to accomplish, and concluded by suggesting a tension between honoring a testator's intention and executing important state policies described in almost patriarchal terms:

> [G]reat indulgence is extended to the declared wishes of testators, touching what they would have done with their property after their death. If it be true, however, that *families* are the original of all societies, and contain the foundation and primitive elements of all other social institutions, and as such deservedly claim the front rank in the protection of Courts, *Wills*, which are calculated practically, to disregard and set at nought this divine ordinance, worth more than all that man in his wisdom has ever devised, cannot claim to be regarded with peculiar tenderness and favoritism by Courts of Justice.

By 1855, divisions began to appear. The court enforced a will that provided for domestic emancipation if possible and for foreign emancipation otherwise.[91] Because Judge Benning had, in a parallel case, argued for the total illegalilty of manumission by will, Judge Lumpkin wrote an extensive opinion on the question. He began, as before, with the proposition that the testator could have sought legislative approval of domestic manumission or could have sent the slaves elsewhere during his life, and said that, although there might be some qualifications, in general a person had the same powers over his own property in his will as he had had during his life. Then Judge Lumpkin ran through the objections. First, the will provided only that the slaves could choose their new place of residence; it did not give a choice between slavery and freedom in terms, although of course that choice followed directly from the one actually given. Even more, the "no election" rule was "too technical" and "prove[d] too much" because it would preclude all manumissions. A slave could not even be allowed to choose the new master.

> True, slaves are property—*chattels* if you please; still, they are rational and intelligent beings. Christianity considers them as such, and our municipal law, in many of its wise and humane provisions, has elevated them far above the level of the brute. We should deeply regret to be compelled to decide that a benevolent disposition like that referred to, and others that might be put, involving to some extent the volition of the slave, was nugatory. Our examination has furnished us with no such rule, applicable to slavery. It is at war with the whole train of adjudications in this and our sister States, as well as of every other civilized country. . . . In the absence of all legal restraint, and upon a point affecting the owner and his slaves only, and where no considerations of public policy intervene, we do not see the paramount necessity of establishing a doctrine so stringent.

Second, Judge Lumpkin faced a conflict-of-laws argument. He vigorously disagreed with the rule in *Somerset* and similar cases[92] that residence in a free state conferred freedom. Indeed he called the rule a "fungus" caused "by the foul and fell spirit of modern fanaticism." But he recognized that if the slaves were sent to a state that followed *Somerset*, and if their status were decided in litigation there, the slaves would be found free. He concluded, apparently disregarding the problem that the status was precisely at issue in Georgia, that it would be pointless to deny effect to the will.

The last objection was that the provisions were void because no one could enforce the will, the slaves lacking legal capacity. Judge Lumpkin granted that and conceded that if the executors refused to comply with the provisions of the will, little could be done about it, but the executor, as "an honorable man," had "a high duty" to carry out the testator's wishes. The court would not premise its rules on an expectation that he would disregard that duty. But Judge Lumpkin had already fired his largest guns, in an extended discussion of the wisdom of laws allowing foreign emancipation. Although he was convinced that state law permitted such emancipation, he was equally convinced that

the best interests of the slave, as well as a stern public policy, resulting from the whole frame-work of our social sysem, imperatively demand that all *post mortem* manumission of slaves should be absolutely and entirely prohibited. Slavery is a cherished institution in Georgia—founded in the Constitution and laws of the United States; in her own Constitution and laws, and guarded, protected and defended by the whole spirit of her legislation; approved by her people; intimately interwoven with her present and pemanent prosperity. Her interests, her feelings, her judgment and her conscience—not to say her very existence, alike conspire to sustain and perpetuate it. We may not be able to prevent expatriation of the living—to restrain the master in his lifetime from removing whithersoever he pleases with his property, but when the owner has kept them as long as he can enjoy them, shall he, from an ignorance of the scriptural basis upon which the institution of slavery rests, or from a total disregard to the peace and welfare of the community which survive him, invoke the aid of the Courts of this State to carry into execution his false and fatal views of humanity? Is not every agitation of these cases in our Courts attended with mischief? Is not every exode of slaves from the interior to the seaboard, thence to be transported to a land of freedom, productive of evil? Can any doubt its tendency? Are there not now in our midst large gangs of slaves who expected emancipation by the will of their owners, and who believe they have been unjustly deprived of the boon? Are such likely to be good servants? On the contrary, are they not likely to sow the seeds of insubordination, perhaps of revolt, amongst the slaves in their neighborhood?

But the statutes, he thought, were absolutely clear, and though he had lobbied for legislation changing the law, Judge Lumpkin believed that, as a judge, he had no choice. "It is not the province of the Court *to make* public policy, but simply *to declare it*, as it exists."

Judge Starnes avoided the problem entirely by construing the will to allow, but not require, the executor to send the slaves to a free state. He was less willing than Judge Lumpkin to condemn at least manumission in Africa, though he distinguished the "bad policy" of "send[ing] the slaves into the free States," which "contribut[ed] to the agitation which engenders so much fanatical sympathy for [the free blacks'] contented and happy kindred in slavery." But "reasons, founded in humanity," might justify Liberian emancipation.

Judge Benning's contrary views were forcefully though repetitively presented in a contemporaneous case.[93] The statutes made it "unlawful . . . to manumit or set free any negro"; they made no distinction between domestic and foreign manumission and were, to Judge Benning, unambiguous. Further, the statute's intent was not, as Judge Lumpkin had contended, to eliminate the intermediate class of free blacks in the state; it was rather to do what the legislature could to eliminate that class everywhere. Even if the purpose were limited to Georgia, it would be best accomplished by prohibiting foreign emancipation and reducing the risk that a free black would illegally reenter the state. Finally, Judge Benning took the quasi-freedom argument to its limit: the slaves were effectively freed in Georgia while they waited to leave. As a matter of policy, too, the evils produced by the different types of will were said to differ only in small degree.

Again Judges Lumpkin and Starnes disagreed on the law, although not on the policy. The case involved the will of Robert Bledsoe, which directed that his executors purchase land in Indiana or Illinois, where he already had extensive holdings, on which his slaves could be settled and thereby freed. For Judge Benning, that provision invalidated the entire will, and the slaves should be transmitted according to the law of intestacy. For the others, the problem was more complicated. Neither Indiana nor Illinois allowed free blacks to come into the state. How were Bledsoe's desires to be carried out? The law of wills had developed a doctrine, called *cy pres*, by which the courts would do the next best thing if a particular intention as expressed in a will could not be carried out. Judge Lumpkin was not happy with the doctrine in general, calling it "revolting . . . to common sense [and] repugnant to our own sense of right," apparently because the doctrine allowed judges to substitute their own preferences for those of the testator. He was willing to accept the doctrine if it were confined to overcoming barriers to some secondary purpose of the testator, however. Was the specification of Indiana or Illinois, then, subordinate to the paramount object of emancipation? Judge Lumpkin thought not: Bledsoe had lived in those states and had "entertained the most inveterate hostility to" Ohio, and he may have preferred to keep his slaves in bondage to having them free anywhere other than Indiana or Illinois. "All beyond [those states] is *terra ignota*, mere vague surmise, upon which we dare not act."

> I will only add that, as a man, I do not regret the failure of this bequest. Look at the stringency of the laws of Indiana and Illinois and other Northwestern States, against persons of color, and reflect upon their thriftlessness, when not controlled by superior intelligence and forethought, and what friend of the African or of humanity, would desire to see these children of the sun, who luxuriate in a tropical climate and perish with cold in higher latitudes, brought in close contact and competition with the hardy and industrious population which teem in the territory northwest of the Ohio, and who loathes negroes as they would so many lepers? Courts should not be astute in so construing wills as to doom them to such a destiny. A stern and inexorable State policy equally forbids it. As to the transpor-

tation of these slaves to Liberia, the wildest and most lat-
itudinous application of *Cy-pres doctrine*, could never, *under
this will*, justify such a project as that.

The slaves, according to the majority, should go to Bledsoe's
nephews and nieces, the recipients of other bequests and the
residuary legatees.

Judges Lumpkin and Benning returned to the battle three
years later.[94] Judge Benning repeated his arguments, and Judge
Lumpkin now gave an extended reply. The statutes aimed at
eliminating the nuisance caused by free blacks in the state,
and the risk of illicit return by freed blacks was trivial. He
again mentioned the desirability of legislation, which, he said,
had recently been overwhelmingly rejected by the state legislature. He returned to the theme in his conclusion:

> For myself, I repeat, I have no partiality for foreign any
> more than domestic manumission. I believe that policy, as
> well as humanity for the negro, forbid both. Especially do
> I object to the colonization of our negroes upon our north-
> western frontier. They facilitate the escape of our fugitive
> slaves. In case of civil war, they would become an element
> of strength to the enemy, as well as of annoyance to our-
> selves. But what of all this? Shall I therefore undertake, by
> my individual opinion, to dictate to more than half a million
> of my fellow-citizens, what shall be the law, by wresting
> these ancient statutes from what I believe to be their true
> and only meaning? A construction adhered to without var-
> iableness or a shadow of turning for a quarter of a century?
> Such is not my understanding of my duty or privilege.

His major argument was directed at Judge Benning's
strongest point, that emancipation by will created quasi freedom. Judge Lumpkin's position was ingeniously stated: consider a will bequeathing slaves to Rufus Choate of Massachusetts. That will could not possibly violate Georgia law
even though its obvious effect would be to free the slaves. So
too for a will directing the executors to take the slaves to New

York, without mentioning, but clearly intending, manumission. Why should a general will for foreign emancipation be any different? Judge Lumpkin here equated the master's powers before and after death, in a way that implicitly contradicted his support for a statutory ban on foreign manumission. For the equivalence arose from the master's right of property, which included a right to emigrate with his slaves. "Any attempt to abridge this right would produce revolution and depopulate the State." Yet wills were made under pressure; plans to send slaves elsewhere might be suddenly aborted by the owner's grave illness, and he or she would write a will to carry out those perfectly lawful plans. However, even Judge Lumpkin would not tolerate a will that transmitted slaves to the widow, to be freed upon her death.[95] In 1859 the state legislature followed Judge Lumpkin's advice and prohibited emancipation by will, but even in the next year the court upheld a foreign-emancipation provision.[96] The opinion was very brief and, as we have seen in other contexts, the Georgia court had no further opportunity to reconcile the statutory provision with the recognition of the master's property right.

Meanwhile another line of attack on manumissions by will had developed, when, in 1857, the court held that the American Colonization Society's charter barred it from accepting bequests of slaves.[97] Again the argument was deceptively simple. The charter authorized the society to colonize, with their own consent, free blacks. Slaves given to the society were not free blacks. In addition, the society was designed to honor the wishes of its beneficiaries, but suppose one of the slaves bequeathed to it did not consent to emancipation in Liberia; if the wish were honored, the society would become an outright owner of a slave, which would violate the charter in one way, and if the wish were not honored, the charter would be violated in another way. Nor could the society, on its own, make them free; only residence in a free territory could do that. The court also rejected, on technical grounds, the society's efforts to have its trustees designated as the recipients of the slaves, but it mentioned too the merits of that effort.

The society differed from its trustees, according to the court, because it had substantial corporate assets, and the testator might not have been willing to leave his slaves to individuals who lacked those assets.

The court, in its conclusion, addressed a peripheral but serious question: could the society sue in Georgia? Probably not, because Georgia had no obligation to open its courts to a society chartered in another state whose purposes were repugnant to Georgia's policy. Judge Lumpkin's opinion quoted extensively from legislative resolutions condemning the Colonization Society by name. He ended his opinion with an oratorical flourish that perhaps indicates the source of the analytical ingenuity of the earlier parts of the opinion.

I was once, in common with the great body of my fellow citizens of the South, the friend and patron of this enterprise. I now regard it as a failure, if not something worse; as I do every effort that has been made, for the abolition of negro slavery, at home or abroad. Liberia was formed of emancipated slaves, many of them partially trained and prepared for the change, and sent thousands of miles from all contact with the superior race; and given a home in a country where their ancestors were natives, and supposed to be suited for their physical condition. Arrived there, they have been for a number of years in a state of pupilage to the Colonization Society, in order that they might learn "to walk alone and by themselves." And at the end of a half a century what do we see? A few thousand thriftless, lazy semi-savages, dying of famine, because they will not work! To inculcate care and industry upon the descendants of Ham, is to preach to the idle winds. To be the "servant of servants" is the judicial curse pronounced upon their race. And this Divine decree is unreversible. It will run on parallel with time itself. And heaven and earth shall sooner pass away, than one jot or tittle of it shall abate. Under the superior race and no where else, do they attain to the highest degree of civilization. . . . Let our women and old men, and persons of weak and infirm minds, be disabused of the false and unfounded notion that slavery is sinful, and that they will peril their souls if they do not disinherit their offspring by emancipating their slaves!

Hostility to the Colonization Society had its limits, though. Judge Lumpkin upheld a will directing that the executors send seven slaves to Liberia and establishing the society as trustee controlling the funds to be used for the slaves' maintenance.[98] The will was a valid one for foreign manumission, and though the society could not act as trustee under the court's prior decisions, the courts would develop ways to effectuate the testator's intention; indeed, Judge Lumpkin spelled out a rather detailed scheme for the support of the emancipated slaves.

Finally, in 1860 the Georgia court adopted the "no election" rule.[99] With Judge Lumpkin curiously silent, Judge Lyon for the court expressed doubt even about foreign emancipation wills, and then adopted the standard "no election" analysis, quoting substantial parts of the relevant Virginia cases. But Judge Lyon added a bizarre wrinkle: a will that allowed a choice between foreign freedom and domestic slavery actually intended to create domestic quasi freedom. After all, he asked, how could a testator wishing his slaves freed desire that their relations with a new master would be the ordinary ones between master and slave? Surely he intended to confer the "bounty" of freedom on them, "wherever they might be."

> The bequest was in fact, placing a charter of the liberty of these negroes in their hands to go throughout the State and trade and traffic on it until such person could be found who would give them the largest liberty for the least consideration; one in whom they could confide, who would hold them nominally as slaves, while for all practical purposes they would be free. There is no time fixed within which they must elect. In the interim, what is their condition, slaves or free? Neither the one or the other—*quasi slave*— *quasi free*.

It would be misleading to call Georgia typical, except in the sense that the array of issues the Georgia court faced was representative. Neither the court's resolution of the issues nor its rhetoric was typical. However, the cases from Georgia and elsewhere establish a rather clear direction of development. None of the states examined in this book moved from a position that limited the master's power to emancipate to a position in which that power was unlimited. Thus, although Georgia was extreme in aborting so many ways that a master could use to manumit by will, nearly every Southern state used at least some of Georgia's techniques. The political pressures displayed openly in Georgia existed elsewhere, of course, and masters always ran the risk that courts in their state would yield to them and would invoke some previously rejected or newly invented rule to bar a manumission by will. And yet a fundamental contradiction remained: a master might find his or her most carefully structured will destroyed by the use of one of the doctrines floating throughout the South, but nothing could prevent a predeath manumission, carried out by sending the slaves to a free state. Of course, even a gravely ill master ran the risk of recovery to a life without slaves. Considering, not the practicality, but the conceptual structure, though, we can see an ineradicable tension between the fundamental tenet that the master had an ordinary, and therefore quite powerful, property right in the slave, and the equally fundamental tenet that slaveowners as a class had an interest in perpetuating the institution even in the face of opposition from individuals within that class. Frequently law and the state attempt to neutralize that sort of opposition by developing rules to override short-sighted individual decisions, but that strategy was probably unavailable in the South because the contradiction in the law arose from the contradiction within slave society in a bourgeois world, where property rights were by definition possessed by uncontrolled individuals.

CONCLUSION

SOUTHERN SLAVE LAW was constructed around the distinctions between regulation according to law and regulation according to sentiment, ultimately grounded in the contradiction between bourgeois and slave relationships. For political and conceptual reasons, the distinction remained latent in most instances. Judges had to appeal to values shared widely in their society, which had not broken completely with the ideology of bourgeois individualism, and so could not easily deny that law was relevant to ordering major social institutions. The force of precedent appeared to limit what the judges could do, though those who, like Judge Ruffin, understood the degree to which precedent is malleable were able to break the bonds of precedent. Finally, many of the transactions that came to the courts in fact involved mixtures of slave and market relationships, and the force of bourgeois ideology and precedent was great enough to inhibit ordinary judges from developing a pure law of slavery.

Yet such a law struggled to emerge from the cases. Cognitive limitations led judges to seek ways of limiting the range of analogy, or, put another way, the force of precedent. The need for slave discipline induced them to try to relax ordinary procedures in ways that posed no threat to free people. Racism, too, affected the scope of the judges' thinking, as they attempted to identify the law of slavery with the affected blacks. All these elements influenced attempts to develop rigid categories into which slave cases could be fit. If such categories could be developed, the range of analogy and the threat to free whites could be limited. Codification represented the clearest form of categorization, but as North Carolina's law showed, that goal could also be reached within a common-law system.

Though categorization was possible, it was at the same time difficult to achieve. In part the problem was temporal; Southern judges were not given the time to work out a pure system of slave law. But the difficulties went deeper. So long as the common-law method of reasoning by analogy was allowed, talented judges would repeatedly break down the categories that their less talented brethren had built. Most important, there was a fundamental contradiction between the idea of a law of slavery and a social structure that provided the basis for the idea that slave relationships should be regulated by sentiment, not law.

One emerges from the maze of Southern slave law with a feeling of dissatisfaction, as if one has heard a progression of chords that ended before reaching a resolution. The incompleteness of the efforts to categorize slave law and the simultaneous assertions of individual choice and social control illustrate the continuing efforts to sustain fundamentally incompatible approaches to the law. These tensions did not have to be eliminated, of course; after all, Southern law tolerated them for a very long time. But maintaining the bifurcated structure of law clearly called for some rather careful maneuvering. It is a measure of the talent of some judges that they were able to pick their way through the problems, but, as I argued in Chapter III, it seems unlikely that many judges with such talents would populate Southern courts. In addition, the increasing politicization of the courts' environment caused by the sectional crisis was likely to make the delicate job even harder, both directly, through appointments and elections to the bench, and indirectly, by making it increasingly clear to the judges what the consequences of their choices were.

To say that the tensions would probably have been resolved, however, does not mean that any particular resolution was likely, at least when attention is confined to the law. The source of the difficulty for slave law was that it was ultimately rooted in a society whose premises contained contradictions. The manumission cases suggest that Southern law was moving in the same direction as Southern politics, and it may be useful to sketch, in conclusion, what a rationalized law of slavery might have looked like. The primary alteration would have been a transformation in the notion of property. It would no longer be defined as the expression of individual will, subject to regulation only for the most pressing social goals. Instead, property, at first only in slaves but eventually in everything, would be defined as the delegation by society as a whole of certain limited authority to "owners," who would be charged with exercising that authority only in socially prescribed ways. Once the master-slave relation was thus generalized, other anomalies would disappear. In particular, once social control was embodied in all relationships rather than being superimposed on them, there would be no need to distinguish between some relationships governed by market or individualistic notions and others governed by other notions; the strain toward categorization and its cognate problem, the attempt to define rigid racial rules, would be eased.

The pressures of the sectional conflict give us a chance to see what a rationalized law of slavery might have looked like. In 1859 the Mississippi Supreme Court tried to limit a master's property rights in his slaves, invoking social ends as its justification.[1] Nancy Wells was owned by her father Edward. In 1846 Edward took her to Ohio, as a result of which she became free. Eighteen months later Wells returned to Mississippi and married Samuel Watts, a barber. Shortly after Wells came back to Mississippi, her father died, leaving her $3,000. After spending three years in Mississippi, Wells and her husband moved back to Ohio. When William Mitchell, the executor of Edward Wells' estate, refused to pay Nancy Wells the $3,000 legacy, she sued him in the Mississippi court.

Judge Harris for a divided court denied relief. Because it was not an "ordinary case" but involved "great questions of public policy," he regarded precedent as less constraining than it would otherwise be. He concluded that slaves could "acquire no right, civil or political, within Mississippi, by manumission elsewhere." He could not keep citizens of Mississippi from taking their slaves elsewhere, there to be freed, but he could deny any domestic effect to their actions. The precedents were in conflict, and no statutes bore on the problem, but Judge Harris thought it appropriate for a court to decide what public policy was by examining "the nature and character of our institutions." He concluded with an attack on Ohio, "forgetful of her constitutional obligations to the whole race, and afflicted with a *negro-mania*, which inclines her to *descend*, rather than elevate herself in the scale of humanity."

Yet even here the limits of a pure law of slavery in a bourgeois world are apparent. The law could not stop emigration but could only deny legal rights within Mississippi to freed slaves. The assertion of control over a master's choice was therefore weak, for it was manumission elsewhere that was the real issue, not the incidental problem posed in *Mitchell* v. *Wells*. Further, the court's opinion was countered by a dissent from Judge Handy, who criticized Judge Harris for talking about "the abstract policy of slavery." I need not rehearse the dissent in detail, for it is the fact of dissent that matters. It shows that a Southern judge as late as 1859 had the materials available—in the decided cases, in the statutes, and most important in notions of the proper judicial role—that made it possible to deny that a pure slave law was consistent with "the nature and character of our institutions," for those institutions were internally contradictory.

The Southern master class chose to wage a "civil" war in order to break free from its political and economic ties within a bourgeois national state. Other choices were open, and even the one taken need not have produced a totally rationalized body of slave law. The world economy remained bourgeois and the heritage of bourgeois thought and law was powerful. In the event, however, it did not matter that choices within the legal system were available, for the decision to wage war turned out to be a decision to become fully integrated into the bourgeois system.

Notes

ACKNOWLEDGMENTS

1. "The American Law of Slavery, 1810-1860: A Study in the Persistence of Legal Autonomy."
2. "Approaches to the Study of the Law of Slavery."
3. "Book Review of Higginbotham, *In the Matter of Color*."

INTRODUCTION

1. The facts and quotations are taken from *Gorman* v. *Campbell*, 14 Ga. 137 (1853).
2. A. E. Keir Nash, "Understanding the Judicial Role in the Institution of Slavery, Part Two," p. 17.
3. For a good discussion of how ways of understanding the world work their way into legal doctrine, see Peter Gabel, "Intention and Structure in Contractual Conditions: Outline of a Method for Critical Legal Theory," p. 601.
4. Eugene Genovese's use of the name "War for Southern Independence" is designed to promote this understanding. See Eugene Genovese, *The Political Economy of Slavery*, pp. 35, 43.
5. Eugene Genovese, *The World the Slaveholders Made*, pp. 111, 129-30, 211-13.
6. The reliance on appellate opinions is justified in Chapter I.
7. Helen Catterall, *Judicial Cases Concerning American Slavery and the Negro*.
8. I have been told that the compilation omits some early cases, but for the period between 1810 to 1860 there is no reason to believe that she omitted anything significant. The patterns are so well supported that discovery of a few additional cases could not substantially alter my conclusions.
9. The exclusions were based on my judgment that the states examined covered the range of variation in Southern law, from the well-developed to the frontier, from common law to civil law, and so on. The volume of the material from Tennessee and South Carolina was, I must confess, another reason for its exclusion.
10. See Chapter II below.

CHAPTER I

1. Helen Catterall, *Judicial Cases Concerning American Slavery and the Negro*, vol. 3, pp. 300-301.

2. Kenneth Stampp, *The Peculiar Institution*, p. 94. See also p. 264, using a litigated case as a dramatic illustration of human "tragedy."

3. Ibid., pp. 351-60.

4. This argument turns on the relative utility of legal and other materials, not on the rate at which facts relating to miscegenation are revealed in legal materials.

5. Fourteen of the nineteen cited cases fit this description, and two others involve different forms of breakdown in social relations.

6. P. 19.

7. Ibid., pp. 107-108

8. See, e.g., John Blassingame, *The Slave Community: Plantation Life in the Antebellum South*, pp. 77-82, 90-91; Robert Fogel and Stanley Engerman, *Time on the Cross*, vol. 1, pp. 126-44; Eugene Genovese, *Roll, Jordan, Roll*, pp. 450-58.

9. Goodell, p. 17.

10. *State* v. *John*, 30 N.C. (3 Ired.) 330 (1848).

11. See *State* v. *Samuel*, 19 N.C. (2 Dev. & Bat.) 177 (1836); *Smith* v. *State*, 9 Ala. 990 (1846).

12. *William* v. *State*, 33 Ga. Supp. 85 (1864).

13. Goodell, p. 108.

14. See, e.g., ibid., pp. 141-48.

15. See, e.g., ibid., pp. 138, 157-59; Stroud, *A Sketch of the Laws*, pp. 13-14.

16. Stroud, *A Sketch of the Laws*, p. 18, citing *State* v. *Bowen*, 3 Strob. 574 (S.C. 1848).

17. See, e.g., *State* v. *Will*, 18 N.C. (1 Dev. & Bat.) 121 (1834).

18. Stroud, *A Sketch of the Laws*, pp. 19-20.

19. See Chapter II, §D for my effort in this direction.

20. See Thomas R. R. Cobb, *An Inquiry Into the Law of Negro Slavery*, pp. 83-84, 100.

21. Michael Hindus, "Black Justice Under White Law: Criminal Prosecutions of Blacks in Antebellum South Carolina," p. 575.

22. For a suggestive example, see Leslie H. Owens, *This Species of Property*, p. 120.

23. Arthur Howington, " 'According to Law': The Trial and Punishment of Black Defendants in Antebellum Tennessee."

24. This point was made by Sanford Levinson in his comments on Howington, " 'According to Law.' "

25. For an explicitly Whiggish view, see A. E. Keir Nash, "Understanding the Judicial Role in the Institution of Slavery."

26. Winthrop Jordan, *White Over Black: American Attitudes Toward the Negro, 1550-1812*, p. 588; Genovese, *Roll, Jordan, Roll*, p. 48.

27. *Anthony v. State*, 9 Ga. 264 (1851).

28. *Jim v. State*, 15 Ga. 535 (1854).

29. *Barclay v. Sewell*, 12 La. Ann. 262 (1857).

30. 4 Ga. 445 (1848).

31. See Nash, "Understanding the Judicial Role."

32. See, e.g., *Bivens v. Crawford*, 26 Ga. 225 (1858).

33. See, e.g., George Fitzhugh, *Cannibals All!*, pp. 15-20; Erik L. McKitrick, ed., *Slavery Defended: The Views of the Old South*, pp. 57-68, printing excerpts from William Grayson's *The Hireling and the Slave*, pp. 21-45.

34. *Peter v. Hargrave*, 46 Va. (5 Gratt.) 12 (1848).

35. See, e.g., A. E. Keir Nash, "Fairness and Formalism in the Trials of Blacks in the State Supreme Courts of the Old South"; Daniel Flanigan, "Criminal Procedure in Slave Trials in the Antebellum South"; Howington, " 'According to Law.' "

36. If this were a biographical study, such variations might be of interest. Nash, "Understanding the Judicial Role," moves toward such a study, but his insistence on the relevance of the liberalism-conservatism dimension to an overall evaluation of the law, rather than of individual judges, makes his concern for law puzzling.

37. James White, *The Legal Imagination*, pp. 469-70.

38. See, e.g., A. Leon Higginbotham, *In the Matter of Color*; Ronald Dworkin, "The Law of the Slave-Catchers." The political argument in the text is developed in Mark Tushnet, Review of "In the Matter of Color."

39. Stanley Elkins, *Slavery: A Problem in American Institutional and Intellectual Life.*

40. Ibid., pp. 37-52, 71.

41. For a collection of materials, see Ann Lane, ed., *The Debate Over Slavery: Stanley Elkins and His Critics.*

42. This is essentially the model used by Marvin Harris, *Patterns of Race in the Americas*. It has been criticized as offering "three collective forms of economic man." Eugene Genovese, "Materialism and Idealism in the History of Negro Slavery in the Americas."

43. Genovese, *Roll, Jordan, Roll*, p. 47.

44. The argument in this section is of course related to Genovese's, ibid., pp. 25-49, but reduces his emphasis on the role of the law in mediating between the master and slave classes and increases emphasis on the role of the law in mediating conflicts within the master class.

45. Peter Gabel, "Intention and Structure in Contractual Conditions: Outline of a Method for Critical Legal Theory," pp. 629-35.

46. For a useful collection of these writings, see Thomas Luckmann, *Phenomenology and Sociology*.

47. Karl Marx, *Capital*, vol. 1, chap. 1, §4.

48. Once concrete examples are introduced, so too are the contradictions of any specific social formation. See text, pp. 230-32 below.

49. See generally C. B. MacPherson, *The Political Philosophy of Possessive Individualism*.

50. "The assumptions which comprise possessive individualism may be summarized in the following seven propositions.

(i) What makes a man human is freedom from dependence on the wills of others.

(ii) Freedom from dependence on others means freedom from any relations with others except those relations which the individual enters voluntarily with a view to his own interest.

(iii) The individual is essentially the proprietor of his own person and capacities, for which he owes nothing to society.

(iv) Although the individual cannot alienate the whole of his property in his own person, he may alienate his capacity to labour.

(v) Human society consists of a series of market relations.

(vi) Since freedom from the wills of others is what makes a man human, each individual's freedom can rightfully be limited only by such obligations and rules as are necessary to secure the same freedom for others.

(vii) Political society is a human contrivance for the protection of the individual's property in his person and goods, and (therefore) for the maintenance of orderly relations of exchange between individuals regarded as proprietors of themselves." Ibid., pp. 263-64.

51. See generally Genovese, *Roll, Jordan, Roll*.

52. Eugene Genovese, *The World the Slaveholders Made*, pp. 125-26.

53. See, e.g., Edmund Morgan, *American Slavery/American Freedom*.

54. A failure to consider the issue of penetration flaws Professor Genovese's otherwise profound analysis of the "hegemonic role of the law." See Genovese, *Roll, Jordan, Roll*, pp. 25-49.

55. Max Rheinstein, ed., *Max Weber on Law in Economy and Society*, pp. 63, 349-56.

56. See also Duncan Kennedy, "Form and Substance in Private Law Adjudication."

57. See John Noonan, *Persons and Masks of the Law*.

58. Cf. Samuel Warren & Louis Brandeis, "The Right to Privacy."

CHAPTER II

1. *Ponton* v. *Wilmington & Weldon R. Co.*, 51 N.C. (6 Jones) 245 (1858).

2. *Farwell* v. *Boston & Worcester R. Co.*, 45 Mass. (4 Metc.) 49 (1842).

3. 35 N.C. (13 Ired.) 305 (1852).

4. See generally Roberto Unger, *Knowledge and Politics*.

5. Roscoe Pound, *The Formative Era of American Law*, pp. 4, 30 n. 2.

6. 14 Ga. 137 (1853).

7. 13 N.C. (2 Dev.) 263 (1829).

8. Stanley Elkins, *Slavery*, pp. 56-57 and n. 53.

9. Eugene Genovese, *Roll, Jordan, Roll*, p. 35.

10. William Goodell, *The American Slave Code in Theory and Practice*, p. 174.

11. Harriet Beecher Stowe, *Key to Uncle Tom's Cabin*, p. 78.

12. Goodell, p. 175.

13. Robert Cover, *Justice Accused*, pp. 197-256.

14. Ibid., pp. 229-32.

15. See Mark Tushnet, Review of Cover, *Justice Accused*.

16. *State* v. *Hale*, 9 N.C. (2 Hawks) 582 (1823).

17. Cover, p. 77 n.

18. Genovese, p. 36.

19. See Morton Horwitz, *The Transformation of American Law, 1780-1860*, pp. 253-66.

20. *Jourdan* v. *Patton*, 5 Mart. O.S. 615 (La. 1818).

21. See Goodell, p. 163.

22. For a lucid explication, see C. B. MacPherson, *The Political Philosophy of Possessive Individualism.*

23. If the damage award included some amount for scrap value, it would make sense to transfer title so that the defendant could recapture that amount, but such a system would clearly be rather awkward.

24. I owe this suggestion to Richard Markovits who also suggested (without endorsing) another possible rationale for the transfer. The trial court's remedy, continuing maintenance costs plus a lump sum, might be more expensive to administer than the transfer, since it called for the continuing threat of judicial enforcement.

CHAPTER III

1. 1 Miss. (Walk.) 83 (1821).

2. 28 Miss. 100 (1854).

3. The statutes are quoted in *Ike* v. *State*, 23 Miss. 525 (1852).

4. See, e.g., *Russell* v. *United States*, 369 U.S. 749 (1962).

5. 21 Miss. (13 Sm. & M.) 263 (1850).

6. *Ike* v. *State*, 23 Miss. 525 (1852).

7. *Sarah* v. *State*, 28 Miss. 267 (1854).

8. See Meredith Lang, *Defender of the Faith: The High Court of Mississippi, 1817-1875*, pp. 160-61.

9. *Mitchell* v. *Wells*, 37 Miss. 235 (1859). Compare *Shaw* v. *Brown*, 35 Miss. 246 (1858).

10. The procedure is described in *Minor* v. *State*, 36 Miss. 630 (1859).

11. *Minor* v. *State*, 36 Miss. 630 (1859).

12. Thomas R. R. Cobb, *An Inquiry Into the Law of Negro Slavery in the United States of America*, pp. 85-90.

13. *Neal* v. *Farmer*, 9 Ga. 555, 579 (1851).

14. Cobb, pp. 84, 91.

15. *George* v. *State*, 37 Miss. 316 (1859).

16. Cobb, p. 84.

17. *Wesley* v. *State*, 37 Miss. 327 (1859).

18. Eugene Genovese, *Roll, Jordan, Roll*, pp. 35-36.

19. The best recent discussion is Stephen Presser, "A Tale of Two Judges."

20. For an overview, see Note, "*Swift* v. *Tyson* Exhumed," pp.

297-305. A more general discussion is Perry Miller, *The Life of the Mind in America: From the Revolution to the Civil War*.

21. *State* v. *Jowers*, 33 N.C. (11 Ired.) 555 (1850).

22. *State* v. *Weaver*, 3 N.C. (2 Hayw.) 54 (1798).

23. Weaver was acquitted by the jury.

24. *State* v. *Boon*, 1 N.C. (Tay.) 246 (1801).

25. The statute also declared that the first offender must pay the value of the slave to the owner. It was silent about civil damages to be paid if the crime was not a first offense.

26. Quoted in *State* v. *Boon*, 1 N.C. 246 (Taylor's Reports, 114 n.) (1801).

27. 8 N.C. 210 (1 Hawks) (1820).

28. *State* v. *Reed*, 9 N.C. (2 Hawks) 454 (1823).

29. *State* v. *Hoover*, 20 N.C. (4 Dev. & Bat.) 365 (1839). For a case with similar facts, see *State* v. *Robbins*, 48 N.C. (3 Jones) 249 (1855), where the court again affirmed a conviction of a master for murdering his own slave.

30. *State* v. *Reed*, 9 N.C. (2 Hawks) 454, 456 (1823). See also *Morgan* v. *Rhodes*, 1 Stew. 70 (Ala. 1827); *State* v. *Flanigin*, 5 Ala. 477 (1843); *State* v. *Jones*, 5 Ala. 666 (1843); *Souther* v. *Commonwealth*, 48 Va. (7 Gratt.) 673 (1851); *Bailey* v. *State*, 20 Ga. 742 (1856), *Bailey* v. *State*, 26 Ga. 579 (1858); *Jordan* v. *State*, 22 Ga. 545 (1857); *Camp* v. *State*, 25 Ga. 689 (1858).

31. 9 N.C. (2 Hawks) 582 (1823).

32. 18 N.C. 121 (1834).

33. 23 N.C. (1 Ired.) 76 55 (1840).

34. Cobb, pp. 94, 95; *State* v. *Caesar*, 31 N.C. (9 Ired.) 391 (1849).

35. *State* v. *John*, 30 N.C. (3 Ired.) 330 (1848).

36. A general summary is in Kenneth Stampp, *The Peculiar Institution*, pp. 224-27. Michael Hindus, "Black Justice Under White Law: Criminal Prosecutions of Blacks in Antebellum South Carolina," pp. 576-77, provides detail on a typical system.

37. See, e.g., A. E. Keir Nash, "Fairness and Formalism in the Trials of Blacks in the State Supreme Courts of the Old South," pp. 79-81.

38. *State* v. *Clarissa*, 11 Ala. 57 (1847).

39. *Laura* v. *State*, 26 Miss. 174 (1853).

40. See also *Peter* v. *State*, 4 Miss. (3 How.) 433 (1839) (murder conviction reversed because prosecutor's name did not appear on indictment), after retrial, 12 Miss. (4 Sm. & M.) 31 (1844).

41. *State* v. *Kentuck*, 8 La. Ann. 308 (1853).

42. *State* v. *Jackson*, 6 La. Ann. 593 (1851).

43. *State* v. *Jerry*, 3 La. Ann. 576 (1848). See also *State* v. *Bob*, 11 La. Ann. 192 (1856).

44. 3 La Ann. 359 (1848).

45. *State* v. *Henderson*, 13 La. Ann. 489 (1858).

46. *State* v. *Lethe*, 9 La. Ann. 182 (1854).

47. *State* v. *Nelson*, 3 La. Ann. 497 (1848).

48. See also *State* v. *King*, 12 La. Ann. 593 (1857).

49. 32 Miss. 382 (1856).

50. The essay concluded with the following sentence: "To hold otherwise would not unfrequently expose the accused to the excited passions or fury of that class of population who in all countries are the subjects upon whom the criminal jurisprudence of the government can be most beneficially employed." The class referred to is surely the poor underclass generally, not specifically the white underclass to which reference was made in *State* v. *Jarrott*, note 33 supra.

51. 11 Ga. 225 (1852).

52. *State* v. *George*, 50 N.C. (5 Jones) 233 (1858).

53. *Simon* v. *State*, 37 Miss. 288 (1859).

54. See also *Dick* v. *State*, 30 Miss. 593 (1856) (confession made after hearing person say "it would be better for the guilty ones to confess, that the innocent might not be punished," should be excluded if objected to).

55. *Peter* v. *State*, 12 Miss. (4 Sm. & M.) 31 (1844). Peter's initial conviction had been reversed because the prosecutor's name was not on the indictment. 4 Miss. 433 (1839).

56. 39 Ala. 359 (1864).

57. Other illustrative cases that, because they come from Louisiana, are less illuminating, are *State* v. *Gilbert*, 2 La. Ann. 244 (1847) (attempted rape; confession given during corporal punishment inadmissible); *State* v. *Isaac*, 3 La. Ann. 359 (1848) (murder; improper to admit voluntary confession when slave had not been allowed to complete it and perhaps offer justification); *State* v. *George*, 15 La. Ann. 145 (1860) (arson and larceny; involuntary confessions to private persons inadmissible).

58. *State* v. *Jonas*, 6 La. Ann. 695 (1851).

59. See also *Stephen* v. *State*, 11 Ga. 225, 235 (1852) (citing with

Chapter III ★ 241

approval Scottish practice of admitting all confessions and leaving
credibility to jury); *Seaborn* v. *State*, 20 Ala. 15 (1852) (magistrate's
failure to warn and statement that "it was a bad business they were
in" did not render confession of murder inadmissible; "the facts that
they were slaves, and ignorant, and to some extent unacquainted
with the consequences" of confession, go to credibility).

60. See *Peter* v. *State*, 12 Miss. (4 Sm. & M.) 31, 38 (1844) (confession repeated to magistrate inadmissible; "Being a slave, he must be
presumed to have been ignorant of the protection from sudden violence, which the presence of the justice of the peace afforded him,
and he saw himself surrounded by some of those before whom he
had recently made a confession").

61. *State* v. *Clarissa*, 11 Ala. 57 (1847). For the facts in the case,
see text accompanying note 38 supra.

62. 32 Ala. 560 (1858).

63. *Simon* v. *State*, 5 Fla. 285 (1853).

64. *Wyatt* v. *State*, 25 Ala. 9 (1854).

65. *State* v. *Nelson*, 3 La. Ann. 497 (1848).

66. *Wyatt* v. *State*, 25 Ala. 9 (1854).

67. Cobb, p. 272, urged the adoption of a flat rule excluding
confessions to masters.

68. *Isham* v. *State*, 7 Miss. (6 How.) 35 (1841). See also *Spence* v.
State, 17 Ala. 192 (1850) (master could be compelled to testify on
behalf of slave; testimony would have established that master had
a practice of whipping accused slaves until they confessed, and that
slave's confession occurred while tied in anticipation of whipping);
State v. *Peter*, 14 La. Ann. 521 (1859) (attempt to commit rape;
masters would have provided alibi).

69. *State* v. *Jim*, 48 N.C. (3 Jones) 348 (1856).

70. *State* v. *Hannah*, 10 La. Ann. 131 (1855).

71. 36 Ala. 211 (1860).

72. *Jim* v. *State*, 15 Ga. 535 (1854).

73. See, e.g., *State* v. *Adeline*, 11 La. Ann. 736 (1856); *State* v.
Kitty, 12 La. Ann. 805 (1857).

74. *Frank* v. *State*, 39 Miss. 705 (1861).

75. *Sam* v. *State*, 33 Miss. 347 (1857).

76. See, e.g., the quotations from *State* v. *Tackett*, note 27 supra,
and from *Isham* v. *State*, note 68 supra.

77. *State* v. *Harrison*, 11 La. Ann. 722 (1856).

78. The conviction of Harrison, a slave, for murdering another slave was nonetheless affirmed because the unconstitutional statute did not repeal the prior statutes that it codified.

79. *State* v. *Philpot*, Dudley 46 (Sup. Ct. Ga. 1831).

80. See also *State* v. *Alford*, 22 Ark. 386 (1860) (presumption inapplicable in murder trial of person identified in indictment as "a negro"; defendant therefore could be convicted of second degree murder even though statutes recognized no degrees of murder when committed by slaves and though evidence showed defendant was a slave).

81. See also *Field* v. *Walker*, 17 Ala. 80 (1849) (freedom suit by black held in bondage must preserve master's right to jury trial, so habeas corpus unavailable).

82. See Cobb, p. 67 (collecting cases).

83. 19 Ark. 580 (1858).

84. *Adelle* v. *Beauregard*, 1 Mart. (O. S.) 183 (La. 1810). See also *State* v. *Cecil*, 2 Mart. (O. S.) 208 (La. 1812) (testimony of "woman . . . of color" admitted; presumption of freedom destroyed by former owner's declaration that she had been a slave but freedom established by his testimony that he had manumitted her).

85. Dudley 224 (Sup. Ct. Ga. 1830).

86. 46 N.C. (1 Jones) 32 (1853).

87. *Daniel* v. *Guy*, 19 Ark. 121 (1857).

88. *Daniel* v. *Guy*, 23 Ark. 50 (1861).

89. The case returned to the supreme court when Guy sought damages for unlawfully being held as a slave from 1856 to 1861. *Daniel* v. *Roper*, 24 Ark. 131 (1863). The court held that the suit was barred by the three-year statute of limitations; because Guy was a white woman, as the prior cases had established, she was never under any disability that prevented her from suing within the limitations period. This is slightly less silly than it seems; the effect of the rule would have been to induce claimants to freedom to join their damage action in the same proceedings.

90. *State* v. *Boyce*, 32 N.C. (10 Ired.) 536 (1849).

91. See also *Henry* v. *Armstrong*, 15 Ark. 162 (1854) (reversing judgment for master in damage action against patrollers from neighboring town who whipped slaves for attending orderly religious meeting, because no damage shown).

92. *Scranton* v. *Demere*, 6 Ga. 92 (1849).

93. *State* v. *Lane*, 30 N.C. (3 Ired.) 256 (1848). See also *State* v.

Jacobs, 47 N.C. (2 Jones) 52 (1854) (personal service required of notice to free black to leave city; "the Legislature never intended to act so oppressively towards a race to whom stern necessity had compelled it, in other respects, to deny so many of the privileges of freemen").

94. *Pleasant* v. *State*, 15 Ark. 624 (1855). The slave's conviction was reversed because the trial judge had refused to allow his owner to testify in his favor and had excluded questions about the woman's reputation for chastity.

95. *Heirn* v. *Bridault*, 37 Miss. 209 (1859).

96. *Bryan* v. *Walton*, 14 Ga. 185 (1853).

97. *Ewell* v. *Tidwell*, 20 Ark. 136 (1859).

98. *Pendleton* v. *State*, 6 Ark. 509 (1846).

99. 2 Del. (2 Harr.) 441 (1838).

100. R. H. Clark, T.R.R. Cobb and D. Irwin, *The Code of the State of Georgia*.

CHAPTER IV

1. See Anthony Kronman, "Specific Performance."

2. 24 Va. (3 Rand.) 170 (1825).

3. The fourth judge discussed only the question of fraud.

4. An earlier case had applied something of the converse rule, holding that where slaves conveyed by will could not be divided in equal portions without separating infants from their mothers, monetary compensation would be allowed: *Fitzhugh* v. *Foote*, 7 Va. (3 Cal.) 13 (1801).

5. *Bowyer* v. *Creigh*, 24 Va. (3 Rand.) 25 (1825).

6. *Randolph* v. *Randolph*, 27 Va. (6 Rand.) 194 (1828).

7. *Harrison* v. *Sims*, 27 Va. (6 Rand.) 506 (1828).

8. *McRae* v. *Walker*, 5 Miss. (4 How.) 455 (1840).

9. *Sevier* v. *John M. Ross & Co.*, Fr. Chanc. Rep. 514 (Miss. 1843).

10. *Murphy* v. *Clark*, 9 Miss. (1 Sm. & M.) 221 (1843). The only Arkansas case also followed *Randolph*. *Sanders* v. *Sanders*, 20 Ark. 610 (1859).

11. *Baker* v. *Rowan*, 2 Stew. & P. 361 (Ala. 1832).

12. 3 Ala. 747 (1842).

13. For Georgia, see *Dudley* v. *Mallery*, 4 Ga. 52 (1848).

14. For examples, see *Virginia Code* §64.1 (1950).

15. *Williams* v. *Howard*, 7 N.C. (3 Mur.) 74, 80-81 (1819).

16. *Summers* v. *Bean*, 54 Va. 404 (1856).

17. 4 La. Ann. 430 (1849).

18. *Fitzhugh* v. *Foote*, 7 Va. (3 Call) 13 (1801). By statute Louisiana prohibited the separate sale of a mother and a child under ten. La. Digest, *Black Code*, § 9 (1828).

19. *Moore* v. *Dudley*, 2 Stew. 170 (Ala. 1829).

20. *Meeker* v. *Childress*, Minor 109 (Ala. 1823).

21. See also *Watkins* v. *Bailey*, 21 Ark. 274 (1860).

22. *Gibson* v. *Andrews*, 4 Ala. 66 (1842).

23. 6 Ala. 471 (1844).

24. 14 Ga. 259 (1853).

25. *Mitchell* v. *Tallapoosa County*, 30 Ala. 130 (1857).

26. *Lingo* v. *Miller & Hill*, 23 Ga. 187 (1857).

27. *Lennard* v. *Boynton*, 11 Ga. 109 (1852).

28. See also *Outlaw* v. *Cook*, Minor 257 (Ala. 1824), where the court noted that the rule in slave cases was "supported by sound considerations of humanity and policy"; *Perry* v. *Hewlett*, 5 Port. 318 (Ala. 1837) (liable for full rental but not for failure to return slave at end of term, i.e., not liable for damages). Contra: *George* v. *Elliott*, 12 Va. (2 Henn. & Munf.) 5 (1806).

29. *Brooks* v. *Smith*, 21 Ga. 261 (1857).

30. *Curry* v. *Gaulden*, 17 Ga. 72 (1855).

31. See also *George* v. *Elliott*, 12 Va. (2 Henn. & Munf.) 5 (1806).

32. *Berry* v. *Diamond*, 19 Ark. 262 (1857).

33. See also *Walker* v. *Smith*, 28 Ala. 569 (1856) (hirer liable to owner for jail fees for runaways).

34. *Curry* v. *Gaulden*, 17 Ga. 72 (1855), emphasized the specific contract, as did the similar case of *Alston* v. *Balls*, 12 Ark. 664 (1852) (noting that hirer could have excepted risk of running away in contract).

35. 35 Va. (8 Leigh) 565 (1837). See also *Collier* v. *Lyons*, 18 Ga. 648 (1855).

36. See *Seay* v. *Marks*, 23 Ala. 532 (1853) (where written contract provides for hire in general terms, hirer may use slave as a prudent owner would but will be liable if slave is exposed to extraordinary hazard and is injured).

37. *Tallahassee R. Co.* v. *Macon*, 8 Fla. 299 (1859). See also *Wilkinson* v. *Moseley*, 30 Ala. 562 (1857) (medical treatment); *Nelson* v. *Bondurant*, 26 Ala. 341 (1855) (hirer not liable in absence of agreement for injury inflicted in the course of lawful punishment).

38. 4 Mart. (O.S.) 58 (La. 1815).

39. *Hendricks* v. *Phillips*, 3 La. Ann. 618 (1848).

40. *Copeland* v. *Parker*, 25 N.C. (3 Ired.) 513 (1843).

41. *Thompson* v. *Young*, 30 Miss. 17 (1855).

42. 33 N.C. (11 Ired.) 640 (1850).

43. 49 N.C. (4 Jones) 402 (1857).

44. See also *George* v. *Smith*, 51 N.C. (6 Jones) 273 (1859) (not negligent to give hired slave a pass to travel on railroad, even though hirer knew slave was likely to get drunk; slave did and was injured while on train).

45. 21 Ga. 270 (1857).

46. 1 Ga. 195 (1846).

47. The Alabama Supreme Court was divided on the question, *Cook & Scott* v. *Parham*, 24 Ala. 21 (1853), but held the owner liable for negligent selection of a grossly negligent supervisor, *Walker* v. *Bolling*, 22 Ala. 294 (1853).

48. *Forsyth* v. *Perry*, 5 Fla. 337 (1853).

49. In Mississippi, a master received one-half the value of a slave executed for crime, Miss. Rev. Code, chap. 37, art. 20 (1848); in Louisiana, up to two-thirds the value, La. Rev. Stat. 57 (1845). Even a sale at distress prices might realize more than the compensation.

50. *Ingram* v. *Mitchell*, 30 Ga. 547 (1860).

51. *Doughty* v. *Owen*, 24 Miss. 404 (1852).

52. *McConnell* v. *Hardeman*, 15 Ark. 151 (1854).

53. See also *Graham* v. *Roark*, 23 Ark. 20 (1861).

54. *Sarah* v. *State*, 18 Ark. 114 (1856).

55. A. E. Keir Nash, "Reason of Slavery: Understanding the Judicial Role in the Peculiar Institution"; Arthur Howington, "Not in the Condition of a Horse or an Ox."

56. *Prater's Administrator* v. *Darby*, 24 Ala. 496 (1854) (overruling *Trotter* v. *Blocker*, 6 Port. 269 [Ala. 1838]).

57. *Atwood's Heirs* v. *Beck*, 21 Ala. 590 (1852), followed in *Abercrombie's Executor* v. *Abercrombie's Heirs*, 27 Ala. 489 (1855); *Pool's Heirs* v. *Pool's Executor*, 35 Ala. 12 (1859).

58. See also *Ross* v. *Vertner*, 6 Miss. (5 How.) 305 (1840).

59. James Johnston, *Race Relations in Virginia and Miscegenation in the South, 1776-1860*, uses petitions to the legislature for such permission to great effect in analyzing the scope of miscegenation and the nature of the personal relations between masters and slaves.

60. 41 Fla. 445 (1852).

61. 9 Va. (5 Call) 311 (1804).

62. 21 Ga. 21 (1857).

63. 28 Ala. 514 (1856).

64. 18 N.C. (1 Dev. & Bat.) 260 (1833).

65. *Thornton* v. *Chisholm*, 20 Ga. 338 (1856).

66. *Leary* v. *Nash*, 56 N.C. (3 Jones Eq.) 356 (1857).

67. *Myers* v. *Williams*, 58 N.C. (5 Jones Eq.) 362 (1860).

68. *Elder* v. *Elder*, 31 Va. (4 Leigh) 252 (1833).

69. 31 Va. (4 Leigh) 289 (1833).

70. 38 Va. (11 Leigh) 616 (1841).

71. These cases are discussed in great detail in A. E. Keir Nash, "Reason of Slavery."

72. *Cameron* v. *Commissioners of Raleigh*, 36 N.C. (1 Ired. Eq.) 436 (1841).

73. *Cox* v. *Williams*, 39 N.C. (4 Ired. Eq.) 15 (1845).

74. *Thompson* v. *Newlin*, 41 N.C. (6 Ired. Eq.) 380 (1849).

75. *Alvany* v. *Powell*, 54 N.C. (7 Jones) 35 (1853). The court also noted the informality of slave marriages, as it upheld a bequest to a child whose father was unknown.

76. See Thomas R. R. Cobb, *An Inquiry Into the Law of Negro Slavery in the United States of America*, pp. 283-84.

77. *Leech* v. *Cooley*, 14 Miss. (6 Sm. & M.) 93 (1846).

78. *Ross* v. *Vertner*, 6 Miss. (5 How.) 305 (1840).

79. *Wade* v. *American Colonization Society*, 15 Miss. 663 (7 Sm. & M.) (1846).

80. *Lusk* v. *Lewis*, 32 Miss. 297 (1856).

81. See, e.g., *Cox* v. *Williams*, 39 N.C. (4 Ired. Eq.) 15 (1845); *Wade* v. *American Colonization Society*, 15 Miss. 663 (1846).

82. *Carroll* v. *Brumby*, 13 Ala. 102 (1848).

83. *Bailey* v. *Poindexter*, 55 Va. (14 Gratt.) 132 (1858).

84. *Williamson* v. *Coalter*, 55 Va. (14 Gratt.) 394 (1858).

85. 37 Ala. 229 (1861).

86. *Redding* v. *Findley*, 57 N.C. (4 Jones Eq.) 216 (1858).

87. *Reeves* v. *Long*, 58 N.C. (5 Jones Eq.) 355 (1860). See also *Harrison* v. *Everett*, 58 N.C. 163 (1859).

88. "Reason of Slavery," p. 104.

89. *Jordan* v. *Bradley*, Dudley 170 (Ga. Superior Ct. 1830).

90. *Vance* v. *Crawford*, 4 Ga. 445 (1848).

91. *Cleland* v. *Waters*, 19 Ga. 35 (1855).

92. See David B. Davis, *The Problem of Slavery in the Age of Rev-*

olution, 1770–1823 (Ithaca: Cornell University Press, 1975), at pp. 469-501.

93. *Adams* v. *Bass*, 18 Ga. 130 (1855).

94. *Sanders* v. *Ward*, 25 Ga. 109 (1858).

95. *Bivins* v. *Crawford*, 26 Ga. 225 (1858).

96. *Myrick* v. *Vineburgh*, 30 Ga. 161 (1860).

97. *American Colonization Society* v. *Gartrell*, 23 Ga. 448 (1857).

98. *Walker* v. *Walker*, 25 Ga. 420 (1858).

99. *Curry* v. *Curry*, 30 Ga. 253 (1860).

CONCLUSION

1. *Mitchell* v. *Wells*, 37 Miss. 235 (1859).

List of Works Cited

Blassingame, John. *The Slave Community: Plantation Life in the Antebellum South*. New York: Oxford University Press, 1972.

Catterall, Helen. *Judicial Cases Concerning American Slavery and the Negro*. 5 vols. Washington: Carnegie Institution, 1932.

Clark, R. H., Cobb, T.R.R., and Irwin, D. *The Code of the State of Georgia*. Atlanta: n.p., 1961.

Cobb, Thomas R. R. *An Inquiry Into the Law of Negro Slavery in the United States of America*. 1858. Rpt. New York: Negro Universities Press, 1968.

Cover, Robert. *Justice Accused*. New Haven: Yale University Press, 1976.

Davis, David B. *The Problem of Slavery in the Age of Revolution, 1770-1823*. Ithaca: Cornell University Press, 1975.

Dworkin, Ronald. "The Law of the Slave-Catchers." *Times Literary Supplement*, Dec. 5, 1975, p. 1437.

Elkins, Stanley, ed. *Slavery*. New York: Grosset & Dunlap, 1963.

————. *Slavery: A Problem in American Institutional and Intellectual Life*. Chicago: University of Chicago Press, 1959.

Fitzhugh, George. *Cannibals All!* Edited by C. Vann Woodward. Cambridge: Harvard University Press, 1960.

Flanigan, Daniel. "Criminal Procedure in Slave Trials in the Antebellum South." *Journal of Southern History* 40 (Nov. 1977): 537-564.

Fogel, Robert and Engerman, Stanley. *Time on the Cross*. Vol. 1. Boston: Little, Brown, & Co., 1974.

Gabel, Peter. "Intention and Structure in Contractual Conditions: Outline of a Method for Critical Legal Theory." *Minnesota Law Review*. 61 (April 1977): 601-643.

Genovese, Eugene. "Materialism and Idealism in the History of Negro Slavery in the Americas." *Journal of Social History* 1 (1968): 371-394.

————. *The Political Economy of Slavery*. New York: Pantheon Books, 1966.

————. *Roll, Jordan, Roll*. New York: Pantheon Books, 1974.

————. *The World the Slaveholders Made*. New York: Pantheon Books, 1969.

Goodell, William. *The American Slave Code in Theory and Practice.* 1853. Facsimile rpt. New York: New American Library, 1969.

Harris, Marvin. *Patterns of Race in the Americas.* New York: Walker, 1964.

Higginbotham, A. Leon. *In the Matter of Color.* New York: Oxford University Press, 1978.

Hindus, Michael. "Black Justice Under White Law: Criminal Prosecutions of Blacks in Antebellum South Carolina." *Journal of American History* 63 (Dec. 1976): 575-599.

Horwitz, Morton. *The Transformation of American Law, 1780-1860.* Cambridge: Harvard University Press, 1977.

Howington, Arthur. " 'According to Law': The Trial and Punishment of Black Defendants in Antebellum Tennessee." Presented at the annual meeting of the Organization of American Historians, New York, April 13, 1978.

————. "Not in the Condition of a Horse or an Ox." *Tennessee Historical Quarterly* 34 (Fall 1975): 249-263.

Johnston, James. *Race Relations in Virginia and Miscegenation in the South, 1776-1860.* Amherst: University of Massachusetts Press, 1970.

Jordan, Winthrop. *White Over Black: American Attitudes Toward the Negro, 1550-1812.* Chapel Hill: University of North Carolina Press, 1968.

Kennedy, Duncan. "Form and Substance in Private Law Adjudication." *Harvard Law Review* 89 (June 1976): 1685-1778.

Kronman, Anthony. "Specific Performance." *University of Chicago Law Review* 45 (Winter 1978): 351-382.

Lane, Ann., ed. *The Debate Over Slavery: Stanley Elkins and His Critics.* Urbana: University of Illinois Press, 1971.

Lang, Meredith. *Defender of the Faith: The High Court of Mississippi, 1817-1875.* Jackson: University Press of Mississippi, 1977.

Luckmann, Thomas. *Phenomenology and Sociology.* New York: Penguin, 1978.

McKitrick, Eric L., ed. *Slavery Defended: The Views of the Old South.* Englewood Cliffs, N.J.: Prentice-Hall, 1963. Printing excerpts from William Grayson. *The Hireling and the Slave.* Charleston: McCord & Co., 1858.

MacPherson, C. B. *The Political Philosophy of Possessive Individualism.* Oxford: Clarendon Press, 1962.

Miller, Perry. *The Life of the Mind in America: From the Revolution to the Civil War.* New York: Harcourt, Brace & World, 1965.

Morgan, Edmund. *American Slavery/American Freedom*. New York: Norton, 1975.

Nash, A. E. Keir. "Fairness and Formalism in the Trials of Blacks in the State Supreme Courts of the Old South." *Virginia Law Review* 56 (Feb. 1970): 64–100.

———. "Reason of Slavery: Understanding the Judicial Role in the Peculiar Institution." *Vanderbilt Law Review* 32 (Jan. 1979): 7–218.

———. "Understanding the Judicial Role in the Institution of Slavery, Part Two." Presented at the Annual Meeting of the Organization of American Historians, April 13, 1978, New York.

Noonan, John. *Persons and Masks of the Law*. New York: Farrar, Straus & Giroux, 1976.

Owens, Leslie H. *This Species of Property*. New York: Oxford University Press, 1977.

Pound, Roscoe. *The Formative Era of America Law*. Boston: Little, Brown Co., 1938.

Presser, Stephen. "A Tale of Two Judges." *Northwestern University Law Review* 73 (March–April 1978): 26–111.

Rheinstein, Max, ed. *Max Weber on Law in Economy and Society*. New York: Simon & Schuster, 1967.

Stampp, Kenneth. *The Peculiar Institution*. New York: Random House, 1956.

Stowe, Harriet Beecher. *Key to Uncle Tom's Cabin*. Boston: J. D. Jewett, 1853.

Stroud, George. *A Sketch of the Laws Relating to Slavery*. 2d ed. 1956. Rpt. New York: Negro Universities Press, 1968.

Tushnet, Mark. Review of Robert Cover. *Justice Accused*. In the *American Journal of Legal History* 20 (April, 1976): 168–171.

———. Review of "In the Matter of Color." In the *University of Chicago Law Review* 45 (Summer, 1978): 906–918.

———. "Swift v. Tyson Exhumed." Yale Law Journal 79 (Dec. 1969): 284–310.

Unger, Roberto. *Knowledge and Politics*. New York: The Free Press, 1976.

Warren, Samuel and Brandeis, Louis. "The Right to Privacy." *Harvard Law Review* 4 (Dec. 1890): 193–220.

White, James. *The Legal Imagination*. Boston: Little, Brown & Co., 1973.

Table of Cases

The names of the cases listed below are followed by the conventional form of legal citation. That form has four parts. Case reports are issued in a series of volumes, usually identified simply by the abbreviated name of the state in which the cases were decided. The number of the volume precedes the abbreviated name, and the number of the first page of the opinion follows it. Thus, *Abercrombie's Executor* v. *Abercrombie's Heirs* is found in the 27th volume of the reports from Alabama and begins on page 489. The final part of the citation is the year in which the case was decided.

Variations work from this basic form. Occasionally the conventions require that an abbreviated version of the name of the reporter of decisions appear in the citation. Thus, *Allen* v. *Freeland* is found in volume 24 of the Virginia reports, which is the third volume of the series of decisions reported by Randolph. Sometimes, especially with the earliest cases, the series is identified only by the name of the reporter, in which event the state name appears with the date of decision. Finally, a few volumes include decisions from courts other than the state's highest court. When the case that is cited was decided by any court other than the highest court included in the volume, the court is named with the date of decision. Thus, *Hunter* v. *Shaffer* appears in the volume of Georgia cases reported by Dudley, and was decided by the Georgia Superior Court in 1830.

Index

abolitionists, 56-57; analysis of law by, 15-16, 27; attention to Southern law by, 19

Alabama slave law: confessions, 131, 134, 137; manumission by contract, 191-93; medical care, 170-71, 171-72; murder, 123, 137 (of owner by slave, 132); poisoning, 130; quasi freedom, 198-99; slave consent to manumission, 208-209, 213-15; uniqueness of slaves, 165-66; valuation of slaves, 168

Allen, John, 204

American Colonization Society, 21, 205, 207-208, 218, 225-27

Arkansas slave law: freedom suit, 143-44, 146-47; hirer's liability for runaway, 175-76; limitations on free blacks, 152-54; presumption of slavery from race, 146-47; rape, 149; torts, 190

arson: Florida, 133; Louisiana, 124; Mississippi, 76-77, 138

assaults: generally (North Carolina), 106-107; justifications, 95; on slave (North Carolina), 54-65, 94, 104; by slaves on whites (Georgia, 20; Louisiana, 124; Mississippi, 77-78, 78-79; North Carolina, 108-20); by stranger on slave, 59, 71

autonomy of law, 28-30, 42-43

battery, by white on free black, 94

Benning, Henry, 219, 222, 224

bourgeois law, 26-27, 29, 43, 54, 157, 169, 188, 229

Brooke, Francis, 161, 164, 204-205

burglary (Mississippi), 138

Cabell, William, 164

Carr, Dabney, 159, 161-63, 204

categorization, 8, 10, 63-64, 67, 71-72, 73, 108, 111, 120, 137-38, 213, 215, 217, 229-30

Catterall, Helen, 10, 12-13

Chilton, William, 192

Coalter, John, 164

Cobb, Thomas, 82, 85, 115, 156, 214

codification, 72, 73, 75-76, 79-80, 84, 85, 89-90, 91-93, 126, 156

common law, 73, 75, 76, 101-102, 104, 105, 110-111; in Mississippi, 72

confessions, 127-37; in Alabama, 123; in Louisiana, 126, 136-37; to masters, 134-37 (North Carolina, 136)

contracts of slave hire, 47, 51-54

contributory negligence, 183

courts for trial of slaves, 122

Cover, Robert, 57-61

criminal defense, duty to provide, 172

criminal law: Mississippi, 72-90; South Carolina, 17; Tennessee, 17-18

criminal procedure, 24, 122-39; Louisiana, 124-26; Mississippi, 82-84

cy pres, 223

Daniel, William, 209-210

Delaware, freedom suit in, 155-56

94; and quasi freedom (North
Carolina, 199-200, 201-202;
Georgia, 200-201, 202-203; Virginia, 203-205); by will (Georgia,
196-98; Virginia, 195-96)
marriage, slave, 120-21
medical care: Alabama, 170-72;
Georgia, 171, 182-83
mediocrity, judicial, 7-8, 29, 35,
37, 38-39, 42, 50, 96
miscegenation, 13-14, 140, 155, 200
Mississippi slave law, 12-13; arson,
76-77, 138; assault by slave on
white, 77-78; burglary, 138;
criminal law, 72-90; criminal
procedure, 82-84; foreign emancipation, 207-208; larceny by
slave, 83; limitations on free
blacks, 149; murder, 72 (by
slave, 79-82, 86-89, 135; by
slave, of slave, 127, 129; by
slave, of white, 123, 129-30);
property in slaves, 231-32; rape,
72 (of slave, 85-86); sale of slave
to avoid prosecution, 189-90;
uniqueness of slaves, 165
Moncure, Richard, 210-11, 213
murder: attempt, by poisoning (Alabama), 123; justification (North
Carolina, 96; Louisiana, 130, 135;
Mississippi, 72); of owner by
slave (Alabama), 132; by slave
(Georgia, 137; Louisiana, 125;
Mississippi, 79-82, 86-89, 123,
127-28, 129-30, 135; North Carolina, 120-21, 128-29); of slave,
84 (Mississippi, 73-75; North
Carolina, 96, 97-99, 100-102,
102-103, 103-104)

Nash, A. E. Keir, 9, 10, 191, 218
Nash, Frederick, 116-17, 145
Nisbet, Eugenius, 19
North Carolina slave law, 90-121;
assault on slave, 54-65; confes-

sions, 136; fellow-servant rule,
45-49; foreign emancipation,
205-207; liability of hirer, 180-82;
limitations on free blacks, 148-
49; manumission by will (quasi
freedom), 199-200, 201-202;
murder of master, 128-29; presumption of slavery from color,
145-46; slave celebrations, 147-
48; slave consent to manumission, 215-16; slave marriage, 15

overseers, 16, 20, 48-49, 178-79

paternalism, 36
Pearson, Leonard, 94, 115-16, 128-
29, 182, 206-207
phenomenology, 31
pluralist analysis of law, 27-28
poisoning (Alabama), 130
Pound, Roscoe, 50
precedent, role of, 8, 24-25, 29, 35,
44, 63-65, 71-76, 89, 94-96, 108-
10, 116-17, 121-23, 217-19, 229
Preston, Isaac, 131
presumption of slavery from race,
142-47

quasi freedom, 197, 198-205, 218-
20

race, 139-56
rape: Arkansas, 149; Georgia, 128,
188-89; Mississippi, 72; of Mississippi slave, 85-86
Roane, Spencer, 196
Ruffin, Thomas, 39, 42, 45-48, 49,
55-65, 103-104, 117-20, 147, 180-
81, 186, 187, 200, 206, 215, 229

Sartre, Jean-Paul, 31
Schutz, Alfred, 31
sentiment, 31, 36-37, 49, 53, 54, 62

Library of Congress Cataloging in Publication Data

Tushnet, Mark V   1945-
    The American law of slavery, 1810-1860.

    Bibliography: p.
    Includes index.
    1.   Slavery in the United States—Southern States
—Law and legislation—History.   I. ʻ Title.
KF4545.S5T87   342.75ʻ0873   80-8582
ISBN 0-691-04681-6
ISBN 0-691-10104-3 (lim. paper ed.)

Mark Tushnet *is Professor of Law at
the University of Wisconsin.*